The
Arabs
in
Israel

The
Arabs
in
Israel

Sabri
Jiryis

**Translated from the Arabic
by Inea Bushnaq**

**Monthly Review Press
New York and London**

Library of Congress Cataloging in Publication Data
Jiryis, Sabri.
   The Arabs in Israel.
   Updated translation of ha-Aravim be-Yisrael.
   Includes bibliographical references.
   1.   Palestinian Arabs—Israel.   I.   Title.
DS113.7.J813   323.4'095694   75-15347
ISBN 0-85345-377-2

First Printing

Monthly Review Press
62 West 14th Street, New York, N.Y. 10011
21 Theobalds Road, London WC1X 8SL

Manufactured in the United States of America

Contents

Foreword by Noam Chomsky   vii
Preface   1
Introduction   3

I: The Military Government

1. "For Security Reasons"   9
2. Toward a New Policy, 1959–1966   36
3. The Velvet Glove   56

II: The Seizure of Arab Land

4. "Redeeming" the Land   75
5. "Liberating" the Land   102

III: The Strong-Arm Policy

6. From Deir Yasin to Kfar Kassim   137

IV: Strangers in Their Own Land

7. Political and Societal Circumstances   161
8. Education, Economics, and Services   203

V: Conclusion   235

Notes   243
Appendix: Tables   289

Foreword

Noam Chomsky

The literature in English on Zionism and Israeli society is extensive, but there are some striking gaps. Within the "green line" (pre-June 1967 borders), one-seventh of the population is Arab. But as the American political scientist Leonard Fein points out, "Unhappily, social scientists have devoted little attention to the Arabs in Israel." This is not to say that American social scientists and other commentators refrain from allusions to the status of the Arab minority. Quite the contrary. One of the great achievements of Zionism is commonly held to be its achievement of the democratic ideal of equality of rights for all citizens. Harvard sociologist Nathan Glazer, a specialist on ethnic minorities with a long-standing interest in Israel and Zionism, writes that "The state created by Zionism is a modern secular state in which civil rights are granted to all people of whatever origin and religion." His colleague, political scientist Michael Walzer, scoffs at Palestinian propaganda in favor of a democratic secular state on the grounds that such a state "already exists in substance" in the former Palestine, namely, the state of Israel. These observations are not untypical of left-liberal commentary on Israel. There is admiration of Israel's secularism and equitable treatment of the Arab minority. Such general acclaim is matched only by the no less general ignorance of the facts.

Perhaps ignorance is not quite the right term. Those who extol Israel's "secularism" can hardly be unaware of the degree of religious control over personal life, and they even sometimes allude to the excessive power of religious authority, a minor departure from the ideal. It is well known that there can be no interdenominational marriage in this "secular" state. In the Jewish community, the Orthodox rabbinate imposes its interpretation of religious law, with its "black book" of citizens who are not permitted to marry because of "sins" of earlier generations, and so on. To be recognized as a Jew is no small matter in the Jewish state. Where one can live or work, even the opportunity to play in the Israeli basketball league, depends on the decision of the Orthodox rabbinate as to who is a Jew, by the criteria that they have established, which require either conversion or a proper genealogy going back four generations. Were similar principles to apply to Jews elsewhere, we would not hesitate to condemn this revival of the Nuremberg laws. But Israel, somehow, remains a secular state by the standards of many liberal American social scientists.

In fact, Israel makes no pretense to being a secular state. Nor is it committed to equal rights for citizens. There is no such thing as "Israeli nationality" in the state of Israel. There is a "Jewish nation" but no "Israeli nation." Citizens are Jews, Christians, or Muslims; their lives are governed by religious authority and religious law. In this respect, Israel is not unlike its neighbors, which no one would dream of calling secular states. Syria and Jordan are, by law, Islamic states. Correspondingly, as the Israeli courts have held, Israel is the "sovereign state of the Jewish people," not of its citizens. It is as if the Supreme Court were to proclaim that the United States is the "sovereign state of the White people" or the "Anglo-Saxon people," assigning to some religious or ethnic authority the power to determine who qualifies to enter this circle of privilege. As for democratic rights, quite apart from restriction of access to land, work, and public funds, Arabs are still controlled by British Mandatory laws that were condemned by the first Israeli Knesset (Parliament) as "incompatible with the principles of a democratic state." Nevertheless, Israel is ranked high by left-liberal American commentators, such as Irving Howe, as an "ebullient democracy" progressing "toward socialism" and "about as good a model as we have for the democratic socialist hope of combining radical social change with political freedom." Meanwhile, its neighbors are quite properly condemned for their religious coercion and adherence to the fundamental principle of discrimination and domination by a selected group.

This disparity in judgment can be placed in a more general context. The American press is regularly disgraced by racist caricatures of "Arab sheikhs" who are bent on destroying Western civilization by raising the price of oil—prominent among them are such "Arab sheikhs" as the Shah of Iran and the government of Venezuela, while Sheikh Yamani of Saudi Arabia, for reasons of his own, hews close to the American line. Comparable references to Jews would be denounced as a reversion to Goebbels and Streicher. We read learned discussions of the "Arab mind," the "shame culture" the prevents Arabs from coming to terms with reality, of Arab trickery and deceit and violence, of the corruption of the Arab language, in which, we are informed, one can barely tell the truth. It is inconceivable that Jews or Israelis could be discussed in similar terms outside of the literature of the Ku Klux Klan. In contrast, Israel is lauded for its democratic virtues, openness, high cultural values, secularism, equitable treatment of minorities, and progress toward socialism.

Since the overwhelming Israeli military victory of 1967, support for Israel—which in practice generally means support for the more intransigent chauvinistic elements within Israel—has taken some remarkable forms in the United States, particularly among liberal intellectuals. The reasons for the phenomenon may be debated; the facts are plain enough. Even on elementary questions of civil liberties and human rights, Israel enjoys a special immunity, as anyone involved in protest against authoritarian and repressive practices throughout the world will quickly discover. Nothing is easier than to publish a letter in support of a victim of the totalitarian regimes of Eastern Europe. It is quite a different matter when Arab intellectuals are expelled from their homes in Israel or the occupied territories or confined to prison under onerous conditions for many months without charge. To cite

just one example of Israel's special status for American civil
libertarians, consider the interesting case of the Israeli League
for Human and Civil Rights, which has been attempting to
make public charges of repressive practices within Israel and
the occupied territories, and calling for an investigation,
exactly as a civil rights organization should do. In late 1972,
the governing Labor Party attempted to take over the group.
A secret memorandum headed "Internal—not for publication" called on members of the party to appear at the regular
meeting of the League, vote its leadership out of office, and
control its activities; the Labor Party would pay membership
dues. The courts, to their credit, declared the outcome of the
meeting where this farce was enacted null and void, although
they did require that the League admit the mass membership
organized by the Labor Party. Evidently, no small civil rights
organization can long survive such tactics, which would be
condemned out of hand in any other state in the world. The
response in the United States was indicative of the general
mood. Well-known civil libertarians publicly defended the
action of the Labor Party while grossly distorting the factual
record (see letters to the *Boston Globe,* April 29, May 17,
May 25, and June 5, 1973). The International League for the
Rights of Man, based in New York, suspended its Israeli affili-
ate, with no comment on the action of the governing party.
Again, the example is quite typical. Given the mood of general hysteria regarding Israel among large circles of liberal
intellectuals, it is perhaps not surprising that well-informed
and respected commentators can speak of the "modern secular state" of Israel, with its concern for equality of rights of
citizens and its fair treatment of the Arab minority.

In fact, in the "sovereign state of the Jewish people" there
is little hope that Arab citizens will gain equal rights. For the
Jewish majority, Israel is comparable in its civil liberties and
inequities to Western democracies. But Arabs have no place
in the Jewish state, except as a tolerated but essentially foreign element, just as Jews can look forward to no other status
in an "Islamic state." In part, the discriminatory structure of
the state of Israel is embedded in law and institutions. In

part, it is based on administrative practice. There is no substantial segment of Israeli society that opposes or seriously questions the fundamental principle of discrimination, nor is it an issue within World Zionism. As for American "supporters of Israel," they resort to the simplest and most familiar of all techniques: to deny the facts.

The Zionist dream is to construct a state which is Jewish as England is English and France French. At the same time, this state is to be a democracy on the Western model. Evidently, these goals are incompatible. Citizens of France are French, but citizens of the Jewish state may be non-Jews, either by ethnic or religious origin or simply by choice, because they would prefer to regard themselves as merely Israelis. To the extent that Israel is a Jewish state, it cannot be a democratic state. If the respects in which the state is Jewish are marginal and symbolic, the departure from democratic principle may be dismissed as insignificant. But the state is Jewish in respects that are quite fundamental.

Consider the matter of land use and development, a question of major importance for the Arabs of Israel, largely a peasant population before 1948. Within the green line, over 90 percent of the land is owned by the state or the Jewish National Fund (Keren Keymeth Leisrael—JNF). Under Israeli law, the JNF controls the Land Development Authority. In its official publications, the JNF describes itself as the "exclusive instrument for the development of Israel lands." Under its charter, recognized by Israeli law, the JNF is restricted to actions that are "directly or indirectly beneficial to persons of Jewish religion, race, or origin." Arabs are not permitted to live or work on lands owned by the JNF. These lands are owned in perpetuity by the Jewish people (not the Israeli people, which does not exist as a legal entity). The extent to which the JNF applies its discriminatory doctrines is difficult to ascertain. Surely, they are taken seriously. For example, ten settlements were recently heavily fined "for illegally leasing agricultural lands to Arabs," the Israeli press reported, while the Ministry of Agriculture is undertaking an "energetic campaign" to eliminate the "plague" of leasing lands to Arabs (see *Haaretz*, July 21, 1975; *Maariv*, July 3, 1975).

Similarly, responsibility for development is assigned in large measure to the Jewish Agency, a quasi-official body that operates in the interests of Jews with a budget on roughly the scale of the development budget of the government. By such means as these, the state has succeeded in directing resources to Jewish citizens without technically introducing legal discrimination—though in part, as noted, segregation and other discriminatory practices are founded in the legal system itself.

Such principles and practices go a long way toward explaining the systematic deprivation of Arab settlements, including those of the Druze, who serve in the Israeli military forces, with regard to such matters as electrification, water resources, and general disbursement of public funds. The extreme inequities introduced by the reliance on quasi-official bodies devoted solely to the interests of Jewish citizens is enhanced by discriminatory distribution of tax funds, a matter that has been brought to light by Knesset member Shulamit Aloni, among others (see *Yediot Aharonot*, October 10, 1975).

In defense of Israeli secularism, it is commonly argued that Arabs participate in government ministries and agencies and that the General Federation of Workers, (Histadrut), long restricted to Jews, now accepts Arab members and participation. It is less frequently noted that Arab officials are to be found predominantly (until recently, and perhaps even today, only) in ministries and agencies dealing with Arab affairs and that Histadrut programs are overwhelmingly organized for the benefit of Jews. In a recent study, Ian S. Lustick comments that "of the thousands of Histadrut-owned firms and factories not one is located in an Arab village," and that there are still no Arab members of the eighteen-man Central Committee of the Histadrut and no Arabs among the more than six hundred managers and directors of Histadrut-controlled industry (see "Institutionalized

Segmentation," a paper delivered at Middle East Studies Association Conference, November 1975).

These matters might be considered in relation to the recent United Nations resolution identifying Zionism as a form of racism. This resolution has been universally denounced in the United States. It has been branded "a lie" by commentators who speak of the "racism of the Arab states," referring to their discrimination against Jews and other minorities, and has been condemned as signalling the virtual demise of the United Nations as a "moral force" in the world. There are ample grounds for condemning the UN resolution, but not those emphasized in the condemnations expressed here. Thus, one might note that states voting for the resolution are no less guilty of racist practices, in the sense of the resolution, which interprets "racial discrimination" as discrimination based on "race, color, descent, or national or ethnic origin," as in international conventions. And one might add that Zionism has historically taken many forms, and in an earlier period explicitly condemned the kinds of institutionalized discrimination now practiced by the state of Israel. But there can be no doubt that the text of the UN resolution is technically accurate, in the sense of "racism" in which we may speak of the "racism of the Arab states." The unending flow of lies and distortion concerning these matters in the United States can only be described as shameful. It amounts to defense of entirely intolerable practices.

If American Jews were excluded from "all-Christian cities" or lands owned and administered by a quasi-official "Christian National Fund," or deprived of development funds, electricity, water, etc., for reason of religious origin, no one would hesitate to denounce these racist practices. The reaction would be no different if the United States government or some quasi-official agency responsible for development were to institute a program of "making New York White," modelled on the recently revived program of "Judaization of the Galilee" (the phrase is commonly used, without comment, in the Israeli press, and in publications of the Jewish

Agency). I do not even speak of the policies pursued in the occupied territories—for example, in the region west of Gaza where thousands of Arabs were expelled, their villages destroyed, the area restricted to all-Jewish settlement, including agricultural cooperatives and the new all-Jewish city of Yamit recently opened on the Egyptian side of the internationally recognized border. In these areas, Arab political activity or organization is suppressed, people are jailed or expelled without charge, there is collective punishment, etc. Within Israel, there has been protest against these actions. In the United States, again, the reaction on the part of "supporters of Israel" is quite different.

An international consensus is developing in support of a two-state settlement in the former Palestine, with a Palestinian state in the West Bank and Gaza strip. The UN Security Council resolution of January 26, 1976, vetoed by the United States, called for the establishment of an "independent state in Palestine" beyond the green line, with a guarantee for the "sovereignty, territorial integrity, and political independence of all states in the area and their right to live in peace within secure and recognized boundaries"—including both Israel and the Palestinian state. Within the Palestine Liberation Organization (PLO) there has evidently been considerable debate about the merit of such a settlement. Various opinions have been publicly expressed. Sabri Jiryis is one of those who have advocated a two-state solution; others have expressly rejected it. A joint Moscow-PLO statement in November 1975 called for a "national state" for the Palestinian people, established "according to UN resolutions," which uniformly call for the security and integrity of all states in the region. The Jordanian press has commented that the Palestinian reaction to the January 1976 Security Council resolution constituted an "implicit recognition of the right of an Israeli state to exist," and the same might be said of the Moscow communiqué. Within Israel, there is some articulate support for a settlement along these lines, though the government has not modified its adamant and total rejection of any political settlement that grants the Palestinians national rights and national independence, and flatly rejects any political negotiations with Palestinians.

The United States is now quite isolated in opposition to the general international consensus, but it is likely that American government policy will shift. The United States government has no abiding commitment to the current policy of Israel, with its dual aims of maintaining control of substantial parts of the occupied territories and crushing Palestinian nationalism. It is an open question whether Congress will continue to authorize the substantial aid that Israel requires to preserve its economy under the conditions of military confrontation, though the matter is complicated by the fact that the "costs" of the Middle East arms race bring substantial "benefits" to American arms producers.

Suppose that in the course of time a political accommodation is achieved, along the lines of the emerging international consensus. This is not impossible, though a realistic estimate might assign it a lower probability than continued military confrontation and an eventual destructive war. If a two-state settlement is imposed by external force (it is difficult to conceive of another mechanism, under current conditions), there will be two small states in the former Palestine: Israel, by the standards of the region, a powerful and advanced industrial society; and a Palestinian state, virtually a dependency, contained within a tacit Israeli-Jordanian military alliance. It is plausible to suppose that the Palestinian state will be a mirror-image of Israel in its internal structure and practices. If so, there will be two states, one weak and the other powerful, each founded on the principle of discrimination against a national minority.

The prospect is hardly an attractive one, though one might argue that there is no preferable alternative under current conditions. It is possible that under conditions of peace, the problems of discrimination and oppression may be faced by groups within the two hostile societies that are committed to civil rights and socialist principles. Such groups might seek to establish relations along other than national lines, specifically along class lines. They might try to find a way to work together to combat oppressive institutions and to develop new political forms, within a socialist framework, that will permit national self-determination without domination of one group by another. In such an attempt, they can find historical antecedents, for example within the pre-World War II Zionist movement and Palestinian Communist Party of that period.

There was a time when Zionist leaders could warn against a realization of Zionism "in the form of the new Polish state with Arabs in the position of the Jews and the Jews in the position of Poles, the ruling people," a "complete perversion of the Zionist ideal" (These words were spoken in 1931 by Berl Katznelson of Mapai, since 1948 the governing party in Israel). This "complete perversion" has in fact been the historical realization of Zionism. It has, quite naturally, been accompanied by a relative decline in the socialist institutions of the pre-state Jewish settlement, exactly the opposite of the "progress toward socialism" perceived by American observers. Perhaps it is not too much to hope for a revival of the bi-nationalist socialism of an earlier day, if the bitter national conflict recedes. It is surely the task of the left—among Israelis, Palestinians, and internationally—to work for that end, whatever the strength of the forces committed to oppression, exploitation, exclusivism, and domination.

The problems of multi-ethnic societies are enormously complex. In most parts of the world they have defied satisfactory resolution, seriously impeding the development of socialist internationalism. Under conditions of war and national conflict, they are virtually insuperable. Partisans of one or another side take comfort in denouncing the crimes, often real enough, of their enemies, constructing an imaginary world in which their favored group is merely the victim of forces beyond its control and enemies that seek to destroy it. Israel faces real and undeniable problems of security. I believe that the policies of the government since 1967 have contributed significantly to what may prove a national catastrophe. But as any rational observer must agree, the Palestinian people have already suffered a national disaster. In their former home they are an oppressed minority; elsewhere they are scattered refugees. Many crimes have been committed on all sides. Continued national conflict simply leaves the fate of the warring parties in the hands of the imperial powers, which will be concerned, as always, with the interests of their own ruling groups. In the Middle East, the United States is by far the dominant external force, as it has been since World War II. Policies that it undertakes are of crucial importance.

Without succumbing to pluralist mythology, we must nevertheless recognize that popular opinion and organization do play some role in influencing state policy, or at least the manner of its execution. At certain historical moments they can exert a significant influence. The stakes, in this case, are extraordinarily high. For Israeli Jews and for Palestinians, the stakes are no less than survival. Others in the region have suffered bitterly in the course of the conflict and can look forward to a fate still more grim, if it persists. Given the strategic and economic significance of the neighboring regions, the international ramifications will continue to be profound and far-reaching. Whatever one's attitude and commitments, it will not hurt to become acquainted with some of the basic facts.

Sabri Jiryis has done work of unique significance in presenting some of the basic facts that are generally little known and often willfully ignored. His work is careful, documented, and judicious. He deals with that central and crucial domain that has been so neglected by social scientists and others who have produced the extensive literature dealing with the state of Israel. The appearance of his study on the Arabs in Israel, in a new and much expanded version, is an occasion of great importance for those who hope to go beyond propaganda to an understanding of the world of social and historical fact. While his study of course by no means exhausts the important questions it addresses, it should raise discussion and understanding of these issues to an entirely new level. If there is a political accommodation along the lines of the two-state settlement that Jiryis has advocated, then his study will gain new and greater significance as attention turns, we may hope, to the basic problems of discrimination and oppression which are submerged in the violence of national conflict and preparation for war.

January 31, 1976

The
Arabs
in
Israel

Preface

This second edition of my book appears ten years after my first interest in the subject and seven years after the first edition, which was originally published in Hebrew in Haifa in 1966. There have been several translations of that first version. In 1967 the Arab League office in Jerusalem mimeographed an Arabic translation and the Research Center of the Palestine Liberation Organization published the book in Arabic, in two parts, and then in French. An English translation was published by the Institute for Palestine Studies. A summarized French version later appeared in Paris and was translated into German and Swedish.

One of the reasons I prepared a second edition was that none of these translations was complete; Israeli military censorship forbid the publication of parts of the original Hebrew work. The present edition follows the plan of the Hebrew edition, keeping the same chapter divisions and covering the same subject matter. Some changes were necessary, however. Censored parts have been included, as has a study of developments since 1966; and some events have been reappraised in light of newly published material. The book has been completely rewritten and expanded to twice the size of the first edition.

Concerning the sources I have used, there is almost too much material available. This subject has been of interest to a variety of groups both inside and outside Israel, with the result that there have been numerous books and hundreds of articles and studies, especially in the Israeli press. As far as possible, I have tried to rely on the most important sources and the most relevant authors. I have paid special attention to official Israeli sources, in the belief that they play an important part in making a number of points clear.

This book does not claim to be a comprehensive history of the Arabs in Israel but rather a study of most of the fundamental aspects of their situation.

I would like to thank all those who have helped to produce it, those who read and commented on its outline, and the editors and printers.

—S.J., March 1973

Introduction

The experience of the Arabs living under Zionism in Israel for the quarter century from 1948 to 1973 is unique and of special importance, both in terms of the Palestine question and of the Arab-Israeli struggle. For the Zionists it has been their first contact with Arabs living under their control. It was an opportunity for crystalizing their position, both practically and ideologically, over a period of time. In view of the latest stages in the Arab-Israeli struggle—the occupation of Palestine in its entirety and parts of neighboring Arab states, whereby half of the Arabs originally living in Palestine have come under the shadow of Israeli rule—this experience gains further significance.

The Arab presence in Israel helped bring into focus many Zionist attitudes toward the Arabs in general, and toward Palestinian Arabs in particular. At the beginning the Zionist movement did not follow any clear or comprehensible policy. Many of its founders, thinkers, and leaders considered the Arab question of no importance. Some were even surprised to learn that Arabs still lived in Palestine. Various organizations suggested projects and advanced ideas, however, concerning what the movement's attitude should be, especially after the Balfour Declaration and the later imposition of the British Mandate over Palestine. Unfortunately, these efforts were tentative and belated and in many cases lacked sincerity. At this time Zionist policy was restricted to strengthening and supporting the Zionist presence in Palestine, in particular by creating faits accomplis at every opportunity.

Indeed, the Zionist leadership does not seem to have had any clear image of even the nature of relations between Zionists and Arabs, including Palestinian Arabs, until after the creation of the Zionist state. That event in 1948 dramatically relieved them of the nightmare of an Arab majority in Palestine, for they were able to establish a predominantly Jewish state on that part of the land where the Arabs who stayed formed a minority. But the presence of that minority, and the fact that the government had to deal with it eventually forced a definition of the Israeli position.

A look at the various early measures concerning the Arabs clearly shows that the Israeli authorities did not feel comfortable with them and that many considered their very presence a contradiction. Apparently there were many who hoped to be rid of the Arabs, if not by "sending" them after their brothers beyond the borders, then at least by "exchanging" them for Jews from the Arab nations. International events stifled such hopes, however, and it finally became clear that an Arab minority was definitely staying on. Then the Israeli authorities did not hesitate: they very quickly decided to adopt a tough policy, exemplified by the imposition of military rule, the confiscation of property, and the neglect of living conditions—the subjects of the following chapters.

The Arabs who remained in Israel were a microcosm of the Palestinian Arab people. How many there were, especially during the first years, cannot be exactly determined. On November 8, 1948, a census was taken in preparation for the election of the Knesset, but it cannot be considered complete as far as the Arabs were concerned because it did not include Arab areas later added to Israel, the Negev, or some of the Bedouin tribes in Galilee. The continual movement of the Arab inhabitants within Israeli borders contributed to the difficulty in assessing their numbers. In addition to those who came back as a result of the family reunification program, many refugees "infiltrated" and some were allowed to stay. On the other hand, the Israeli authorities occasionally expelled Arabs to neighboring countries, even after they had been registered in the census. Thus the figures remained approximate until a second census on May 22, 1961, which included all the Arab inhabitants (see Table 1, Appendix).

It is clear from the census that up to the present the Arabs in Israel have remained at somewhere between 11 and 13 percent of the total population. In spite of the continual increase in the Jewish population—a result of immigration—the Arabs have been able to maintain this percentage because of their rate of population growth, said to be one of the highest in the world. At the same time, the number of Arabs leaving Israel has been low. In 1955, population increase among the Arabs reached 37.8 per thousand, compared with 26.3 per thousand among the Jews. In 1960 it rose to 44.8 per thousand, compared with 18.4 among the Jews; in 1965, 44.6 compared with 16.2; and in 1970, 39.1 compared with 16.9. Within the Arab population, the rate of increase is highest among the Moslems—43.7 per thousand in 1970—followed by the Druze, 37.5 per thousand, and then the Christians, 19.7 per thousand.

The Arab inhabitants of Israel live in three main areas. The majority, some 60 percent, are in Galilee in the north. "The Triangle" in the center of Israel is the home of about 30 percent. Though rectangular in shape, this area is called the Triangle because it was part of the Jenin-Nablus-Tulkarm Triangle, which was outside the boundaries of Israeli occupation. It was added to Israel after the ceasefire agreement with Jordan in April 1949. The remaining 10 percent live in the Negev in the south (see Appendix, Table 2). The density of settlement parallels the distribution of population (see Table 3): some 60 percent live in villages, 30 percent in cities, and 10 percent are nomadic. There are two Arab cities, Nazareth and Shafa Amr, in Galilee; six cities of mixed population, Acre, Haifa, Lydda, Ramle, Tel Aviv/Jaffa, and New Jerusalem; and 104 Arab villages, mostly in Galilee and the Triangle. There are also twenty-four Bedouin tribes, half living in the Negev and half in Galilee.

Table 4 shows the division of Arabs by faith: more than 70 percent are Moslem (Sunni), 20 percent are Christian, and 10 percent are Druze. Of the Christians, about 40 percent are

Roman Catholic and 30 percent Greek Orthodox.

Although every Arab in Israel is considered a citizen, he or she is not an Israeli national because to the Zionists Israel is before all else a Jewish state. This is made clear by the fact that every immigrant Jew is granted rights that exceed those of an Arab, even though the Arabs and their ancestors lived in Palestine before the state of Israel existed. This inevitably affects the Arabs. The announcement that "every Jew has the right to immigrate to Israel" was followed by the right to Israeli nationality with all the privileges it entails, almost by way of welcome. The Arab who stayed in Israel could not attain Israeli nationality unless he or she fulfilled various conditions, which were established with the purpose of rendering a considerable number ineligible. As many as a quarter could not meet the requirements.

With the passage of time these rulings have lost much of their edge, but their very existence is a testament to the fact that it is Israeli policy to regard even the highest status Arab under Israeli control as a second-class citizen.

I
The Military Government

"They take our land. Why? For security reasons! They take our jobs. Why? For security reasons! And when we ask them how it happens that we, our lands and our jobs threaten the security of the state—they do not tell us. Why not? For security reasons!"

—Walter Schwarz,
The Arabs in Israel (London, 1959), p. 15

"A dairy refused to employ an Arab recommended for a job because 'in times of war, milk is a strategic item and a disloyal Arab could do much damage.' "

—Ernest Stock,
From Conflict to Understanding (New York, 1968), p. 92

1
"For Security Reasons"

Security measures were probably the most significant aspect of Israel's policy toward the Arab minority after 1948. The military rule imposed from the early days of the newly created state affected all official dealings with the Arabs and contained their presence in the country. In spite of periodic changes and improvements, and eventually official elimination of the military government, the spirit of military rule remains. It would be difficult to appraise Israel's internal policy and its influence on the lives of the Arabs without first studying that government.

Military rule in Israel had its legal foundations in the British Mandatory Defense (Emergency) Regulations, 1945[1] and the Israeli Emergency (Security Zones) Regulations, 5709 of 1949.[2] The history of the 1945 regulations goes back to 1936 and the outbreak of the Arab Revolt in Palestine (1936-39).[3] At that time, the British High Commissioner gave special orders—in the form of Emergency Regulations, 1936—granting the British forces in Palestine the power to take all necessary steps to quell the revolt.[4] By 1937, with the revolt in full swing and likely to continue, the Mandate government felt the need to further extend those powers and passed the Palestine (Defense) Order in Council, 1937.[5] Article 6 entitled the High Commissioner to "make such ... 'defense regulations' as appear to him in his unfettered discretion to be necessary or expedient for securing the public safety ... and for maintaining supplies and services essential to the life of the community."

The same article provided that the High Commissioner could bring anyone disobeying these orders before a military court established by the regulations whether the offenses were made before or after such courts were established. Furthermore, the decisions of the military courts could not be appealed. The High Commissioner was also to be able to give instructions for detention, expulsion, or banishment from Palestine, seizure and control of property and land, or the imposition of fines. His orders could "amend any law, suspend the operation of any law, and apply any law with or without modification." Moreover, "any provision of a law which may be inconsistent with any defense regulation ... shall ... have no effect as long as such regulation ... shall remain in force." Finally, the validity of the provisions of the defense regulations were not to be questioned in any court or "in any other manner whatsoever."

In short, the Palestine (Defense) Order gave the Mandate government the legal and administrative freedom to carry out any action it might choose, however harsh or irregular. The population had no means of opposing or challenging such acts.

In 1937, using his power under the new act, the High Commissioner issued the Defense (Military Courts) Regulations, 1937, which were amended and added to until they were replaced by the Defense Regulations, 1939.[6] These too were modified to meet the needs of the situation, the quelling of the Arab Revolt. The Mandate government condemned many Arab insurgents to death, had thousands of Palestinians interned or banished, expropriated their property and blew up their houses. Many others were killed in clashes with the British forces.

In the short period of relative quiet between the end of the Arab Revolt and the outbreak of World War II in 1939, the Mandate government had no need to resort to the defense regulations. Shortly after the beginning of the war, however, they were used again, this time against the Jews in Palestine, whose Lehi organization (*Lochmei Herut Israel*—Fighters for the Freedom of Israel, otherwise known as the Stern Gang) had begun its activities against the British. By the end of the war, the defense regulations had proved to be the Mandate government's main weapon against Zionist military organizations. They made it possible to banish members of Lehi and I.Z.L. (*Irgun Zvai Leumi*—National Military Organization— which followed Lehi) to Eritrea and to intern dozens there for years; to search Jewish settlements for weapons; to arrest Jewish leaders and force them into the prison camp at Latrun; and to impose a curfew on the Jewish towns and settlements.[7] The defense regulations were continually modified and developed until they were published in their present form in 1945, although the British continued to introduce small changes until 1947.

Jewish opposition to the laws was intense and openly expressed on a number of occasions. One such protest was voiced at a conference of the Lawyers' Association in Tel Aviv on February 7, 1946, attended by about four hundred Jewish lawyers. Dr. Moshe Dunkelblum, who later became a Supreme Court judge, made the following comments:

> It is true that these laws threaten every Jewish settler, but, as lawyers, we are especially concerned because they violate the basic principles of law, justice, and jurisprudence. They give the military and administrative authorities absolute power which, even if it had been approved by a legislative body, would create a state of chaos ... The defense regulations abolish the rights of the individual and grant unlimited power to the administration. The aim of this conference is to express our position, both as settlers and as lawyers, on these laws which rob every settler of his basic rights, in violation of law, order, and justice.[8]

A more vigorous statement was that of Dr. Bernard Joseph, later Dov Joseph, of the Jewish Agency:

> As for these defense regulations, the question is: Are we all to become victims of officially licensed terrorism or will the freedom of the individual prevail? Is the administration to be allowed to interfere in the lives of the people with no protection for the individual? As it is, there is no guarantee to prevent a citizen from being imprisoned for life without trial. There is no protection for the freedom of the individual: there is no appeal against the

decision of the military commander, no means of resorting to the Supreme Court . . . while the administration has unrestricted freedom to banish any citizen at any moment. What is more, a man does not actually have to commit an offense; it is enough for a decision to be made in some office for his fate to be sealed. . . . The principle of collective responsibility has become a mockery. All of the six hundred thousand [Jewish] settlers could be hanged for a crime committed by one person in this country.

A citizen should not have to rely on the good will of an official, our lives and our property should not be placed in the hands of such an official.

There is no choice between freedom and anarchy. In a country where the administration itself inspires anger, resentment, and contempt for the laws, one cannot expect respect for the law. It is too much to ask of a citizen to respect a law that outlaws him.[9]

On a subsequent occasion Joseph described these laws as having "deprived [the country] of the elementary protection which the laws of any civilized country afford its inhabitants. . . . the regulations expressly reintroduce provisions such as were known in Europe before the era of liberty and, in recent times, in totalitarian states."[10]

Mr. Yaacov Shimshon Shapira, who was to become a legal advisor to the new government, was even more emphatic:

The established order in Palestine since the defense regulations is unparalleled in any civilized country. Even in Nazi Germany there were no such laws and the [Nazi] deeds of Mayadink and other similar things were against the code of laws. Only in an occupied country do you find a system resembling ours. They try to reassure us by saying that these laws apply only to offenders and not to the whole of the population, but the Nazi governor of occupied Oslo also said that no harm would come to those who minded their own business. . . .

It is our duty to tell the whole world that the defense regulations passed by the government in Palestine destroy the very foundations of justice in this land. It is mere euphemism to call the military courts "courts." To use the Nazi title, they are no better than "Military Judicial Committees Advising the Generals."

No government has the right to draw up such laws . . .[11]

At the close of the conference the following resolutions were passed:

1. The powers granted the authorities under the emergency regulations deprive the Palestinian citizen of the fundamental rights of man.
2. These regulations undermine law and justice, and constitute a grave danger to the life and liberty of the individual, establishing a rule of violence without any judicial control. [The conference] demands the repeal of these laws. . . .[12]

With the establishment of the state of Israel, one might have expected one of its first steps to have been the repeal of these oppressive imperialist laws. Not only did they remain in effect (with the exception of one part relating to illegal immigration to Palestine), but the new regime employed them as extensively as the old—as if nothing had happened.[13] The leaders changed their tune overnight. The lawyers, too, seemed to have forgotten their earlier resolutions, since it was they who, as judges or legal advisors to the government, developed and interpreted the emergency regulations in such a way as to increase the power of the authorities.

There was in fact some attempt by members of Israel's judicial apparatus to repeal the regulations by refusing to be bound by them. For example, Shalom Kassan, a judge of Israel's Supreme Court of Justice, reviewed the first appeal after the establishment of the state (a request for the repeal of an administrative arrest order) and refused to apply the regulations because in his judgment they were illegal.

Everyone knows that all groups and classes of Jewish settlers in this country, and the Jewish people in exile, have protested violently against the defense regulations and have submitted petitions against them in the strongest language on every possible occasion. Why? Because these laws abolish the rights of citizens and, in particular, the control of the competent courts over the actions of the authorities. . . . These emergency regulations cover dozens of pages with their 14 chapters and some 150 articles, most of them long and complicated with a variety of clauses, but all of them sharing the single aim of suspending the building of a national home. . . . These laws and their aims are well known to Israel's defense minister [David Ben-Gurion] . . . as they are known to the government's legal advisor [Yaacov Shimshon Shapira, whose position is equivalent to that of an attorney general]. . . . Both these gentlemen were among the first to fight these laws. . . . I cannot act and pass judgment in accordance with the defense regulations which are still on the statute book. Believing as I do that these laws are essentially invalid, I should not be asked to act against my conscience merely because the present government has not yet officially repealed them, though its members declared them illegal as soon as they were passed. . . . If the courts of the British Mandate did not cross these laws off the statute book, this court is honorbound to do so and to utterly eradicate them.[14]

This remained a minority view without influence, coinciding with neither the opinions of other judges nor with the political leadership. Nevertheless, the debate over whether it was legal or moral for Israel's government to continue to enforce laws that had been so violently opposed during the Mandate went on until Ben-Gurion cut it short with this statement: "We opposed this law of the Mandate government because a foreign government, neither elected by us, nor responsible to us, had given itself the right to detain any one of us without trial. In the present instance the law is being applied by the state of Israel, through a government chosen by the people and responsible to them."[15]

Although the emergency regulations have generally been applied only against the Arab population, the Israeli government has not refrained from using them against Jews. Less than six weeks after the establishment of Israel, on 30 June 1948, the authorities ordered the administrative arrest of some members of I.Z.L. on the charges that they were connected with bringing the munitions ship *Altalena* to Tel Aviv.[16] Similar orders were given to dissolve Lehi and arrest its members after the assassination of Count Bernadotte, a United Nations mediator, during the summer of 1948.[17] Yet very few people were actually arrested and by the summer of 1949 only eight were still in prison under the emergency regulations.[18]

Then, in 1951, the government found itself in a situation so embarrassing that it immediately stopped the practice. At the beginning of that year Israeli intelligence had traced a plan to bomb members of the Israeli government during a Knesset session to a conservative group of Orthodox Jews who wanted to protest the government's approval of recruiting women into the army. As a result, administrative arrests were made and the police took members of the group from Jerusalem to an army camp in the north. Their ill-treatment there brought an investigation of the entire incident onto the Knesset's agenda.

The case had wide repercussions. The government came under severe criticism in the Knesset from most members of the opposition, and its own members were forced to remain neutral. For seven months the case remained under investigation; fourteen sessions were held to discuss it; and it was not until the end of 1951, after committee findings had been published in detail, that it was removed from the agenda.[19] Those responsible for the ill-treatment were brought to trial.

After this no Jews in Israel suffered the effects of the emergency regulations until after the 1967 War, when some of the less important restraints were enforced (for example, Jewish women married to Arabs needed written permits, as did their husbands, to visit the newly occupied territories). The laws were almost exclusively applied against the Arab population.

In 1950, two years after the state's establishment, the Israeli government organized a system of military government to handle its relations with the Arabs in Israel. Before that, the Israeli army had dealt directly with the Arab population in the areas it occupied, both within the state of Israel, as defined by the 1947 United Nations Partition Plan, and outside it. Army treatment of the Arabs did not differ very much from that of any occupation force in an occupied territory: Arabs were attacked, their property was confiscated, and they were forcefully expelled. When the Israeli government was established, early in 1949, a commission was appointed to study the situation and, on its recommendation, the military apparatus was instituted.[20] All matters relating to Arabs living in the cities were handled by the police; military governors were put in charge of Arabs elsewhere. Simultaneously, the emergency regulations began to be officially enforced. "The military government was formally and legally established in January 1950, based on the Defense (Emergency) Regulations, 1945, which gave the military governors the power to appoint military commanders, while the judicial powers were entrusted to military courts appointed by the army chief of staff."[21]

After the formal adoption of the emergency regulations, the minister of defense used the powers granted him to appoint military governors for the three principal regions in Israel inhabited by Arabs: Galilee (military government in the north), the Triangle (military government in the central area), and the south (military government of the Negev).

The defense regulations themselves, worded in great detail, are a typical example of the traditional imperialist attitude in dealing with the native population of a colony. They give the authorities extensive and extremely rigorous powers, and their enforcement can destroy individual freedom and individual rights to property almost completely. They cover every aspect of life, from control over the freedom of speech, movement, and the press to the regulation of the possession of arms, the expropriation of property, and the control of means of transportation. Some of their more important provisions are as follows.

Concerning freedom of expression, Article 142 states that "any person who endeavors, whether orally or otherwise, to influence public opinion in a manner likely to be prejudicial to public safety, defense or the maintenance of public order" shall be considered as having committed a crime. Similarly, Article 109(I)(d) says that restrictions can be imposed on any person "in respect of his employment or business, in respect of his association or communications with other persons, and in respect of his activities in relation to the dissemination of news or the propagation of opinions." In addition, "no notice, illustration, placard, advertisement, proclamation, pamphlet or other like document containing matter of political significance . . . shall be printed or published in Israel" without first obtaining a permit. The district commissioner can grant or refuse the permit "without assigning any reason therefore" (Articles 94 and 96). The press censor has the right to prevent the publication of any material he considers harmful to the security of the nation or the welfare of the people; he can forbid the importation or distribution of such material and force editors, printers, writers, and journalists to submit all articles for his approval before publication.

Articles 122 and 126 empowered the military governor to "prevent, limit, or supervise . . . the use of specific roads or roads generally"; Article 129 enabled him to "order the owners or foremen of stores and workshops . . should he have reason to believe that they have been shut as a result of a general or organized strike . . . to reopen them and work as usual . . . or conversely . . . order the shops shut for a determined period"; Article 119 allowed him to "order the confiscation . . . of any house, building, or piece of land if he has reason to suspect that guns have been fired . . . or bombs, explosives, or fire illegally set off from that property; and the confiscation of any house, building, or piece of land lying within a region, town, village, neighborhood, or street if he is convinced that the inhabitants of that region, town, village, neighborhood, or street have committed, attempted, or aided and abetted a crime or were accessories after the fact to a crime."

The Israeli authorities did not, in fact, use the above-mentioned powers against the Arabs except in rare cases and in emergencies.[22] For reasons to be explored later, they preferred other articles. The most notorious was Article 125, which "grants the military governor the power to proclaim any area or place a forbidden [closed] area . . . which no one can enter or leave without . . . a written permit from the military commander or his deputy . . . failing which he is considered to have committed a crime." Thus all the Arab villages and settlements in Galilee, the Triangle, and the Negev were divided into small pockets called "closed areas,"

usually consisting of one or more Arab villages, which no
Arab could leave or enter for any reason without first obtaining a written permit from the military governor of the area.[23]

Two other articles were popular with the military government. Article 109 gave it the power to force any person to
live in any place designated by the military governor (banishment) or to remain at his or her place of residence for an
appointed length of time, "reporting his movements to the
authorities or to appointed persons . . . at set times according
to instructions. . . ." Restrictions could also be placed on a
person's "purchase and use of certain materials or he could
be forbidden the purchase or use of any determined
material." Article 110 allowed the military governor "to have
any person . . . placed under police supervision for any length
of time not exceeding one year," a period subject to renewal
at its expiration. A person under police supervision had to
comply with restrictions imposed by the military governor:
"he must reside within any area in Israel that may be designated in the military governor's order . . . being unable to
move to any police precinct within the same district without
written permit from the chief of police in that district, or to
any police precinct outside the district without written
authorization from the inspector of police. He cannot leave
the town, village, or district in which he resides without obtaining written authorization from the district chief of police;
he must always inform the police officer assigned to him of
his address . . . and he must remain at his residence from one
hour after sunset until sunrise, being subject to a police
checkup at his place of residence at any time."

The military governor also implemented Article 111,
which permitted the "detention of any person named in the
[military governor's] order for a period not exceeding one
year [subject to renewal] at any detention camp mentioned
in the order," without bringing charges against the detainee
and without a trial.

Other articles invoked were Article 124, to impose total or
partial curfew in any village or area, and Article 137, to
control the sale, use, and possession of firearms; to forbid,

restrict, and regulate the purchase or sale of arms, ammunition, and explosives; and to withdraw or limit all permits to carry arms.[24]

To ensure compliance with these articles, a special network of military courts was established. Military courts are of two kinds: (1) Military courts that consist of a president, "who must be a senior officer, and two other members of officer rank. These are appointed by the army chief of staff . . ."— previously the General of the British Forces in Palestine (Article 13). This court is empowered to try all offenses against the defense regulations and, in practice, to impose any penalty that the district court can impose, including life imprisonment and death (there are twenty offenses punishable by death in the regulations). These courts do not exist on a regular basis but are convened periodically for specific cases.[25] (2) Summary military courts, consisting of one officer (Article 156). These courts can impose prison sentences not exceeding two years or fines up to £3000 (Israeli) (later increased to £5000). Three such courts were established and still function regularly: one in Nazareth, attached to the military government in the north (Galilee); another in Kfar Yonah for the military government in the central area (the Triangle); and the last in Beersheba for the military government in the Negev.

When the defense regulations were passed, Articles 30, 46, 47, 48, and 50 stipulated that there was no appeal to any other court, military or civil, from the judgments of the military courts, but that the highest military authority, represented by the army chief of staff, had the power to reduce or even quash the sentences passed by these courts or to order a retrial. In 1963 some provision for repeal was made, as will be discussed.

The decision to enforce the restrictions on movement (Article 109), police supervision (Article 110), administrative detention (Article 111), curfew (Article 124), closed areas and travel permits (Article 125), and weapons licenses (Article 137) was left to the military governor, who could impose them, under Article 108, at any time he considered it necessary "for securing the public safety, the defense of Israel, the maintenance of public order, or the suppression of mutiny, rebellion, or riot." This extremely wide definition in practice enabled the military government to interfere in every aspect of the lives of the citizens under its rule. It formed a state within a state, with its own "legislative," judicial, and executive powers. The mere enforcement of these powers, quite apart from their abuse, could be extremely prejudicial to the citizen against whom they were used.

The military government quickly became an absolute power in the areas it controlled, with the freedom to act exactly as it chose, unhampered by administrative restraints. Judicial control was restricted to the possibility of appealing to the Supreme Court of Justice to challenge the legality of the military government's actions. Time proved that there was no practical advantage in doing this, since the Supreme Court made it a rule not to interfere with the military government when its actions were based on "security reasons." It was impossible even to question the military governors, or their representatives, about the nature of the "security reasons" since that could be prejudicial to the state's security. Thus with the passage of time the Supreme Court in fact extended the powers of the military government, while claiming that its own supervisory powers were progressively diminishing.

This principle was established and vindicated in a long series of judgments. For example, in Appeal 53/197, the court's ruling included the following: "The object of the defendant's order [to impose police supervision on the plaintiff] was to ensure the safety of the people and public order. We have no right to express an opinion on the efficacy of this method. It is left to the absolute discretion of the defendant [the military governor] . . . and we see no justification for interference in the matter."[26]

In the ruling on Appeal 50/46 the statement appeared that:

The power of this court to criticize the competent authority when acting in accordance with the Defense (Emergency) Regulations, 1945 is extremely limited. When an article of the law grants the competent authority freedom of action as regards the individual, in all cases in which "it thinks" or "is of the opinion" that the circumstances warrant such action, the competent authority in effect becomes the final judge of the matter, being the sole authority in possession of the details of the case ... while the Supreme Court's restricted powers do not allow it to inquire into the competent authority's motives in issuing the order in question.[27]

In Appeal 59/126 the ruling included the following: "It should be noted that this power [to order banishment, detention, etc.] is very extensive. It is the [military] commander and not the court who can, at his discretion, issue an order on the mere grounds that it appears to be desirable."[28]

These rulings granted immunity to the military government, especially the decision that it is not possible to question the governors in court, which made it impossible to discover the true motives behind their actions. Any effort in this direction was firmly rejected by the Supreme Court in Appeal 50/46:

The responsibility for protecting the higher interests of the state rests on the *military commander* [italics in the original] and it is up to him to decide whether these interests prevent him from revealing any additional details explaining the basis for his orders. In other words, the justification for imposing supervision (which is subject to criticism by this court only within the narrow limits allowed) is the same as that used to justify the strict secrecy surrounding the details of such matters.

Another appeal, 53/111, states:

A public authority must not be obliged to submit to the court verbal or written proofs, the disclosure of which might endanger vital affairs of state, including security matters ... in particular, it is forbidden to reveal the public authority's source of information ... and the same degree of caution is required not only with regard to sources of the information, but also its significance.[29]

With these and similar precedents, it became the practice of the military government, whenever its conduct was challenged, to submit to the court a certificate signed by the minister of defense stating that the reasons for the action were related to "security," thus guaranteeing that, even had it been so inclined, the court would not interfere. These certificates became such normal procedure that the Supreme Court found it appropriate to state in a ruling:

> We must here establish that there is no magic in the words "for security reasons," or "state of security," or other such expression that can justify the actions of the competent authority or prevent this court from inquiring into the justice of such actions. If it appears to the court that these words are being used merely to cover harsh or arbitrary and illegal action, it will not hesitate to say so openly, for the sake of truth and to ensure that justice is done.[30]

How the court was to be sure that "such expressions" were not abused is found in the same ruling: "We have only two alternatives: either we believe that what the military governor says is the truth, and that security considerations were uppermost in his mind when he gave the expulsion order, or we reject what he says completely and say that we do not believe it."[31]

This became the established principle. As it was impossible to disclose the "security reasons" or to investigate them, the Supreme Court had merely to decide whether to believe the word of the citizen or that of the military governor—and of course in most cases the scales were weighted in favor of the latter.

As a result of the Supreme Court's attitude, arbitrary conduct was reinforced. Using the excuse that it needed freedom of action to protect the nation's security, the military government went beyond all effective control. The Supreme Court increasingly identified with the military government, at times almost adopting that government's position and doing its best to legally justify its actions. In several rulings the Supreme

Court implicitly accepted the extension of the military government's sphere into situations that had no bearing on security. For example, Appeal 56/146 involved "mediation" by the military government in the affairs of a local council; Appeal 57/92 challenged the military government's denial of a permit to enter a closed area: a farmer wanting to farm the land was turned down until he had established ownership or lease of the land.[32] Appeal 59/126 had requested repeal of an expulsion order against a villager from Tayba in the Triangle who had distributed leaflets in his village.[33] All these cases quite clearly come under the jurisdiction of the civil courts. As a direct result of the Supreme Court's attitude, most of the Arabs suffering damage from military government action have not even appealed, considering it a useless procedure.[34]

Thus, armed with all these powers and protected by the cover of "security reasons," the military government was able to deal with the Arabs in Israel with immunity from almost all interference in its decisions and conduct.

Since Article 125, which deals with closed areas, is particularly notorious and has been used a great deal, it merits a more detailed discussion. The precise frontiers of the military government areas and the closed areas were known to no one but the staff of the military government, which alone had the relevant maps. The military government never published the extent of the areas under its control and very rarely disclosed anything about its activities.[35] Anyone wanting to find out which areas he or she could visit without a permit had to go to one of the few military government offices or to a police station, which could rarely provide the information. Anyone entering or leaving a closed area without a permit is liable to prosecution for breaking the emergency regulations, despite the fact that he or she does not, and cannot, know the boundaries. Ignorance is not a valid excuse before a military court.

With the passage of time, however, most citizens have come to know the boundaries, either through daily contact with the military government, from information leaked to the press, or from various government documents. Perhaps the most reliable description of the administrative composition of the military government was one published in a report by the state controller.[36]

According to Article 6 of the Defense Regulations, military governors have been appointed to the following areas:

1. The north, including the whole of Galilee, Acre, the plain of Beisan, and Marj ibn Amer, including the town of Afula, but not the Carmel area and the Zebulun Plain [the coastal plain between Haifa and Acre].[37]

2. The central region, including the Triangle and Wadi Ara.

3. The Negev, including the whole of the Negev and Wadi Arava.

These areas are subdivided into a number of smaller areas, in each of which a branch of the military government acts as liaison with the local inhabitants on matters relating to the functions of the military government.

The branches are as follows:

(a) In the military government in the north there are five branches in the following places: (i) Nazareth: serving the city of Nazareth and the neighboring villages. (ii) Nazareth: serving eastern Galilee, that is, the villages on Mount Tabor as far as Safad. (iii) Shafa Amr: serving Shafa Amr and the villages nearby, the villages of the Battuf Plain and Sachnin. (iv) Tarshiha-Ma'una: serving the villages of western Galilee. (v) Majd al-Kurum: serving the Kurum Plain and the village of Jish. [An additional branch was later set up in Acre.]

(b) The military government in the central area has the following three branches: (i) Ara: covering the area around this village and Umm al Fahm. (ii) Baqa al Gharbiya: covering Baqa, Jatt, and the surrounding villages. (iii) Tayba: covering Tayba, Tira, and Jaljulya.

(c) In the military government area in the south there are two branches: (i) Shuval: including the tribes of (a) Huzayyel, (b) Asad, (c) Aqabi, (d) Atauni, (e) Abu Bilal, (f) Afunish, (g) Qulaiq, and (h) Talaliqa, whose migration area lies east of the Beersheba road to the [1949] armistice lines with Jordan, and as far south as the Beersheba–Tel Yeroham road and west to Wadi Utayyir.

There are in the northern military government area . . . Arabs living in 65 villages and small towns . . . in the central area . . . 28

villages [in all, 93 villages out of a total of 104 Arab villages are in these areas], while in the south there . . . are the Bedouins, eighteen tribes altogether.

Of the areas declared closed the state controller's report goes on to say:

In accordance with Article 125, large parts of the areas under military government have been declared closed areas:

1. The area under military government in the north is divided into fourteen areas [previously fifteen]. . . . Details of the northern area follow:

(a) Area no. 1. This is a Jewish area consisting of Jewish colonies stretching along the whole of the frontier with Lebanon, Syria, and Jordan.[38]

(b) Areas no. 2, 4, and 5 (Area no. 3 has been abolished). These areas are inhabited by Bedouin tribes living near the frontiers with Lebanon, Syria, and Jordan.

(c) Areas no. 6 to 14. These are of mixed population, though the majority is Jewish. They run parallel with Area no. 1 [on the frontier] and include the towns of Safad, Afula, and Nahariya.

(d) Area no. 15. This is an Arab area covering the rest of Galilee, including the town of Nazareth. Most of the Arab population of the northern area is concentrated here.[39]

2. The whole of the central area under military government [the Triangle] constitutes a single closed area.

3. The area under military government in the Negev has one closed area stretching north and east of Beersheba. It is the area inhabited by the Bedouins and does not include the city of Beersheba.[40]

It should not be assumed that these statements are strictly accurate: it is well known, for instance, that in the area controlled by the military government in the north (Galilee), there are more than ten other closed areas, small ghettos within the larger closed area. Some of these consist of demolished Arab villages which were declared closed to prevent those of the inhabitants who live inside Israel from returning. The rest are used for training the Israeli army or have been declared closed to facilitate their expropriation from their Arab owners, as happened in the villages of

Sachnin and Araba in the Battuf Plain, where the canal diverting Jordan River water to the Negev passes, or in the lands of the villages of Deir al Asad, Bi'na, and Majd al Kurum, which were confiscated so that the Jewish town of Carmiel might be built (see Chapter 5). In December 1955 some seventy-four thousand dunums of land in central Galilee and in June 1959 an area near Baqa al Gharbiya in the Triangle were declared closed for army maneuvers. According to some estimates, until 1954 there were fifty-four closed areas in Galilee, after which only one-third remained.[41] But, as indicated previously, it is difficult to obtain precise information.

The defense regulations were, in theory, in effect throughout Israel, but in fact until the end of 1966 they were most frequently enforced in the areas subject to the military governors. Indeed, they were enforced in their full rigor against the Arabs alone, whether they lived under military government or not. And although Arabs outside military government areas were subject to travel restrictions (including entry into military government areas without special authorization), the Arabs under military government endured the full effect of liability to police supervision, banishment, administrative detention, and so on. The Jews, on the other hand, whether inside or outside the areas, are not touched by the regulations. This policy was described in the state controller's report:

> An order from the military governor declaring an area closed is, in theory, applicable to all citizens without exception whether living in the area or outside it. Thus anyone who enters or leaves a closed area without a written permit from the military governor is in fact committing a criminal offense. In practice, however, Jews are not expected to carry such permits and in general are not prosecuted for breaking the regulations in Article 125 ... There is something wrong in this law, which was drafted to apply to all citizens in the country but is in fact enforced only against some of them.[42]

The practice of making distinctions between Arabs and Jews continued until the end of 1966 when the whole system of military government was dismantled. But the changes made at that time simply resulted in the laws being applied to the entire Arab population, whether living inside an old military government area or not, while the Jewish population continued to enjoy full immunity.

From the outset, the military government was created as an important tool to help the government carry out its policy toward the Arabs. As such, it is not surprising that whenever a particular policy was officially approved, some relevant modification appeared in the military government's style. Policy was seldom stable, but fluctuated according to the government's plans. There have been three major phases so far: the first from 1948 to mid-1959, the second from 1959 to the end of 1966, and the third from 1967 to the present.

The distinguishing feature of the first phase was a clearly aggressive policy of cruelly oppressive measures against the Arabs. Most significant was the seizure of hundreds of thousands of dunums of Arab land and the strict enforcement of the regulations, including Article 125, a sword of Damocles hanging over Arab heads. The mere threat of its use was sufficient to crush the opposition of any Arab peasant, worker, or simple citizen who "dared" resist the military government for any reason. And it is no wonder, since the refusal of a permit to enter or leave a closed area meant that a worker, for example, could not get to his place of work or a peasant to his land.[43] Usually the confinement to a village or a particular area and the consequent inability to go to work continued for an unlimited period. These restrictions were most frequently used against Arabs connected with political organizations or engaged in independent social and cultural activities disapproved of by the military government.

The imposition of travel restrictions was so frequent in Israel's first years that the military and civilian police made a habit of stopping both public and private traffic, especially on the main roads and sometimes daily, in order to check Arab identity cards. Those without travel permits, whatever the explanation, were arrested and driven off to prison, and

from there they were taken before a military court.[44] Dozens,
sometimes hundreds, of Arabs were convicted each month on
charges of having broken the travel restrictions. The large
number of convictions, fines, and prison sentences gives a
clear indication of the extent to which the military government used its powers.[45]

For all their harshness, the travel restrictions proved especially ineffective against political activists who openly condemned and worked against the military government, endur-
ing or even ignoring the restrictions. The military government
was chary of carrying out further punitive measures—such as
banishment, police supervision, and administrative detention
—and only did so after "admonishing," threatening, or otherwise pressuring the "candidate." Then, if he or she still failed
to return to "the straight and narrow path," several measures
were simultaneously enforced. For example, in addition to
ordering banishment, which meant living in some remote
place without a house of one's own and no means of providing for self or family—a person might be forced to stay home
between sunset and sunrise and be required to report to the
nearest police station at least once a day.[46]

Thus, for example, on 19 June 1953, twelve members of
the Shibli Bedouin tribe, which lives near Mount Tabor, were
exiled to the village of Mi'lya in western Galilee and ordered
to report to the police station in Tarshiha twice a day.[47] Nine
inhabitants of the Triangle were banished in January 1957 to
the village of Beisan in Upper Galilee and ordered to report
daily for a month to the police station in Tarshiha, some
twenty kilometers away.[48] Similarly, in September 1957, the
military governor ordered five men from Baqa al Gharbiya in
the Triangle to report twice a day to the police station in
Bardas Hanna, fifteen kilometers away. A particularly cruel
and "amusing" order was issued in August 1958 in the case
of a Bedouin named Ahmad Hasan from the Al-Wadi tribe
near the village of Arava in Galilee. The military governor
ordered him to sit every day for six months, from sunrise to
sunset, under a large carob tree which stands to the west of

the village of Deir Hanna. The purpose was to prevent him from contacting smugglers.

Other examples abound for the years 1953 to 1958 when banishment was frequently used. Those described were "normal" incidents in which the military government used its power to protect "national security." The punitive measures were noticeably more vicious in cases where a political point was to be made or where awe and respect for the authorities was desired. For example, in August 1953 three young men were banished from the village of Mazra'a, near Acre, to Beersheba for a year, while seven others were ordered to report to the Acre police station twice a day for three months because they had "made fun" of a portrait of Theodor Herzl, the proponent of a Jewish state, when it appeared on the screen during a film in a Nahariya cinema.[49] At the end of March 1954, when the villagers of Arava in Galilee began a protest against paying certain taxes, the military governor ordered the imprisonment of four village elders for one month as a way of "influencing" the younger men and inducing them to temper their opposition. Eight others were ordered to make a daily appearance at the police station in Majd al Kurum, and when one of these failed to do so he was sentenced to three months' imprisonment.[50] In May 1956, Muhammad Al Sharidi of Umm al Fahm and Othman Abu Ras of Tayba were sentenced to twelve and fifteen months' imprisonment respectively for having "insulted the military governor and caused a disturbance in his office."[51] No doubt these heavy penalties for relatively petty misdemeanors were not unconnected with the fact that each man worked as Communist Party secretary in his village.

Besides banishment and police supervision, the military government used administrative arrest, under Article 111, to detain any person without trial or charges beyond the vague one of being a "security risk." In effect, it had the power to hold any person for as long as it chose. Only the army chief of staff could order detention for a year, renewable at the end of the year, but the military governors were allowed to order detentions of one month, also renewable at expiration. The detainee in these circumstances could appeal to an advisory committee of three persons headed by a judge of the Supreme Court (the Vitcon Committee or the Sussman Committee or the Mani Committee, from the names of the three Supreme Court judges who have been heads of the committee thus far). But the decisions of the committee, as the name indicates, were merely advisory and the military government was not bound by them. It became customary for the detainee to be sent out of the room, after stating his case, while the committee heard the response of the military governor or his representative. The detainee was not allowed to hear why he has been detained; nor was he allowed to reply in his own defense, for reasons of "security." Under such conditions the committee made its recommendations.

The military government always made frequent use of Article 111. From the sparse information available, it appears that during the period 1956-57, 315 administrative detention orders were issued, an average of almost one every two days.[52] Dozens of banishment and detention orders were issued after the 1958 May Day demonstrations and again after the establishment of the (Arab) Popular Front that summer.

Article 124 was equally popular with the military government and for a period of fourteen years was employed to impose curfews in all the Arab villages of the Triangle for most of the night. On entering the Triangle after the armistice agreement with Jordan in 1949, the Israeli forces "imposed a curfew on all roads and thoroughfares from sunset to sunrise and inside the villages from 8 P.M. until 5 A.M. Then in January [1953] ... the curfew on all roads, thoroughfares, and villages was reduced to the hours between 10 P.M. and 4 A.M."[53] The curfew was not lifted until February 1962. In other areas subject to military government there was no permanent curfew, but it was imposed for short periods according to circumstances.

In addition to inequitable enforcement of the regulations, Arab citizens received unfair adjudication of offenses by the military courts. The judges, army officers appointed by the chief of staff and legally subject to his authority, are neither personally nor objectively independent. Hence the courts become administrative institutions attached to the military government, implementing the instructions of its various branches and perhaps even making dictated decisions. The procedure followed differs from that in all other Israeli courts, civil or military. Since the original judges were British officers, the Mandate government decided that it would be simpler to employ the British rules of evidence; even after the establishment of Israel no change was made.[54] Arabs appearing before these courts seem to be expected to be familiar with these rules of evidence. In addition, when appeal was finally provided for, on July 18, 1963, it was only to the Military Court of Appeals attached to the Israeli army. (It should also be pointed out that this amendment was made through the military justice law, not by changing the "sacred" and inviolate defense regulations.)

Most of the offenses the military courts are empowered to try, and for which they inflict extremely severe sentences, are also within the jurisdiction of the civil courts. The attorney general must decide whether cases shall be tried in civil or military courts, but in the great majority of cases he chooses the latter.

From the beginning, the military government had met with criticism from many different groups and for very different reasons. Arab opposition was continuous. The harshness and pettiness with which restrictions were enforced drew criticism from every political party except the dominant Mapai (Party of the Workers of the Land of Israel), which had used the military system to obtain its political objectives among the Arabs. Ideological opposition came from parties and groups who disapproved of discrimination against those Arabs in Israel who were officially considered Israeli citizens. It was felt that such open and shameless discrimination would inevitably have a harmful effect on the nature of the Israeli government in general, and would eventually affect Jews also.

The first blow against the military government, though spiritual rather than real, came from the government itself. In July 1949 a defense and security bill was introduced in the Knesset, which, among other things, aimed at repealing the emergency regulations. After using a number of less than complimentary epithets to describe the regulations, the minister of justice said that they would be replaced by a number of clauses in the proposed bill.[55] In the end the bill was not approved "because of objections to it in the Knesset and among the people," according to the minister.[56] His derogatory description continued to ring in people's ears, however, and the opponents of military government continued to bring the matter to the attention of the government.

Not more than ten months after the bill's rejection, in May 1950, Aharon Zisling of Mapam (United Workers' Party) proposed the repeal of the defense regulations within three months. The suggestion was turned over to the Knesset Committee on Constitution, Law, and Justice for study, after the minister of justice had declared his support.[57] The committee's findings proved inconclusive, and Zisling again proposed that the military government be abolished in one year, by May 1951, on the grounds that "its existence is not in the best interests of the nation nor conducive to its security and does not contribute to the better administration of the areas under its control, being a restriction on the freedom of the people."[58] This time his proposal was turned over to the Knesset Foreign Affairs and Security Committee. After only one week's discussion, amidst the flurry of investigation into the ill-treatment of the Orthodox Jews detained on conspiracy charges, the Knesset declared that "the Defense (Emergency) Regulations, 1945, which have been effective since the time of the British Mandate, are incompatible with the principles of a democratic state" and asked that "the Committee on Constitution, Law, and Justice . . . present a new bill on the defense of the state, within two weeks."[59] Indeed, two weeks later the Knesset did come back to the subject, but the new bill had not been prepared. The whole question was then abandoned until the end of 1951 when the

Foreign Affairs and Security Committee, commenting on Zisling's proposal, declared (over the objections of the Mapam representative on the committee) that "as long as the present security situation between the state of Israel and its neighbors continues, the military government has to be maintained for the protection of the nation."[60] This conclusion was approved by the Knesset in February 1952.[61]

After this temporary victory, the military government's treatment of the Arabs was especially severe, and between the years 1953 and 1956 many restrictions were imposed.[62] In heated, behind-the-scenes struggles about Israel's attitude toward the Arab world and its interalliances, the Arabs inside Israel seem to have become a scapegoat for conservative elements. Although Ben-Gurion formally resigned as prime minister during this period, his presence continued to be felt in the ruling party, and his supporters, who eventually restored him to his position, maintained his policy of open hostility toward the Arab world and oppressive measures against Arabs in Israel. The hostility reached a climax during the triple attack on Egypt in 1956.

At the same time, opposition to the military government seemed at its weakest. When Meir Vilner proposed to the Knesset, in the name of the Israeli Communist Party, that Article 125 of the emergency regulations and the system of closed areas be abolished on the grounds that "the military governors have lately made a habit of declaring whole villages and stretches of land 'closed areas' within the larger closed area under military government, in order to prevent Arab peasants from working their land," his proposal was crossed off the agenda.[63] In October 1955 the military government went further and the governor for the northern region ordered all Arabs in his area to stay out of the Jewish colonies, giving as his reason that "he could not control the increasing infiltration of the agricultural colonies by minority laborers who were becoming permanently employed in various fields."[64] In other words, he was forbidding Arabs to work in Jewish colonies. In periods of unemployment it was usual for the military government to resort to withholding travel permits to prevent Arab laborers from reaching their places of work in the cities, thus ensuring work for the Jews.[65]

Another factor that was eventually to check the career of the military government and turn public opinion against it began to come into focus at this time. This was the "discovery" by the other Zionist parties, as well as the ruling Mapai party, of the possibility of winning Arab votes in Knesset and local elections. Indeed, during the first six months of 1955 the General Zionist Party was noticeably active among the Arabs, preparing the ground for the third Knesset elections, which took place on July 26, 1955. This led to conflict between the ministry of interior, then headed by a General Zionist, and the military government, and to mutual accusations by Mapai and the General Zionists of hindering the abolition of the military government, or, at least, the alleviation of its restrictions. In the midst of this, the Israeli Communist Party and Mapam each proposed a bill to abolish the military government as a way of forcing the parties in the government coalition to show their cards or, in the words of Mapam member Rustum Bastuni, "to make clear the position of the various parties on the Arab question in general and the military government in particular, a matter of considerable importance when every political faction in the country is demonstrating its sympathy for the Arab population."[66] But both bills were removed from the agenda.

These efforts were not wasted. The results of the third Knesset elections showed a loss of support for Mapai, and in order to form a new government Mapai had to form a coalition with Mapam and Achdut Haavoda, both of which insisted on a review of government policy toward the Arabs and on taking whatever action necessary to bring about equality between Arabs and Jews. Thus in early December 1955, Prime Minister Ben-Gurion appointed a three-member committee headed by Professor Yochanan Ratner of the Technion (the Institute of Applied Technology in Haifa) and including Daniel Auster, ex-mayor of Jerusalem, and Jacob Solomon, a lawyer from Haifa, to look into the question of military government and make recommendations. The committee report, presented in March 1956, provided "complete justification for the government's policy."[67] It stated that "the areas under military government and the scope of the activities of the military commander should not be abolished or reduced," because

> these areas are of supreme importance from the security point of view, and need to be kept under control, since they might be made use of by the enemy in an emergency. There is no doubt that the Arab states count on local support from Israeli Arabs when the proper time comes. . . . Even today part of the Arab population in Israel maintains contact with the enemy, though this contact seldom takes the form of obvious sabotage.[68]

There was strong reaction to this report at all levels, but it soon faded in the face of the growing security crisis caused by Arab guerrilla raids into Israel from the West Bank and the Gaza strip in the spring and by the nationalization of the Suez Canal Company in the summer.

A slight alleviation in the system of travel permits was introduced at the beginning of July 1957, when the government announced that Arabs in Galilee could travel to the cities of Nazareth, Acre, and Afula without permits; the curfew in the Triangle was reduced by a few hours a night; and the Tira-Ramat-Hakovesh-Tel Aviv road, the main highway in the area, was opened to free travel. But major changes would have to await the advent of the fourth Knesset elections.

2
Toward
a
New
Policy
1959-1966

During 1959, as the fourth Knesset elections approached in November, there was much concern over the continuation of military government. Bills abolishing it or alleviating it were presented in the Knesset by four different factions: the Israeli Communist Party, Mapam, Achdut Haavoda, and the General Zionists.[1] Obviously, some of these were no more than attempts to attract Arab votes, especially since the government had already appointed a ministerial committee to reappraise the military government.[2] According to quasi-official reports leaked to the press, the committee was about to recommend "extensive improvements for the Arab minority."[3]

Then, on August 5, 1959, Prime Minister Ben-Gurion announced that his government had decided to adopt a new policy with regard to the military government. This was in partial response to the recommendations of the ministerial committee. The most notable changes were in the system of travel restrictions. In Ben-Gurion's own words:

The government has approved a series of resolutions in favor of free travel in the military government areas. (a) In the Negev, the Bedouins now have two days on which they can travel to Beersheba without permits. [Since 1957 they had been allowed to come into Beersheba without permits on only one day a week.] (b) In the Triangle, the population can now travel without permits during daylight hours to the local centers of: Acre, Haifa, Hadera, Natanya, Petah Tikva, Tel Aviv–Jaffa, Lydda, and Ramle. (c) In the north the population can now travel during daylights hours without permits to the local centers of: Afula and Nahariya.

Security areas and Area no. A, near Israel's northeastern borders with Lebanon, Syria, and Jordan, were not included. In conclusion, Ben-Gurion stressed that "these alleviations will enable the people to travel freely for purposes of work, education, trade, and general services, removing the main burden of the system of travel restrictions of the past."[4]

If these improvements seem marginal, they were, in fact, only a token; the new policy, though it appeared to differ from the old, was essentially a continuation.

There were several factors behind the announced change in policy, some related to the internal situation in Israel and to Jewish opposition, some to Arab opposition, and some arising out of the Middle East situation in general.

Inside Israel, the wave of indignation against the military government and its actions was beginning to reach its height. Since criticism came from many established Jewish groups with a record of steadfast Zionist loyalties, the government could not very well discount it. There had been challenges to the very existence of the military government and exposure of the military governors and their activities. For example, on February 11, 1957, the influential newspaper *Haaretz* wrote:

> It is impossible to accept the claim that it is thanks to the watchfulness of the military governors that there has been no political sabotage and no serious attempt by the Arab population to organize an underground movement. If there are extremist groups among the Arabs willing to risk hostile acts against Israel, no military governor will be able to stop them. The military government is not a solid organization and its manpower is limited. The physical presence of military rule in the Arab areas is not on a scale to prevent hostile acts on the part of the local population; it is rather the fear of the state's power to punish that has prevented deeds harmful to the nation, and this fear will remain even if the military government is abolished or its powers curtailed.

On the same subject, the report of the ministerial committee had recommended the following:

It is true that the security problems in the state of Israel have no precedent. Yet even if we assume that sections of the Arab population have not yet resigned themselves to the existence of the state of Israel, it does not necessarily follow that the Arabs in Israel will be prepared to engage in organized mass action against the state. Only such a threat on a mass scale could justify the existence of the military government and the normal resources of the security services are sufficient to control individuals. And even if Arab nationalist elements do exist in the country, these elements are quite different from other extremist nationalist movements in that they look beyond the border and wait for "liberation" forces to come from abroad. This reliance on its neighbors to perform the task gives Arab nationalism in Israel a passive character. If this nationalism, insofar as it exists at all, has not yet exploded, it is not due to the deterrent factor of the military government but to the lack of sufficient motive. Nearly ten years' experience, including the period of the Suez campaign, has taught us that the Arab population is not inclined toward offensive nationalist activity. ... Meanwhile, the number of Arabs who are not ready to assume that Israel can be erased from the map is increasing.[5]

Opposition to the military government was expressed not only by those in political circles but by various other groups as well. For example, in the summer of 1958 a statement signed by representatives of twenty kibbutzim and about two hundred of the most prominent intellectuals in Israel, including seventy professors and lecturers at the Hebrew University in Jerusalem, said the following:

About 200,000 of the inhabitants of Israel, belonging to another religion and with a different nationality, do not enjoy equal rights and are the victims of discrimination and repression. The overwhelming majority of Arabs in Israel live under a system of military government which deprives them of their fundamental rights as citizens. They have neither freedom of movement nor of residence. They are not accepted as members with equal rights and obligations in the Histadrut [the main trade union] or as employees in most concerns. Their whole life is dependent on the whims of the military governor and his assistants. ... The state has other means at its disposal, in the civil laws and the ordinary security forces, to protect the security of the nation without discriminating against the Arab population.

Ten years of discrimination and repression have created and fostered feelings of despair and bitterness, and the Arab population becomes a prey of those wishing to exploit the situation for their own political purposes. The continuation of this situation could seriously endanger the security of the nation.[6]

Poets, artists, and men and women of letters also took their turn at criticizing the military government. One group made a public appeal for the immediate abolition of the system with a statement that: "The last ten years have increased the bitterness of the Arab population, which has, time and again, protested against acts of injustice and repression, against the fact that it does not enjoy the same rights as its Jewish fellow-citizens, against the arbitrary closure of its agricultural land . . . and against the restriction of movement and the frequent arrests."[7]

During the period leading up to the new policy in 1959, the military government also suffered a blow from a recognized moral authority. In one of his reports, the state controller confirmed the charges that, without the power to do so, the military government had interfered in affairs falling within the jurisdiction of other departments.

The military government handles numerous matters which are within the competence of the civil administration, either by making recommendations or objecting to the department concerned, about granting permits to buy agricultural equipment, renting land, or offering work. . . . [It] often handles matters falling within the competence of government departments, with no urgent security reasons to justify such interference. It has been suggested to the military government that it restrict its activities to cases in which the security factor demands its intervention. . . . Furthermore, reform of the legal and administrative system governing the closed areas is essential. Every detail of this system must be clarified to ensure that the letter of the law is carried out exactly.[8]

The state controller's criticism was perfectly accurate, but it "modestly" refrained from going into details. The military governors had until then enjoyed the powers of most government departments without any of their obligations. One governor once said:

> [The military government] interferes in the life of the Arab citizen from the day of his birth to the day of his death. It has the final say in all matters concerning workers, peasants, professional men, merchants, and educated men, with schooling and social services. It interferes in the registration of births, deaths, and even marriages, in questions of land and in the appointment and dismissal of teachers and civil servants. Often, too, it arbitrarily interferes in the affairs of political parties, in political and social activities, and in local and municipal councils.[9]

It would be wrong to assume that such disapproval by itself, or even the atmosphere which led to its expression, was enough to convince the Israeli government to change its policy. Even a casual familiarity with the mentality of the authorities and their methods would persuade one that these murmurings were not given much weight. It was other developments—Arab opposition inside and outside Israel—that swung the pendulum toward change.

Never known for its moderation, government policy toward the Arabs was most severe in 1958, ten years after the establishment of the state. It seemed as if land expropriation, police supervision, restrictions on employment, and limitation of sources of income were destined to become progressively worse. Arab opposition intensified as a result. During the 1948–58 period the Arabs had seized every opportunity to express their anger and disapproval, whether through meetings and protests or small-scale clashes with the authorities. Then, in 1958, the dissatisfaction came to a head and found expression in Nazareth, the "capital" of the Arabs in Galilee and in some ways the capital of the Arabs in Israel. The immediate cause was a demand that the time set for a Communist Party-organized demonstration be changed to the afternoon. The party refused and insisted on holding the demonstration in the morning, as it had done in previous years. This led to clashes between the demonstrators, many of them Arab workers who had come from their villages in

Galilee for the demonstration, and the police. But what began as a clash soon turned into an open fight between the Arabs of Nazareth and the auxiliary police that had been hurriedly called to the city. The fighting went on for most of the day, leaving twenty-six policemen and many civilians injured.[10] More than 350 people were arrested.[11]

What added to the anger of the authorities was that 1958, Israel's tenth anniversary, had been planned as an occasion for displaying the state's achievements to the world, including the "progress" enjoyed by the Arabs in Israel. Now they were unexpectedly confronted with the hostility of the Arab workers, interpreted in Israeli circles as a blatant insult to the military government. To make matters worse, two days later clashes with the police much like those in Nazareth were repeated on a smaller scale in Umm al-Fahm, the largest Arab village in the Triangle.[12]

Making the most of the incidents in Nazareth and Umm al Fahm, dissenting elements among the Arabs spent the following months working to set up a permanent body to oppose official policy. The result was the formation of the (Arab) Popular Front in July 1958 (see Chapter 7). What caused special concern among the Israeli authorities was that the front included Arabs with different political leanings, including Communists and nationalists. Renouncing all ideological differences, they had united to pursue clear-cut goals, namely to resist government policy toward the Arabs and to protect their rights. The government interpreted this as a threat to the military government and a demonstration of its failure. The front had been formed under the military government's very nose, despite the stern restrictions imposed on its leaders and supporters.

Both the Arabs and the Israeli authorities were also affected by events taking place in the Middle East. In February 1958 Egypt and Syria had joined forces as the United Arab Republic (UAR), which fired the enthusiasm of the Arabs in Israel. The July revolution in Iraq coincided with the formation of the Popular Front, giving it moral support. At the same time, the Israelis uncovered several spy networks set up by eager young Arabs driven by nationalist sentiments. Further, many young Arabs were secretly leaving for neighboring countries, then returning to engage in activities hostile to the Israeli regime. Most of these young men had some education but were unable to continue their studies and could only find employment as unskilled laborers.[13]

These developments—opposition by both Israelis and Arabs—had forced the government to reappraise its policy. Not only had containment led to a dead end, but it seemed to have endangered the very existence of Israel.[14] Under these conditions, there were no objections to introducing ways of absorbing the Arabs into Israeli society and freeing them from their ghettos. These were the circumstances that led to the changes announced in 1959.

The new policy was not as liberal as it appeared at first, however. It was based on several dubious assumptions, which were described by Ben-Gurion as he introduced it. Four premises had been accepted by every member of the ministerial committee: First, that the Arabs in Israel constituted a security problem because of the "absence of peace" between Israel and the Arabs, and especially because "some of the Arab population in Israel have personal relations with Arabs in the neighboring enemy countries." Secondly, that "certain elements among the Arab minority pose a threat to the security of the nation." Thirdly, that "the government must prevent infiltration from across the borders."[15] And lastly, and most dangerous of all, that the thorn of Arab settlements must be removed from Israel's side by increasing the number of Jewish settlements in areas with a predominantly Arab character, like Galilee. This opened the door to further expropriation and "absorption" of Arab land, as will be seen.

Nor did the new policy silence the opposition. When the government announced changes that it had persistently resisted as extremely dangerous to national security, the doubts of those opposing military rule were confirmed. They were convinced that government claims that the military government was essential to the nation's safety were simply a way of disguising Mapai's exploitation of that government for strictly political ends. If it was possible, from the point of view of security, to introduce changes that formally stripped the military government of most of its content, it was surely also possible to take the final step and completely abolish the system, or at least replace it with a civil system based on new and more democratic "Israeli laws" rather than the emergency regulations.

That the opposition wanted more significant change became obvious six months later, in February 1960, when the government had to enlist all its supporters in the Knesset to defeat three bills, all calling for the repeal of the emergency regulations (or their replacement with a new Israeli law) and the abolition of the military government.[16] This time the traditional opponents of military rule, the Israeli Communist Party and the General Zionists, were joined by the influential Herut Party, successor to I.Z.L., whose proposal was presented by Menachem Begin, its leader.[17] Then Pinhas Rosen, a Progressive who had served as minister of justice for several years, used a legal maneuver to undermine the emergency regulations. He introduced a bill to treat the laws as if they had been originally promulgated by the Knesset, in which case they would have to be reviewed and confirmed every three months in order to remain valid.[18] But this, too, was rejected.

Opposition to military rule, both popular and political, reached a peak between 1961 and 1963. On the popular level, individual factions joined in a concerted effort to abolish the system. After a mass demonstration against military rule in Tel Aviv on December 2, 1961, the Jewish-Arab Committee for the Abolition of Military Government was formed. Among its members were the Israeli Communist Party, Matzpen (the Israeli socialist organization), the Arab Students' Committee at the Hebrew University in Jerusalem, and the Al Ard movement, a successor to the Popular Front. Most of the mass rallies and other activities protesting the military government were organized by this committee until it was dissolved three years later.[19] These years also saw significant action by Mapam, which had decided to act independently. On its initiative, a call for the abolition of the military government was published in the press in February 1963. It was signed by, among others, twenty university professors, seventeen employees of the Weizmann Institute, thirty-nine lawyers, twenty-five secondary school teachers, twenty-three writers and poets, and thirty-six artists.[20]

At the same time, on the political level, there was heated debate in the Knesset over bills proposed by almost all the parties, including some in the government coalition (though not Mapai), to repeal the emergency regulations and eliminate the military government altogether.[21] The results of the voting after the two main debates on February 20, 1962, and the same date in 1963, neither supported the government position nor gave it cause for celebration: the first vote was 59 to 54 in favor of retaining the military government and the second was 57 to 56. Even this slim margin was only achieved by applying every kind of pressure, including bribes, to some of the parties.[22]

Much of the debate was in reaction to the policy of Prime Minister Ben-Gurion, who responded to his critics in a long speech in February 1963. He expressed his determination to maintain the military government. Although he added nothing new to the arguments of the system's supporters, he was remarkably frank. In his view, military rule was indispensable because "three regions, Galilee, the Triangle, and the Negev, are hotbeds of hate and conspiracy, and therefore always a potential danger. Acting openly or under cover of communism, there are elements in these areas who could instigate disturbances among the Arabs themselves, or between Arabs and Jews, in any moment of tension." Furthermore, he thought the situation could become explosive if there were incidents or demonstrations hostile to Israel in the Arab countries, when Israel celebrated its Independence Day, when new Jewish settlements were founded in some desolate area with a non-Jewish population (and Ben-Gurion did not acknowledge that those "desolate" areas were mostly agricultural land expropriated from the Arabs), if an attempt was made to expand into the Gaza strip or other areas beyond the borders, or, conversely, if spies and killers infiltrated from the strip or a neighboring country. He went on: "There are in this country two organizations which resent Israel, one called 'the Front' [the Popular Front] ... a communist organization in disguise, and the other a nationalist group called 'Al Ard,' both of which periodically distribute poisonous propaganda in the form of leaflets and pamphlets."[23]

In the same speech Ben-Gurion spoke of "a minority among the Arab population with no thought for the economic or cultural situation, who are robbed of their sleep by the mere existence of Israel. The military government is there ... to restrain this minority, which would be prepared to help the rulers of the neighboring Arab countries, in any way possible, to destroy Israel. The military government, with its power under the defense regulations to arrest, imprison, and banish such people, acts as a deterrent."[24]

Ending on a bitter note, Ben-Gurion said that military government was necessary because the circumstances of the Arab minority in Israel differ from those in any other country:

> Many members of the minority here do not look upon themselves as a minority but rather consider us a minority—a foreign, usurping minority. This is the difference between the Arab minority here and minorities elsewhere. In our case the facts make it possible for people to think that it is not the minority but the majority who constitute a minority, since the minority is surrounded by tens of millions of its fellow-countrymen beyond the borders.[25]

Despite this strongly stated position, there were prominent Israeli officials who opposed it and could not be ignored or easily challenged, in view of their past positions and experience. For example, Yigal Allon, a leader of Achdut Haavoda, had written the following:

> It would be fanciful to assume that the military government can, through the powers it exercises, prevent secret contacts between Israeli Arabs and their brothers over the border. ... It is only

through army security control, assisted by the frontier guard and the frontier colonies, that we can make such contacts less common. ... There is absolutely no connection between effective control of the borders and the existence of the military government. ... It is an error to believe that the existence of the military government can prevent espionage or that it can prevent the Arab population from harboring infiltrators. This task can only be undertaken by a competent security department and an intelligence network worthy of the name. ... whenever such actions have been uncovered it has been through the security services, not through the military government. ... Because it has no direct security tasks, the military government concentrates on internal politcal activities, such as the ... establishment of a counterforce to prevent the formation of undesirable political organizations.[26]

Israel Bar-Yehuda, a fellow member of Achdut Haavoda, who had come into conflict with the military government when he was minister of the interior, stated during the 1962 debates:

The present situation does not mean that the military government must be abolished because there are no dangers at home or abroad, but that it must be abolished because, for a long time, it has performed no real security function and has indeed become a factor greatly increasing the insecurity of the state. The military government has become a private body, which to justify its existence has to find a range of new duties unrelated to security ... it has ceased to be concerned with security, and for a long time now has increased the threat to security. It must be abolished.[27]

A third member of Achdut Haavoda, Moshe Carmel, had similar views:

This institution is no longer essential to the security of Israel, and its continued existence may well harm the establishment of healthy relations between Israel's Jewish and Arab inhabitants, the growth of a genuine democratic government based on the equality of all citizens, and the development of progressive democratic awareness. It blocks any genuine feeling of citizenship among the Arab population, and it damages Israel's reputation abroad. The military government ... no longer performs any positive functions in protecting the country from within, and its existence does more harm than good.[28]

Mapam adopted the same attitude. According to the second man in the party, Yaacov Hazan:

We are convinced that the military government does no service to the security of the state of Israel and that it is incompatible with the principles of justice and law. . . . The military government has isolated the Arab population through its discrimination against them in various fields, and by reducing them to second class citizens has greatly increased the risk of their domination by negative elements. The military government is making the Arab minority feel more and more strongly that it is despised, rejected, and discriminated against as a race apart, and this can only breed hatred.[29]

Aharon Cohen, one of Mapam's experts on Arab affairs and one concerned about Arab-Jewish relations, had the following to say concerning the military government's effect on the Arabs: ". . . the military government is a negative factor, causing resentment and creating obstacles, which is bound to poison relations between Arabs and Jews. It is therefore more likely to undermine the security of the nation rather than strengthen it. As Michael Assaf wrote in the periodical *Beterem* on May 15, 1953, 'Whether it wishes to or not, the military government is, every day, simply by its existence and its conduct, forcing every Arab to hate the state or to become a saboteur. This is because the whole structure of the military government, its thinking and its actions, are based on punishing people, not for offenses they have committed or conspiracies they have hatched, but for offenses they may commit (in the judgment of the military government), or merely because they are Arabs.' "[30]

The position of the Herut Party was similar to that of the others. A conference of the Herut movement, held in January 1963, adopted the following resolution: "We demand the repeal of the imperialist emergency regulations, which the Knesset has decided are incompatible with the principles of a democratic state. The military government can and must be replaced with suitable security arrangements all along the armistice lines." The conference declared that the administrative system called the military government no longer fulfilled any real security function.[31]

The leader of the Liberal Party (later part of the Progressive Party), Pinhas Rosen, expressed a similar attitude:

> The military government has a disastrous effect on the moral standards of the masses in the areas under its control. It is bound to lead to the degrading flattery of the authorities, who have the power to grant movement permits and other attractions. This can only undermine the moral standards of the masses and diminish the respect felt by the Arab minority for the state.[32]

As for the Israeli Communist Party, its position on the military government was clear. Having suffered, especially its Arab members, at the hands of the system, the party demanded its abolition shortly after it was established and has not changed its attitude to this day.

Two years of debate were not without effect. In 1962, for example, a series of improvements were introduced. Travel permits became valid for one year, instead of one day or one month, and were automatically renewed unless the holder of the permit was found to be "at fault" in some way. (The military government had been gradually moving in this direction over the previous three years.) The curfew in the Triangle was lifted. Arabs sentenced before a military court gained the right to appeal to a military appeals court of the Israeli army with at least one jurist on the panel. Members of the Druze sect were exempted from having to obtain travel permits in recognition of their services in the army.[33] Committees were set up in Galilee, the Triangle, and the Negev to receive complaints from all those who felt they had suffered as a result of military government action. These committees were to make recommendations for appropriate action to the minister of defense.[34]

Despite repeated calls for the abolition or limitation of the military government, the Israeli authorities persisted in maintaining the system with only these minor changes. The reasons for its longevity varied from time to time as the responsibilities of the military government changed, under the guise of security needs.

In the beginning, from the establishment of the state until the early 1950s, one cannot help accepting the official explanation that the military government was created for security reasons. If a wide interpretation of "security" eventually led to its permeating most aspects of the Arabs' daily life, one must remember that the military government was established while the war between Israel and the Arab countries was still being waged, and the newly established Israeli regime was confronted with grave external problems and an Arab population whose loyalty was open to question. In a very short time, however, the military government was transformed from an organization in charge of security questions into an important tool of the dominant political party, Mapai, or, to be more precise, of small circles with decisive authority within that party.

Since it was formed with the merger of Achdut Haavoda and Hapoel Hatzair in the early 1930s, Mapai had been the dominant party among the Jewish settlers in Palestine and then the ruling party in the new state, a position it still holds.[35] In time Mapai came to act on the assumption that what was good for Mapai was good for Israel, and vice versa. When, in 1948, it became obvious that an Arab minority—just over 10 percent of the Jewish population—would remain in Israel, Mapai concentrated on winning the same prominent position among the Arabs that it had enjoyed among the Jews. There was the further incentive of serving the welfare of the nation by keeping the Arab minority quiet and by creating an Arab leadership loyal to Israel, or at least willing to collaborate. At the same time, of course, the leadership would be more useful to the government if it was politically tied to Mapai. In the long run, such an alliance could affect the whole Palestine question by preventing the formation of any Arab organization not favorable to Israel.

No sooner had Mapai outlined these aims than the military government, which was answerable to the minister of defense (a member of Mapai), began to carry them out carefully and conscientiously. Indeed, the military government was ideally placed for this task, given its direct involvement in the lives of the Arabs, and it scored a remarkable success. In every Knesset election it managed to produce four or five Arab members tied to Mapai and completely controlled by the military system. It also had the means necessary to guarantee Arab votes for the candidates of the ruling party. It could entice the voters with promises of travel permits, with support for the appointment of relatives, and with help in obtaining trade licenses or loans, or by renting out pieces of the "public lands" or absentee property, etc. And it could, where necessary, threaten punishment, such as the withdrawal of travel permits or the imposition of house arrest, banishment, or internment. These methods were not reserved only for Knesset elections but were used during the elections of the local councils in the Arab villages, and were eventually applied whenever the military government chose to interfere in any popular activity among the Arabs, political or social.

The military government had the support of the special duties department of the Israeli Police and the Internal Security Service and its agents at all levels of Arab society. It had recruited these agents using every means from bribery to threats and by exploiting the weaknesses of Arab society. Soon there was no Arab family (in the broad sense) in Israel without some "representation" in the military government. In addition, it received valuable weekly reports from the mukhtars of the Arab villages.[36] This network was devoted to furthering the interests of Mapai, and the Arab circles linked to it, and the interests of the Arab department in the Histadrut, which was totally subject to Mapai influence. These groups soon became the main sources of support for every serious program—positive or negative—related to the Arabs and became in fact the deciding factor in the lives of the Arabs in Israel.

There is no doubt that the other Israeli parties understood the role played by the military government in furthering

Mapai's political interests. Aharon Cohen outlined the situation:

> The refusal of Mapai, the main party in power, to give up this position of strength [the military government] was ... because the party secured for itself in this way both the majority of Arab votes for the Knesset elections and the possibility of exerting pressure on Arab electors supporting contending parties. In elections to the second Knesset (1951), Mapai and its affiliated Arab lists won 66.9 percent of the votes of Arab electors; and in the elections to the Third Knesset (1955), it won 64 percent of votes in Arab localities, almost twice the percentage it won among the Jewish public. Similar results were obtained in subsequent elections.[37]

The military government developed a close relationship with the Arab Knesset members it had helped to elect, to their mutual benefit. The votes of these members in 1963 provided the best indication of the relationship. With opposition at its height and the fate of the military government in the balance, the Arab members voted against its abolition. Jabr Ma'di of Yarka and Diab Ebeed from Tayba openly voted in favor of the military system, while the other two Arab members, Elias Nakhleh of Rama and Kamel al Dhahir of Nazareth, first abstained and then voted for abolition, in an unsuccessful maneuver which, at the end of four rounds, resulted in the 57 to 56 vote in favor.[38] Menachem Begin's comment at the time was that "the military government safeguards a special corner in this house [a place for the Arab members linked with Mapai], and today ... this corner will safeguard the survival of the military government."[39]

However, the military government's success on behalf of Mapai, and vice versa, eventually led to its downfall. In pursuing Arab votes, the military government opposed every other political organization that was active, or trying to be active, among the Arabs. This brought it into direct conflict with the Israeli Communist Party, which has a strong following among the Arabs, and eventually with every independent Arab organization. And when the Zionist parties discovered

the possibility of working politically with the Arabs and
winning their votes, whether through ideological or material
arguments, the military government had to extend itself to
counteract the interests of these parties and their supporters.
In doing this it made its biggest mistake. In a multiparty
government like that in Israel, the votes in the general elections directly elect Knesset members and the number of
members it has in the Knesset determines a party's position
in the government coalition or in the opposition. It is therefore unpardonable for an official body to interfere in the
elections on behalf of a particular party. Being far from the
seat of government, the Israeli Communist Party could only
react on a popular level by criticizing the military government and exposing its methods. The other Zionist parties,
however—especially those regularly voted in and frequently
participating in the government coalition, like Mapam and
Achdut Haavoda—could do much more, when the need arose,
to decide the fate of military rule at the highest government
levels.[40]

Not only did the military government serve the interests of
the ruling party, it was also involved in undertakings benefit-
ing the state. If by helping Mapai it was also helping the
country, it followed that in serving the state it was also
helping Mapai. The military government expended great
efforts to encourage and consolidate Jewish settlement of the
Arab areas inside Israel. By expelling Arabs from their villages
and towns, the military system made it possible for Israeli
authorities to seize their lands. By declaring the ruined Arab
villages and expropriated land "closed," it prevented the
Arab inhabitants from returning and over the years enabled
Zionist groups to colonize the area. It used its powers to
silence Arab resistance to the land expropriations. Indeed, it
is difficult to imagine how the Jewish settlements could have
been established without the military government, whose role
the Israeli government has never denied. On the contrary, as
opposition to the military government intensified, the government frequently mentioned its importance in that respect.

Before the vote in the Knesset in 1962, Shmuel Segev, who was familiar with the work of the security services, wrote:

> The repeal of Article 125 which deals with the "closed areas"—the most important article as far as the military government is concerned—would mean in practice the abolition of the legal power to declare areas closed. . . . The closing of an area by virtue of this Article means that it is being prepared for Jewish settlement, which is becoming more and more urgent with the increasing waves of immigration.[41]

And Shimon Peres, deputy minister of defense, who was enamored of the military government, said:

> It is by making use of Article 125, on which the military government depends to a large extent, that we can directly continue the struggle for Jewish settlement and Jewish immigration. . . . In Galilee . . . today, there are hundreds of thousands of dunums [one dunum equals one thousand square meters] of unsettled land which are earmarked for programmed settlement. But there has been an attempt at unlicensed settlement; hundreds of houses have been built on the hills of Galilee without permit. If we are agreed that settlement has a far-reaching political import, we must prevent the creation of faits accomplis incompatible both with the Zionist concept of the state of Israel and with the law.[42]

This view was confirmed by Ben-Gurion, who said that "the military government came into existence to protect the right of Jewish settlement in all parts of the state."[43]

Despite their defeat by one vote in 1963, opponents of military government continued to express intense disapproval of the system and the government continued to modify the laws regulating it.

The first of these amendments was announced on November 15, 1963, after Ben-Gurion's resignation and Levi Eshkol's appointment as prime minister. It was simply a supplement to the changes approved in 1959, with the one difference that areas formerly open to the Arabs only during daylight hours could be visited day and night. Some of the border areas, however, were put under stricter observation, and the opposition was still unsatisfied

> because the areas that Arabs could not enter without authorization in the past are still forbidden to them even after the "alleviations." We mean work places in the Negev, Tiberias, Jerusalem, and in the settlements and kibbutzim in the north. Even today inhabitants of the Triangle cannot enter Galilee without a travel permit and vice versa. Arabs living in Jaffa, Haifa, Ramle, and other cities will not in future be able to enter areas under military government without permits. The new alleviations, like the announcements about closed areas in Galilee in the past, regrettably are simply alleviations designed to make things easier for the directors of interior and foreign propaganda.[44]

Pointing to a new measure announced at the same time, which soon proved to be the foundation of Israel's security policy regarding the Arabs, Arab Knesset member Emil Habibi said:

> There are also serious cases where the new measures are more strict than the old. For example, the government departments have drawn up lists of Arabs said to be "security risks." These men have been forbidden by the military government to venture outside their villages whether by day or by night, without travel permits. In the past . . . they would have been able to leave their villages during the day to go to their work without any restrictions. Now, with the new alleviations, they cannot do so.[45]

As a result of this measure black lists were initiated; although the general population was treated with increasing leniency, the military government imposed special restrictions on any Arab whose name appeared on these lists.

The Israeli government went on to introduce real improvements. In January 1966 it allowed:

> free travel in and out of Galilee . . . and freedom of travel for the Bedouin tribes of the Negev . . . and free travel to the Negev or Galilee by inhabitants of the Triangle . . . but entry into the Triangle was still forbidden . . . and Arabs were similarly prevented from entering some towns, like Tiberias and Safad, without special authorization.[46]

The single real alleviation for the Arabs was the freedom granted to enter the city of Nazareth and the central part of Galilee.[47] In contrast, there was a simultaneous extension of the military government's powers to include cities that had been immune from military government regulations since the early 1950s. For the first time since the creation of Israel, house arrest and residential restrictions were imposed on Arabs living in those cities—mostly members of the Al Ard movement. A resolution introduced in the Knesset by Communist member Meir Vilner condemning this practice was rejected.[48]

By the mid-1960s, the military government, as it had originally been conceived, had reached its limits. In 1966, following a change in policy toward the Arabs, a series of significant modifications were made.

3
The
Velvet
Glove

During the years between 1964 and 1966 in particular, it was obvious that the Israeli government was searching for a new policy toward the Arabs living under its rule. This policy was formally announced at the end of 1966 and, as in 1959, the motives behind the change were both internal and external.

The 1963 resignation of Ben-Gurion and his decision to retire from politics was a significant event for the Arabs. Ben-Gurion had been known for his unyielding position toward the Arabs, including those living in Israel, and the appointment of Levi Eshkol as prime minister seemed to promise more favorable circumstances for a reappraisal of the government's attitude toward the Arab minority.

Ben-Gurion's resignation did not result in immediate changes, however, since he continued to exert considerable influence. Furthermore, he had left a large number of supporters behind him in sensitive posts and a number of prominent institutions and projects were indebted to him. But through his own actions, he soon lost his hold on the establishment. Shortly after his resignation he launched a savage attack on Eshkol and his government, shocking many Israelis. Since there was no logical reason for the attack, people assumed that he must be regretting the loss of his power or that age (he had just turned 77) had begun to take its toll. His own supporters rallied around him, and eventually they split from the main Mapai party to form a separate party

(Rafi) which entered the lists in the sixth Knesset elections in 1965. But by that time most of Ben-Gurion's supporters, including Moshe Dayan and Shimon Peres, had either retreated or been removed from the government and Eshkol and his supporters were free to review the Arab policy. There was an opportunity for all viewpoints to be expressed and debated before the government selected the most suitable and acted accordingly.

Outside Israel, there were new developments relating to the Palestine question. The Israeli government was well aware of the formation of the Palestine Liberation Organization, the creation of Fatah, and especially the call for armed Palestinian resistance.[1] The Israeli authorities were not as disturbed by all this as one might imagine, especially at the beginning, but soon events among the Arabs inside Israel put a new light on the matter. After the dissolution of the (Arab) Popular Front in 1959, the Al Ard movement formed and became politically active, making no secret of its Palestinian character. The Israeli government was unprepared for this and eventually decided on the formal liquidation of the movement in 1965.

Although the Israeli authorities could not discover any direct link between Palestinian activists inside and outside Israel, and although Israeli intelligence was confident that it could counter any attempt at "coordination" between the two halves of the Palestinian people, these new factors required immediate attention. To some extent, Al Ard was the result of oppressive Israeli policy and the neglect of Arab rights. Most of its support came from the new generation that had grown up after the creation of Israel. This confirmed the feeling among many Israeli leaders and officials that there was something fundamentally wrong with Israel's policy regarding the Arabs that should be corrected before it became uncontrollable. If the Palestinians (and the words "Palestine" and "Palestinian" are not very dear to most Israelis) beyond Israel's influence were trying to organize, it would be unwise, to say the least, to give their leaders reason to speak on behalf of their brothers and sisters inside Israel.[2] It was in the interests of Israel to eliminate—even if only in form—injustices that could become rallying points.

It was not surprising that when a change of policy was contemplated, a review of the military government was, again, one of the first steps. The most suitable man Eshkol could find for the job was Isar Harel. He had been head of Israeli intelligence for years but had resigned while Ben-Gurion was prime minister. He was appointed an advisor as an attempt to silence Ben-Gurion's attack on Eshkol on security grounds.

In the middle of December 1965, Harel presented his recommendations to Eshkol. There was no official announcement, although there were widespread rumors that Harel was proposing to abolish the military government.[3] The rumors were based on a press conference at which Eshkol stated that he had asked Harel to study the possibilities of granting alleviations to the Arabs, "even the abolition of the military government apparatus."[4] The prime minister's office confirmed this impression when a spokesman said that "1966 will be recorded in the history of the Arabs in Israel as the year of the abolition of military government for all practical purposes, and the elimination of all other sources of discontent among the Arab population of the country."[5]

When the Israeli government began to act on Harel's recommendations, there was still no official statement. But contrary to his usual habit, Harel held a press conference in Tel Aviv to explain the basis for his recommendations.

> The military government is not a necessity on security grounds and could be dispensed with. The army should not be concerned with our Arab citizens; it is a blot on our democracy . . . that this is so. Even if there were a need for restrictions, they should be applied individually. This collective restraint is a violation of the feelings of the Arabs. It would be far better to put individuals under stricter observation than to cast doubts on the whole Arab population in the state, and thus humiliate them.[6]

Once the military government was abolished, Harel, as befits a former head of intelligence, felt that:

The remedy for violations of the peace by members of the Arab minority [would be] the creation of an effective and expert security system, alert and on the watch for the threat of hostile underground movements and any failure in security. Neither a strong-arm policy nor a policy of absorption with equal rights can affect the depth of the [Arabs'] loyalty to the state. However elaborate the security mechanism and the restrictions, they will not stop the Arabs from joining the opposition in times of crisis. In the same way, we will not banish these feelings from their hearts even if we pursue a liberal policy. [Therefore the proposed policy should be] a delicate balance between security needs and . . . respect for the rights of the individual. Once it is established that there is no need for the military government, it should not be kept on for a single day. It is up to Israel to consider carefully whether it can rule the villages of Galilee and the Triangle with bayonets alone. And if it decides that law and order can be maintained under civilian rule with the help of the police, then there is no need for the military government. This does not mean that the army will leave the area; it is part of the nation . . . But, where necessary, restrictions will have to be imposed on individuals to prevent their undermining security and to prevent some elements from going too far.[7]

Harel's prestige as former head of intelligence was sufficient to overcome much of the continual hesitation about eliminating the military government. His proposals had the further effect of ending the long hidden struggle between Israeli intelligence and the military government (with the police taking a "neutral" position) over the responsibility for Arab affairs. The intelligence service had secretly accused the military government not only of failing in its security tasks, but of creating problems through its unjustified conduct that exposed Israel to greater danger, by angering the Arabs and driving them to seek "revenge." There are indications that in many instances this appraisal was accurate, especially as the military government had become a typical military bureaucracy, its officers only making a brief appearance in their offices for a few hours each morning.[8] Meanwhile, the intelligence service had been left to undertake duties the military government did not acknowledge on its own.

In any event, a change in Israeli policy toward the Arabs would not come about merely by changing the military government, modifying its clauses, or even abolishing it completely. More was needed than the elimination of military rule or the enforcement of a "moderate" policy, especially with regard to such everyday matters as work, education, and housing. Criticism of the government for its neglect of the Arab minority in this respect had surpassed the objections to military rule in intensity. At the same time, Arab resentment was increasing and a decision was made to bring about a change.

Some of these improvements came through the office of the advisor to the prime minister on Arab affairs. This office was created, as the title indicates, to assist the prime minister in drafting and carrying out government policy regarding the Arabs. Previously, this task had been entrusted to the ministry of police and minorities, which became simply the ministry of police after the minorities division was eliminated.[9] According to the state controller, the duties of the advisor were that:

> He initiates, plans, coordinates, guides, and supervises matters relating to the minorities, which basically have to do with security, land problems, local government, agriculture, industry and trade, banks and development agencies, roads, water and electricity, housing, education, religious sects, health and social welfare, apprenticeships, and trade associations.[10]

The advisor is thus concerned with most aspects of Arab life, but he does not in fact have very much influence.[11] One reason for this was Ben-Gurion. He did not give his advisors on Arab affairs much freedom of action or listen to their advice. One of them, Uri Lubrani, once said that Ben-Gurion offered him more advice than he offered Ben-Gurion.[12] It has also been said that "the advisor's task, as Ben-Gurion defined it, was simply to landscape the ugly side of military government, of the security service and faction leaders. To the outside he had to appear as a benefactor, making himself available to the representatives of the Arabs and listening to their complaints about the institution that handled their affairs. . . . At best, he could occasionally announce some slight gesture of goodwill." [13]

The personality of those holding the position and their inability to follow a constructive policy contributed to the weakness of the office. The first to hold the post (until 1955) was Yehoshua Palmon, a veteran of Haganah's intelligence organization and of its Arab department. [14] In view of his "training," his opinion of the Arabs did not help him achieve anything constructive. [15] He was succeeded by Shmuel Divon (1955-60), another graduate of Haganah who, though he was said to be "friendlier," accomplished no more than his predecessor. But the worst of the advisors was Uri Lubrani (1960-63). His background was very different, but he had the arrogance of the Sabra generation to which he belonged, so that he had no qualms about making merciless attacks on the Arabs, which earned him much hostility and eventually led to his dismissal. [16] The highest qualification of the fourth advisor, Rehebaam Amir (1963-65), was his service as the first military governor of Galilee. With this history, one would not expect him to effect radical changes, but he did try to introduce a few innovations. A dispute between him and other Israeli departments handling Arab affairs seems to have been the cause of his sudden resignation in April 1965. [17]

The government used the opportunity of the vacant position to find a candidate more suited to its newly emerging attitude to the Arabs. The choice fell on Shmuel Toledano (1965—). Born in Tiberias, Toledano has spent much of his life among Arabs and speaks Arabic perfectly, unlike most of his predecessors. He has supervised several construction projects in the Arab sector and has held various posts in the security service, which means, according to one source, "that he combines, in ideal proportions, a sternness in dealing with anyone prepared to threaten the safety of the nation and a sense of justice where peaceful Arabs who recognize Israel and are now prepared to live under its protection are concerned." [18]

It would be wrong, of course, to expect a single appointment, however important, to change government policy regarding the Arabs, but Toledano soon established that he was very different from previous advisors. He had only been in his job for a few months when he found himself in conflict with the guardians of Mapai's party interests among the Arabs, particularly with Abba Hoshi, leader of the Arabs in Mapai, and with the informal political structure among the Arabs and his son-in-law Amnon Lin, chairman of the workers' council in Haifa and an embodiment of that council's pomposity. Obviously these groups disapproved of the new line in the government's policy. They centered their attack on Toledano, while putting pressure on Mapai's leadership. They organized a "revolt" of the Arab Knesset members patronized by Mapai, on the grounds that they had not been "consulted" on the government's new policy—they who had never been consulted on lesser matters.[19] The attack was extended to an "ideological" level, and during a meeting in August 1966 in Haifa attended by several hundred Arab supporters of Mapai, it was decided that an "ideological department" should be created to spread "Arab-Israeli awareness" among the Arabs.[20] In short, "the time has come for plain speaking and to stop this ostrich-like policy . . . it is up to the Arabs in the country to make up their minds with utmost clarity whether to become part of the nation, identify with it, and prove their loyalty or suffer the consequences . . . the 'consequences' [quotation marks in the original] being . . . to pack and emigrate."[21] These opinions were more unpopular with many Jews than with the Arabs.

Toledano responded that the new policy had crystallized around "the need to treat the Israeli Arab according to his deeds, and as long as he does not prove by his actions that he is hostile to the state or helping its enemies, he must enjoy the same freedom as other citizens."[22]

Toledano's definition of "hostility to the state"—which included political activity within some of the opposition parties, objections from the security service that the "personality" of a particular Arab was hostile to the state, and, later, support of an Israeli retreat from the occupied territories—is not very different from Amnon Lin's definition of "loyalty to the state."[23] But his style was better suited to the new Arab policy.[24]

Toward the end of 1966, the Israeli government formally presented the final step in its new policy: as in 1959, it necessitated changes in the military government. On November 8, 1966, Eshkol announced in the Knesset that the government had decided "to consider the military government apparatus abolished as of December 1 of this year, and to transfer the responsibilities it has shouldered until now to civil authorities."[25] Eshkol also said that there would be no need to modify or repeal any law to eliminate the military government, since it had existed and functioned through internal military regulations. The areas formerly under military government would be placed in the charge of the regional military commands, whose officers would no longer be responsible for issuing travel permits once the civilian police took over.

The immediate, practical effect of Eshkol's proclamation was the closing of twelve military government offices, in Galilee, the Triangle, and the Negev, and the transfer of eighty-four soldiers to other divisions of the Israeli army.[26] This was the total military government apparatus. The power to enforce the emergency regulations, which remained in effect, was entrusted to the military commanders of the three regions (north, central, and south). Each commander had the assistance of an advisory officer, who formed the link to the Internal Security Service and the civilian police, who were now in charge of carrying out the provisions of these laws. But the final authority continued to be within the domain of the army chief of staff. Similarly, the post of chief of the military government division of the general staff was kept in order to conclude the coordination of military government tasks. Thus the military government became, in form at least, a body that "observes but is unseen," as its supporters had always described it.

These changes were ostensibly made to support the government's newly proclaimed policy of "integration" and "absorbing" the Arabs into the nation by fostering and encouraging the "positive" elements among them, and by isolating and thus diminishing the influence of the "negative" elements. But in fact the changes were superlatively shrewd. By announcing the abolition of military government, the Israeli government won the first round from the point of view of propaganda. It impressed those sections of domestic and world public opinion that had shown concern over Israel's policy toward its Arab population and reassured the ordinary Israeli Arab, who was relieved to be no longer confronted by military faces and restrictions. But it would be a mistake to think that these changes were as radical or as positive as they appeared at first or that the Israeli regime had changed overnight. Despite the abolition of travel permits and closed areas in principle, many areas in fact remained closed (for instance, border areas and areas being developed). Many of the destroyed Arab villages, which lay deep inside Israel, remained closed to prevent former villagers from returning.

Although there were some improvements, in one area the government regulations were more strict. The new policy excepted those elements considered "security risks" by the authorities. Since the general travel restrictions had been lifted, it was the army commanders who now ordered such individual restrictions. Whereas in the past such orders confined a person to a certain area, he or she could no longer leave a village or town (sometimes a section of town) without special authorization—a hard and bitter confinement.[27]

Not only did the emergency regulations remain in effect, but a new body was created with the power to enforce them at any moment—a special duties department of the Israeli police in charge of counterespionage, aliens, and the Arab population.[28] Its methods are extremely vicious and highly effective. In addition, the whole police apparatus, from municipal police to frontier guard, lends its services. Although military rule in the past imposed restrictions only on extreme "instigators" among the Arab political activists—writers, poets, lawyers, and intellectuals who openly criticized government policy in their writings and work—the special duties department restricts laborers, peasants, and the "general" population. It takes very little—voting for the Communist Party or a party supporting the wrong list in some local council election, or showing general dissatisfaction with official policy—to antagonize the special duties department. Furthermore, restrictions can now be imposed on Arabs anywhere in the country, even in cities with mixed populations; this rarely happened under the military government because only the areas under its control were affected.

These features are not a complete surprise, since in introducing the new policy its proponents announced that they had "caught the tiger and cut its whiskers, they had dyed its skin and were now trying to pass it off as a faithful dog before the people, but the first drop of rain would wash off the borrowed coloring, the whiskers would grow back and the tiger would again show its claws."[29]

It took only eight months for the tiger to show its claws again. When fighting began on June 5, 1967, military government was reinstated, but was withdrawn two weeks later. In the first few hours of the war forty Arabs, most of them well known, were arrested in various parts of Israel, apparently as a warning to the rest of the Arab population not to attempt any hostile action.[30] They were released about two weeks later.

The period immediately following the June War saw an increase in house arrests and residential restrictions, as a result of "the rise in national feelings among the youth . . . of the Arab minority in Israel . . . [who believe] that deep penetration into Israel by saboteurs and strikes against centers of population and military targets would spread fear and panic and undermine the morale of the Jewish population in Israel."[31] During July and August hundreds of Arabs were placed under house arrest. They could not enter the areas occupied during the June War and some could not even leave their towns or cities without authorization lest they somehow influence "negative" elements among Israeli Arabs and those living in the newly occupied territories.[32]

It is difficult to determine exactly how many Arabs were affected because the government has not published any statistics. At the beginning of 1968, when Dayan was asked in the Knesset, he refused to answer on national security grounds and said only that they were 50 percent fewer than in 1967.[33] But Dayan also announced, during a Knesset debate over residential restrictions in October 1968, that there were 157 persons who were not allowed to leave their places of residence (as opposed to 316 in April 1967) and 875 who were not permitted to visit the newly occupied territories.[34] On the basis of available information, the number of Arabs subject to military government restrictions from 1967 to the present appears to be somewhere between one and two thousand.[35] This includes most political activists opposing the government and many intellectuals, poets, writers, and lawyers, people who have always been severely restricted since they are a "negative" element that refuses to cooperate with the government and is always critical.

This period also saw frequent use of administrative detentions, which lasted longer than in the past. For example, at the end of March 1970 there were eighty persons in administrative detention, who had been held for more than two years.[36] Never before in the history of Israel had people been held for this long without charges or trial. The talk about repealing, or at the very least modifying the emergency regulations was no longer heard after 1967. On the contrary, Israeli authorities seem to have been so pleased with their "success" with the Arabs that they imposed similar regulations in the areas occupied in 1967, including house arrest, residential restrictions, curfews, administrative detention, and closed areas.[37]

On the other hand, the Israeli government has been remarkably sensitive, in recent times, to criticism of its use of the emergency regulations, promptly easing restrictions (contrary to past practice) if there is any likelihood of public disclosure of an incident. For example, in April 1970, when seventeen administrative detainees in the Damun prison announced a hunger strike to protest their detention without trial, the newspapers publicized it throughout the country.[38] A protest meeting, attended by hundreds of Arabs, was held in Haifa, and there were demonstrations in front of the Knesset and the prison, with many Arabs and Jews participating, while the government rushed to the relief of the prisoners.[39] Indeed, about two months later most were released. Again in July 1970, when some Arabs in Haifa held a press conference protesting house arrests and residential restrictions and threatening to take "measures" against these restrictions—meaning, in this case, no more than sending protests to local and international organizations—Toledano hastily announced that there had been no change for the worse in the government's policy toward the Arabs.[40] A few days later the Arabs involved were summoned to their local police stations and their restrictions were eased.

Also remarkable was the policy of "self-control" followed by Israel in dealing with Israeli Arabs who had decided to help the Palestinian resistance and to carry out guerrilla operations inside Israel. In October 1968 there were only forty-eight such Arabs; by November 1969 there were 110; in February 1970, 159; 250, in November 1961, and by the end of 1972 there were some 320.[41] But the authorities refused to carry out the measures used against their counterparts in the newly occupied territories, hoping that it would not be forced "to use such methods against citizens of Israel." It did not, for example, blow up their houses, nor did it send them into exile, because "it is impossible to banish an Israeli citizen to a foreign country."[42] But in fact they were treated with severity and with less understanding or tolerance than Arabs from the occupied territories caught in an act of sabotage, since they were granted neither pardons nor light sentences.[43]

This third phase of Israeli "security" policy—from 1966 on—obviously differs very much from that in the past. Whatever restrictions the authorities can impose when necessary, there is no doubt that the change in form—from military to civilian authority—has led to a change in content. Most important has been the easing of restrictions on the general population—while focusing on individual offenders, however large their number—and a less humiliating style of enforcing them.

It is noteworthy that the Israeli government has persisted in carrying out the new policy, announced some six months before the June 1967 War, despite the war and despite the difficult security situation inside Israel, especially during the three years immediately following the war. The attitude of many of the young Arabs who favored Palestinian resistance and operations hostile to Israel, including sabotage in all-Jewish areas, would have been sufficient in the past not only to abolish all improvements but to reinstate military authority and increase its power beyond what it had been during the heyday of the military government. Indeed, there were calls for a return to military government.[44] But they were few and generally disregarded, especially after Toledano's assertion that there was no need to return to those days because

> ... there is a misapprehension among the public over the meaning of the expression military government. A wider use of the defense regulations would be a more effective deterrent than a return of the military government, since without the sanction of the emergency regulations the military government has no deterrent mechanism. It is possible to impose a curfew on an Israeli-Arab village or to close off areas and prevent entry into them, or to arrest and banish people, or to imprison people and blow up their houses, it is possible to bring back the system of [travel] permits and so on, without a return of military government. In other words, a return of the military government could have dangerous political consequences among the people, without achieving the objective of deterrence. This, as I have said, can be realized by a wider use of the emergency regulations.[45]

And this is what the government tried to do from time to time.

Describing the continuing policy in broad outline, Toledano went on to say:

> The government intends to adopt a policy of reward and punishment ... From now onward, the government departments, with

the help of various public agencies, will give every kind of support and assistance, both individual and general, to the positive elements. At the same time, we shall fight every nationalist agitator, directly and indirectly, until he is destroyed. Our hope is to reach the point where every nationalist Arab is isolated in his own village, so that society can regurgitate him easily! Those who want Jewish-Arab coexistence, on the other hand, shall gain in importance and feel more secure. We shall work toward this aim methodically and continually, pulling the rug from under all agitators and preparing a solid base for positive elements among the Arabs.[46]

One reason for the government's attitude was the insignificance of the hostile action by the Arabs inside Israel when compared with other security problems. Confronted with the resistance of the Arabs in the occupied territories and with opposition from the Palestine resistance movement and the Arab nations, the government considered it inevitable and natural that a number of the Arabs in Israel would want to engage in similar activities. They were certain that it would end or decline where the situation along the border and in the other countries changed. This is what eventually happened. Furthermore, both the Israeli government and the Arab population had "matured" in their attitudes to each other, especially when the June War ended with the occupation of vast areas of Arab territory and the addition of one million Arabs to those under Israeli rule. It then became clear that whatever the political settlement, an Arab minority would continue in Israel for an unlimited time. The Israeli government did not think it proper to retreat from its proclaimed policy toward Israeli Arabs because of what it hoped was a temporary security situation. For the same reason, the Arabs in Israel adopted a quiet and cautious attitude and kept the door open between themselves and all government bodies. Finally, the Israeli authorities felt confident after the 1967 victory, and this had something to do with their "tolerance."

The change in the government's attitude toward the Arabs had developed over a period of twenty years. Gradually, the power of the military government faded and various political factions and organs gained strength and authority among the Arabs, as described by Uri Avneri, who had been elected to the Knesset on a new list (New Force):

> A complete government . . . was created in the Arab sector, a secret government, unsanctioned by law . . . whose members and methods are not known . . . to anyone. Its agents are scattered among the ministries of government, from the Israel Lands Administration to the ministry of education and the ministry of religions. It makes fateful decisions affecting [Arab] lives in unknown places without documents and communicates them in secret conversations or over the telephone. This is the way decisions are made about who goes to the teachers' seminar, or who will obtain a tractor, or who will be appointed to a government post, or who will receive financial subsidies, or who will be elected to the Knesset, or who will be elected to the local council—if there is one—and so on for a thousand and one decisions.[47]

This "secret and illegal government"—the ruling party's covert ties to the Arabs—did not spring up overnight; it has existed since the creation of Israel:

> The Jewish people have always, from the establishment of the state until the present, preferred to treat the [Arab] question with indifference, and to leave it to the "experts" [quotation marks in the original] who have over the years earned the title of "Arabists." The people trusted us and gave us a freedom of action that has not been enjoyed by any other group in the country, in any field. . . . Over time we have attained a unique position in the state as experts, and no one dares to challenge our opinions or our actions. We are represented in every department of government, in the Histadrut and in the political parties; every department and office has its "Arabists," who alone act for their minister among the Arabs.[48]

Yet this "government" was not then as powerful as the military government had been in its prime. Its influence and importance began to grow as the concern of government relations with the Arabs shifted from security to day-to-day problems. The government favored its supporters among the

Arabs with both moral and financial aid. It supported a particular group in some local council election, or granted loans and other financial subsidies, helped with the education of members of a person's family or secured them jobs in government offices or with one of the political parties, especially those forming the government coalition. In return it expected political help and support as the need arose, whether in filling an important post in the administration of Arab affairs, or during the local council or Knesset elections.

The party organs finally discovered that the continuation of the military government, with its reputation for viciousness, stood in the way of their interests, as well as being a blot on Israel's good name. With the growth of the "secret government" agencies, the handful of military bureaucrats in charge of the military government were unable to survive. In any case, some of them were alert enough to identify with the "secret government" and enjoy its benefits, knowing that in the event of the military government's elimination, it would continue to function as best and as fully as it could.

II
The Seizure of Arab Land

"It should be clear that there is no room for both peoples to live in this country. ... If the Arabs leave, it is a large and open country; if they stay, it is small and poor. Up to this point, Zionists have been content to 'buy land,' but this is no way to establish a country for the Jews. A nation is created in one move ... and in that case, there is no alternative to moving the Arabs to the neighboring countries, moving them all, except, perhaps, those living in Bethlehem, Nazareth, and the Old City of Jerusalem. Not one village, not one tribe must remain. They must be moved to Iraq, Syria, or even Transjordan."

—Joseph Weitz,
Diaries and Letters to the Children
(Tel Aviv, 1965), 2: 181

"When an [Arab] peasant asked an official at the Israel Lands Administration, 'How do you deny my right to this land, it is my property, I inherited it from my parents and grandparents, I have the *kushan tabo* [deed of ownership],' the official replied, 'Ours is a more impressive *kushan tabo*, we have the *kushan* for the land from Dan [in the north of Israel] to Elat [in the south].

"In another instance, a peasant asked an official, 'What are you offering me? Is my land worth only two hundred pounds per dunum?' The official replied, 'This is not your land, it is ours, and we are paying you "watchman's" wages, for that is all you are. You have "watched" our land for two thousand years and now we are paying your fee. But the land has always been ours!' "

—Abu Issam (Lawyer Hannah Nakkarah),
in *Al Ittihad*, July 15, 1966

4

"Redeeming" the Land

From the beginning, the twin objectives of the Zionist movement have been the acquisition of land in Palestine and the attraction of Jews from all over the world to settle that land. Even before the official founding of the World Zionist Organization, in the last half of the nineteenth century, the Zionist dream had been to own land in *Eretz Israel*. The important difference between land in Palestine acquired by Jews independently and that bought through the Zionist movement is that the first was for private use while the second became public property. The idea of publicly owned land was at the heart of a proposal made at the first Zionist congress at Basel in 1896, to found a company for the specific purpose of purchasing land. The land bought by this company, later called *Ha-Keren Ha-Keymeth Leisrael* (Eternal Fund for Israel) and also known as the Jewish National Fund, would be for the settlement of Jews in Palestine; it would become Jewish property permanently, never to be sold or disposed of, except to be leased.[1]

Though it had been agreed to, for various reasons this proposal was not immediately carried out. Supporters of the Keren Keymeth raised the matter again during the fifth Zionist congress in 1901, and it was not until the sixth congress in 1903 that the company was finally launched. In 1905 the Zionists made their first land purchase in Palestine. Two years later, the Keren Keymeth was formally registered as a company in Great Britain. First in the list of the company's objectives was the acquisition of land or rights to land in the region including "Palestine, Syria or any other parts of Turkey in Asia and the Peninsula of Sinai or any part thereof, for the purpose of settling Jews on those lands."[2]

There were a number of foundations, both public and private, engaged in purchasing land in Palestine, but from its creation, Keren Keymeth was the principal tool of the World Zionist Organization for this purpose. It eventually became the largest company of its kind and enjoyed the support of a wide range of Zionist factions. Two basic principles governed the company's activities: "conquest of the land" and "conquest of labor." First, land was to be acquired by every means possible; company officials were to have no compunction about using persuasion, bribery or deception as long as the end was achieved.[3] A sampling of company bulletins and progress reports or the statements of its executives will impress the reader with their "indignation" at the very presence of Arabs in Palestine, owning the land and living off it, and with the sense that the company's highest aim was to uproot and wipe out all trace of these people to make room for Zionist settlers. Only rarely do company officials speak of buying or acquiring a plot of land; instead, they use expressions like *"liberating," "emancipating,"* and *"redeeming"* land. The slogan "redemption of the land," which the company coined, seems to have served as a war cry for Zionist colonists in Palestine.

After "conquest of the land," Keren Keymeth concentrated on "conquest of labor." Belief in the importance of controlling labor was not peculiar to the company, and "conquest of labor" became the motto of most Zionist activists in Palestine. The two notions are complementary: the "conquest of labor" kept the use of redeemed land exclusively in Jewish hands. The so-called Hebrew labor regulation was the prime tool; it began by preventing Arab laborers from working on land owned by Keren Keymeth and ended with attempts at forbidding them to work for Jewish employers generally. The limits of space prevent further study of these ideas; suffice it to say that the policies of "conquering the land" and "conquering labor" were, and continue to be, crucial to Zionist settlement of Palestine. One must keep in mind the spirit underlying these principles in order to understand Israel's subsequent measures for expropriating Arab land, since it was adherents to these ideas who eventually held the power to realize them. The Zionist movement's land ownership policy involved it in a long and bitter struggle with the Palestinian Arabs, starting some time before the British Mandate and lasting throughout the period of British rule. Its efforts to acquire land were continuous and exhaustive. Toward the end of the Mandate, after the publication of the 1939 White Paper and the subsequent passage of laws controlling sales of land to Jews in Palestine, the Zionists were also forced into a confrontation with the British. But for all their activity, and allowing for the conditions under which they worked, one can hardly describe the Zionists as successful in land acquisition. A former head of Keren Keymeth estimates all the land owned by Jews in 1947 at 1,734,000 dunums, of which his company owned 933,000.[4] After nearly three quarters of a century of both individual and organized efforts, the Jews had acquired only 6.6 percent of the total land area of Palestine.[5]

Once Israel became independent, the situation changed radically. The Israeli government annulled the laws controlling land sales to Jews and took all necessary steps for transferring ownership of the land it had occupied to its own people. Even before the establishment of the state, the heads of Keren Keymeth received a clear indication of the impending change when, on May 13, 1948, they were summoned by Ben-Gurion who made them an offer of 2 million dunums of land yet to be conquered, at half a pound per dunum. Ben-Gurion needed the money for arms.[6] But the heads of the company did not have much confidence in his optimism and politely rejected his proposal. Later they changed their minds and accepted.

The outcome of the 1948 War and the ceasefire agreements between Israel and the Arab countries left Israel in control of some 20.5 million dunums of Palestinian land, much of it originally owned by Palestinians who had either been driven from their towns and villages or left because of the war. The occupation and "absorption" of these lands took place gradually. In March 1948, the Haganah set up a Committee for Arab Property in the Villages, for the appropriation of all Arab possessions falling into the hands of the Israeli forces. In April, after the occupation of Haifa, a custodian for Arab property in the north was appointed, and when Jaffa fell on May 14, 1948, a second custodian, for Jaffa, followed.[7] Then a department for Arab property was created to supervise all Arab property in Israeli hands. Finally, in July 1948, a general custodian of absentee property was appointed.[8] All these measures were looked upon as temporary (which did not, of course, prevent the takeover of the land) until 1950 when the Israeli position opposing the return of Palestinian refugees to their homes finally became clear.[9]

To "absorb" the refugees' land and put it at the disposal of Zionist settlers in Palestine, a development authority was created by special decree of the Knesset. The Development Authority (Transfer of Property) Law, 5710—1950, stipulated that the authority could release property in its control only to the state, to agencies resettling Arab refugees who had stayed inside Israel, or to local governments, on condition that it be offered for sale first to Keren Keymeth.[10] While these formal arrangements were being made, ownership of the land was transferred from one Israeli organization to another and given to Jewish agricultural settlements or individual farmers to use. Arab buildings in the cities were turned over to the Amidar Company, for housing Jewish immigrants.[11] On September 29, 1953, the custodian of absentee property signed over his "rights" to all the land he was responsible for, in return for a "price" to be paid by the development authority.[12] This sum was then returned to the authority in the form of a loan. Three months earlier, on June 26, 1953, the government and the development authority had agreed to the "sale" of 2,373,677 dunums of "state lands" and development authority lands to Keren Keymeth.[13] This was in fulfillment of agreements made in January 1949 and October 1950.[14]

These complicated transactions arouse one's interest. It appears that Keren Keymeth's sense of propriety would not let it accept Arab land until it could be handed over, free of any restrictions and absolutely "legally," by some Israeli agency.[15] "State land" was all the land seized by Israel which did not, or was considered not to, belong to anyone, totaling 15,025,000 dunums. This, together with Keren Keymeth's 3,570,000 dunums, was later declared "national land."[16] Forming more than 90 percent of the total area of Israel, national land has been placed under the direct control of Zionist foundations promoting Jewish settlement in Palestine. Thus in Zionist terms, the movement has indeed "redeemed" most of the land it captured, reserving its use to Jews, without any scruples about the methods by which it was acquired.

A United Nations commission estimates that more than four million dunums of Israel's "redeemed" national land (not including the Negev) was originally the property of Palestinian refugees.[17] Other estimates differ, which is to be expected, given the lack of detailed information on the size and nature of such properties.[18] The Israeli government probably possesses such information or at least has kept some records, but so far it has refused to release them.[19] Some idea of the extent of the disaster suffered by the Palestinian Arabs can be gleaned from the fact that of about 807 towns and villages in Palestine in 1945, only 433 were still standing in 1967.[20] Of these, 328 are in the West Bank and the Gaza strip and 105 more inside the borders of Israel.[21] In other words, 374 Arab towns and villages, or 45 percent of all Arab settlements in Palestine, disappeared after the creation of Israel.[22] They were demolished and their land given to Jewish settlers to farm. Villages in the plains were ploughed over to become agricultural land. On hilly ground which could not be farmed, the sites of villages were covered with trees and soon looked no different from any other forest. By the mid-1960s the Israeli government was carrying out the last of its projects for "cleaning up the natural landscape of Israel" by removing the remaining traces of ruined Arab villages.[23]

By the beginning of the 1960s there was little land left in Israel to be redeemed. Doubts over the need for maintaining Keren Keymeth were expressed and the company's activities were eventually restricted to land reclamation. Before this, as a conclusion to its operations, Keren Keymeth pressed the government to pass a series of laws giving formal recognition to the company's principles of land redemption.[24] On July 19, 1960, the Knesset passed the Basic Law: Israel Lands which, by definition, superseded other laws.[25] One of its provisions was that "lands in Israel of the state, the development authority or the Keren Keymeth Leisrael shall not be transferred either by sale or in any other manner," except in accordance with strict limitations outlined in a second law passed six days later.[26] On the same day, yet another law was passed setting up the Israeli Lands Administration to manage state property, including Keren Keymeth's land.[27] Then on November 28, 1961, the government and Keren Keymeth signed an agreement limiting both sides' powers, though Keren Keymeth reserved the right to break the agreement if the government changed or modified its policy forbidding the sale of state land.[28] Thus ended one phase of the Zionist program for redeeming the land.

This land redemption doctrine had far-reaching effects on the lives of the Arabs. The Israeli government did not confine itself to taking the land of the Palestinian refugees but extended its operations to dispossess the Arabs who had remained in the country, and whose luck was often not much better. The usual method was for the army, immediately after occupying an area, to seize the residents' land. After independence, kibbutzim and agricultural colonies near Arab villages would take over their neighbors' land, very often with the encouragement and approval of the government, simply by building barbed wire fences around it and annexing it. Indeed the eagerness of both individuals and settlements to

seize Arab property reached such extremes that the government had to draw up the Law of Abandoned Territories,
5708—1948 to deal with this phenomenon. As the minister
of agriculture put it, this law was "to regulate the legal status
of the abandoned areas, in the absence of a central government and a legal system which would normally guide action
regarding Arab property in the cities and in the dozens of
villages that have been all but abandoned. I take the liberty
of saying that there are signs of chaos here which are damaging and affect the welfare of the state as a whole and not
only the welfare of its [Arab] inhabitants."[29]

The expulsion of the Arab population and the confiscation
of its land continued despite adverse public opinion both in
Israel and abroad. More than 1 million dunums of land
belonging to Arabs who had remained in Israel was seized
after 1948.

One of the first incidents of the expulsion of Arabs from
their villages was the evacuation of Ikrit in western Galilee
and the transportation of its inhabitants to the village of
Rama, on November 5, 1948. Three months after that, on
February 4, 1949, the inhabitants of Kfar Anan were evicted
from their homes; half were sent to the Triangle where they
were forced to cross the armistice lines into the West Bank.
Three years later, when the villagers who remained in the
country submitted a request to the Supreme Court to be
allowed to return to Kfar Anan, all its houses were destroyed
by the Israeli army.

On February 28, seven hundred refugees were expelled
from Kfar Yasif, to which they had fled from nearby villages
during the fighting in Galilee. Most were loaded onto trucks,
driven to the Jordanian border and forced to cross.

The forced removals continued. On June 5, 1949, the
army and police surrounded three Arab villages in Galilee—
Khasas, Qatiya, and Yanuh—and expelled the inhabitants to
the Safad area. In January 1950 an army unit arrived in the
village of Ghabisiya and told the inhabitants they had to
leave within two days or be expelled across the frontier.
Seeing no alternative, they left their homes and moved to

Sheikh Danun, an abandoned village. On July 7, after a search in the village of Abu Ghosh near Jerusalem, some one hundred residents were rounded up and taken to an "unknown destination."

On August 17, the inhabitants of Mijdal in the south (now called Ashkelon) received an expulsion order and were transported to the border of the Gaza strip over a three-week period. At the beginning of February 1951, the inhabitants of thirteen small Arab villages in Wadi Ara in the Triangle were sent over the border. And on November 17, 1951, a military detachment surrounded the village of Khirbet Buweishat (near Umm al Fahm in the Triangle), expelled the inhabitants, and dynamited their homes.[30]

In addition to these collective expulsions, the Israeli government carried out "selective" expulsions in most of the Arab villages in Galilee between 1948 and 1951. Several dozen men would be chosen and forced to leave—notably heads of families, the eldest sons of large families, and the breadwinners—no doubt in the hope they would soon be followed by their dependents.[31]

Wholesale expulsions continued well into the early years of the Israeli state. In September 1953, the villagers of Umm al Faraj (near Nahariya) were driven out and their village destroyed. In October 1953, seven families were expelled from Rihaniya in Galilee, despite a Supreme Court ruling that the expulsion was illegal. On October 30, 1956, the Baqqara tribe was forced to cross from the northern part of Israel into Syria.

As late as 1959—eleven years after the establishment of the state—Bedouin tribes were expelled to Jordan and Egypt; the action was reversed only after United Nations intervention.[32]

Many other villages were either partly or completely demolished and many of their inhabitants now live as refugees in various parts of Israel.[33] But the incidents described are a fair sample of the "redemption of the land" operations undertaken by the Israeli authorities during the first years after the creation of the state.

While this project was in full swing, the Israeli government was passing a masterly series of laws chiefly aimed at justifying these acts and giving the authorities extensive powers to continue expropriating land that still remained in Arab hands.

The first of these laws was the Absentee's Property Law, 5710—1950.[34] This law first appeared in the form of regulations relating to refugee property that were promulgated by the minister of finance on December 12, 1948.[35] These regulations were renewed periodically until the Knesset replaced them with the new law on March 14, 1950. The purpose of the law was to define the legal status of the property of Palestinian refugees living outside Israel, by transferring it to a "custodian" of absentee property on the assumption that he would protect the rights of absentee owners until their cases were settled.

At first sight, this law seems a normal way of dealing with one of the problems resulting from the 1948 War, with no bearing on Arabs living inside Israel. But anyone defined as an absentee had all his property put in the care of the custodian, and the law's definition of absentee includes the following:

A person who, at any time during the period between ... November 29, 1947, and the day on which a declaration is published ... that the state of emergency declared by the Provisional State Council ... on May 19, 1948, has ceased to exist [and the state of emergency is still officially in effect to this day] was a legal owner of any property situated in the area of Israel or enjoyed or held it, whether by himself or through another, and who, at any time during the said period—

(i) was a national or citizen of Lebanon, Egypt, Syria, Saudi Arabia, Transjordan, Iraq, or the Yemen, or

(ii) was in one of these countries or in any part of Palestine outside the area of Israel, or

(iii) was a Palestinian citizen and left his ordinary place of residence in Palestine

(a) for a place outside Palestine before ... 1 September 1948 or

(b) for a place in Palestine held at the time by forces which

sought to prevent the establishment of the state of Israel or
which fought against it after its establishment. . . .

The significance of the definition becomes clear when one
looks at the dates set as limits. During that period, which
began on the day of the United Nations decision on the
partition of Palestine, all the Arab towns and villages occupied by Israel or later annexed by her, through the terms of
the ceasefire agreements, were far from being under Israeli
control. The residents were, of course, in the habit of leaving
their villages and towns for neighboring Arab countries on
business and other trips. Furthermore, when Israel occupied
these areas the Arabs often moved from their villages to the
neighboring towns or large villages, with the intention of
returning to their homes as soon as the situation returned to
normal. There were also Arabs who were forced to move by
the Israeli army.

Although the Arabs were hoping to return home once
conditions had settled, the Israeli authorities decided otherwise. A very few were allowed to return but the majority
were forced to remain far from their homes and areas they
had lived in, and their property was seized by the government. Thus, in the event that a property owner had left for a
neighboring country some time after the 1947 Partition Plan
was announced—even though he may have returned home
before Israel occupied the area—or had changed his place of
residence through force of circumstances during that period,
or had been forcibly expelled from his home town by the
Israeli army, or had left his house for a few days during the
fighting, the absentee's property law and the regulations
preceding it were enforced for the expropriation of additional land. Indeed,

Every Arab in Palestine who had left his town or village after
November 29, 1947, was liable to be classified as an absentee
under the regulations. All Arabs who held property in the New
City of Acre, regardless of the fact that they may never have
traveled farther than the few meters to the Old City, were
classified as absentees. The thirty thousand Arabs who fled from

one place to another within Israel, but who never left the country, were also liable to have their property declared absentee. Any individual who may have gone to Beirut or Bethlehem for a one-day visit, during the latter days of the Mandate, was automatically an absentee.[36]

Clearly there is no logical reason why an Arab leaving his house for a neighboring country or some other part of Palestine, or even walking over to the next village—all normal and legal actions at the time—should be declared an absentee and have his property confiscated. It is difficult to explain these unreasonable and oppressive acts except as motivated by an insatiable appetite for Arab land.

The absentee's property law is the cruelest of the land expropriation measures, making possible the seizure of tens of thousands of dunums of land, not to mention other forms of property.[37] Once a person is declared an "absentee," not only his land but every other possession is handed over to the custodian.[38] Thus property valued at millions of pounds has been confiscated from Arabs who are regarded as citizens of the country, voting in local and Knesset elections. This is how the absentee's property law came to be dubbed the "law of the present absentee." Indeed the definition of "absentee" applied permanently, so that even after the expropriation of his land any future acquisitions made as a result of the absentee's own labor were also considered the custodian's property. The Israeli authorities later modified the law, however, limiting its application to past possessions.[39]

The enforcement of this law has been merciless. Paragraph 30 empowers the custodian to issue written certificates, as to who is an absentee and what is absentee property; that, once he has signed them, these certificates have the effect of a law. Thus if "the custodian has certified in writing that a body of persons is an absentee," or that "some property is absentee property," then that "person or persons shall be regarded as absentees" and "that property, absentee property, so long as the contrary has not been proved." It has become frequent practice to issue such certificates based on no more evidence than the testimony of a mukhtar or a collaborator. Furthermore, to ensure that these decisions remain in force and to protect them against attacks in the courts, an article in the law stipulates that "the custodian may not be questioned about the sources of information which led him to issue" such certificates. Another article (17) further states that "Any transaction—and by 'transaction' is meant sale, transfer or any other form of disposal—made in good faith between the custodian and another person, in respect of property which the custodian considered at the time of the transaction to be vested property shall not be invalidated and shall remain in force even if it is proved that the property was not at the time vested property." The custodian was also empowered to "release" property in his possession and to return it to its owners if they made a request and obtained the consent of a government committee. But it soon became obvious that to free property from the grasp of the custodian was one of the most complicated undertakings in Israel. Similarly, the custodian has the power to use revenue from the property in his control to assist any person dependent on a former owner of such property or the owner himself, provided the person has no other source of income. The limit set for such subsidies was £50 per month. This was increased to £300 per month in 1967 when the law was modified.[40]

Furthermore, this law has been enforced in the Triangle, which was annexed under the armistice agreement concluded between Israel and Jordan in April 1949, despite the fact that the agreement includes an article clearly stating Israel's obligation to protect the rights of the inhabitants of the annexed areas (paragraph 6): "wherever villages are affected as a result of the [new] demarcation line, the residents of such villages shall be entitled to their full rights . . . as regards their places of residence, their property and their freedom. . . ."[41] Citing this article, a number of villagers in the Triangle brought an action against the custodian of absentee property, before the district court in Tel Aviv, demanding the return of their property, which was in his hands. The court granted their request and ordered it returned. The custodian appealed to the Supreme Court, however, which annulled the decision and denied the protection of the armistice agreement on the grounds that "any decision on matters connected with this agreement does not lie within the competence of the courts of Israel, because the rights conferred by this agreement and the obligations imposed by it, are rights and obligations binding the states that concluded the agreement and their enforcement is in the hands of these states alone."[42] The inhabitants of the Triangle suffered some of the greatest losses under the absentee property law. Half of the land expropriated from the Arabs once belonged to the population of this area, and most of it is the richest and most fertile in Israel.

The absentee property law was severely criticized and opposed by various groups, both Arab and Jewish. As it was debated in the Knesset, more than twenty-five reservations regarding individual articles were voiced. A few of the criticisms were accepted but most were rejected.[43] Even the Arab Knesset members attached to Mapai voted against it. The most fundamental objection was that it gave the custodian extensive powers without sufficient or effective supervision, since he was controlled only by the Knesset finance committee whose sessions are not public. Criticism became especially intense when it was discovered that the custodian was renting much of the land to kibbutzim, companies, and individuals with connections in the government, giving them unfair access to rich profits.[44] Tawfiq Tubi, of the Communist Party, expressed the feelings of the general Arab population when he said:

> This law is a symbol; it is an expression of the discrimination practised against the Arabs of this country. . . . By virtue of the provisions of this law, thousands of the Arab inhabitants of Israel are regarded as "absentees" although they are citizens of the country. They are deprived of their rights to the use of their property. The custodian, with the help of the law of course, is stripping them of their rights as citizens. This law does not allow them to enjoy their rights to their land and their homes and they are quite unjustifiably regarded as "absentees." . . . The real assignment of the honorable custodian is to steal more and more.[45]

Opposition to the law has continued, finding expression in numerous meetings, protests, and petitions, and is still echoed, from time to time, in the Knesset and other official bodies. In December 1952, for example, Rustum Bastuni of Mapam proposed a bill abolishing the term "absentee" for Arabs in Israel and returning their property. In his words, "there are more than twenty thousand such 'absentees' in eastern and western Galilee alone."[46] The bill was rejected. In February 1954, a similar proposal by Moshe Aram of Mapam was turned over for study to the finance committee, which did no more than praise the government's willingness to pay compensation to the absentees.[47] Again in February 1956, Mapam attempted a similar bill proposed by Yusef Khamis. This fared no better, especially after Levi Eshkol, who was then minister of finance, explained that it was impossible to return the land since: "it has been settled in the meantime . . . hundreds of farms and settlements have been built . . . on which thousands of people live. . . . In my opinion it is unthinkable to suggest the possibility of turning back the clock after what has happened."[48] But in July 1957, Mapam found support in its fourth attempt from similar proposals made by Masad Qassis, an Arab member attached to Mapai, and Tawfiq Tubi for the Communist Party.[49] All three suggestions were again referred to the finance committee. After studying the problem for a year, the committee reported that it had noted, again, the government's proposed measures "to pay suitable compensation to land owners whose property was in the possession of the development authority" especially after "the government's approval on February 2, 1958 of the project to resettle Arab refugees and 'absentees' living in Israel in housing projects and agricultural settlements."[50] But this missed the point; the struggle had been for restoration, not compensation. The government had always been prepared to pay compensation, albeit in modest amounts. Thus the land belonging to "absentees" living in Israel suffered the same fate as that of refugees outside Israel: in both cases it was given to Zionist foundations and Jewish settlements.

The second in the series of land expropriation laws is the perennial law on which the military government was based, the Defense (Emergency) Regulations, 1945, or, to be more precise, Article 125. This was the notorious closed areas article, which enabled the military governor to restrict access to those with written permits. The authorities have exploited Article 125 to prevent many Arabs from returning to the villages from which they were expelled during the fighting in 1948. The method was very simple. Villagers were prevented from returning to their villages and offered compensation for relinquishing their property. In most cases, however, they determinedly refused such offers and continued their attempts to return home. To prevent this, and to prepare for taking the necessary steps against them should they persist, the military governor would declare the area closed. After this it would invariably become impossible to obtain permits to enter the village for "security reasons." The approval of the army chief of staff or the minister of defense was needed; the military governor himself was not "allowed" to issue such permits.

There are many "closed" villages in the areas formerly ruled by the military government, especially in Galilee. The village of Ghabisiya is just one example. At the beginning of February 1950, the inhabitants of the village were ordered to leave by the military governor of Galilee, and their village was declared a closed area. A year after their expulsion, faced with the persistent refusal of the authorities to allow them to return, the Ghabisiya villagers submitted a complaint asking that the military governor's orders be repealed and they be allowed to return to the village. The Supreme Court judged that the declaration of an area as "closed" was a "legal act" and could not be considered effective "unless the declaration had been published in the *Official Gazette.*" In view of the fact that there had been no official announcement for Ghabisiya, the villagers should be returned to their homes.[51] This provided a dangerous loophole in the system of expropriation laws, however, and the response of the authorities and the military government was prompt. The villagers were prevented from returning and a few days after the court's decision, Lieutenant-General Na'aman Stavi, military governor of Galilee, published the order declaring Ghabisiya "closed."[52] The villagers made a second appeal to the Supreme Court but were not so fortunate again. The court ruled that villagers who had not returned home before the order could still not return, except, of course, with the written permission of the authorities.[53]

So ended the story of Ghabisiya. Other villages suffered similar fates, and their populations for the most part still live in Israel. In anticipation of future troubles, the order declaring Ghabisiya a closed area also applied in eleven other Arab villages in Galilee: Amqa, Fradiya, Kfar Anan, Saffuriya, Mijdal, Kfar Berem, Mansura, Kuweikat, Barwa, Damun, and Ruweis.

The third land expropriation law, which was also a law on which military rule was based, was originally promulgated by the minister of defense as the Emergency (Security Zones) Regulations, 5709—1949.[54] It was extended periodically by the Knesset until the end of December 1972.[55] Since then there have been no requests for further extensions.

This law enabled the minister of defense, with the approval of the Foreign Affairs and Security Committee, to designate the "protected area" (a strip of land stretching ten kilometers north and twenty-five kilometers south of Latitude 31, for the length of the Israeli border)[56] or any part of it a "security zone." Exploiting his powers to the full, the minister of defense declared almost half of Galilee, all of the Triangle, an area near the Gaza strip, and another along the Jerusalem-Jaffa railway line near Batir as security zones.[57]

Once an area was declared a security zone, no one could live in it permanently, enter or be in it without a special permit from the authorities appointed by the minister of defense. The provisions of the security zones regulations resulted in conditions similar to those in the closed areas, but their real object was to give the minister of defense and Israeli authorities further powers. For example, one of the articles of the security zones regulations says that "the competent authorities may by order require a permanent resident to leave the security zone." Anyone receiving such orders "shall leave the security zone within fourteen days from the day on which the order to leave is served on him" or be forcibly driven out by the army or the police. He can appeal the order before a special appeals committee provided he does so "within four days from the day on which the order is served on him . . . the decision of the committee shall be final."[58] To put it more simply, these articles made it possible for the minister of defense to drive out the inhabitants of any Arab village lying within a security zone. As for the appeal committees, their main purpose was to disguise the arbitrary actions of the authorities; they have never annulled an order. It later became obvious that these articles were formulated to allow the authorities to expropriate land on or near the border and sell it to the Keren Keymeth, in fulfillment of an agreement made with the legal advisor to the Israeli government at a meeting near the end of 1948.[59]

The cited articles were enforced for the first time against the inhabitants of the village of Ikrit in western Galilee, near the Lebanese border. The Israeli army had occupied Ikrit and neighboring villages on October 31, 1948. There had been no opposition or struggle on the part of the population. Six days later, on November 5, the villagers were ordered to leave their homes "for two weeks" until "military operations in the area were concluded." They were advised to take only what they needed for that period. The army provided locks for the houses and the villagers were handed the keys.[60] Within three days the villagers were evacuated to Rama in central Galilee, on the main Acre-Safad road.

Much more than two weeks passed before the villagers were allowed to return. All appeals to the authorities were rejected. After more than two years of negotiations with no results, the villagers realized there was no intent to return them to their homes and they appealed to the Supreme Court. On July 31, 1951, the court announced that "There is no legal impediment to the plaintiffs' returning to their village."[61] The villagers then asked the military governor to implement the decision; he referred them to the minister of defense who referred them back to the governor. This went on for about a month, at the end of which the villagers received formal orders to leave their village, in accordance with the security zone regulations. They appealed at once to the appeals committee, which—after a session lasting until after midnight—ratified the expulsion order. The villagers then appealed again to the Supreme Court, which agreed to consider the case on February 6, 1952.[62] Six weeks before the appointed date, on Christmas Day, the Israeli army blew up all the houses in the village, all of whose inhabitants were Christian Arabs.[63] After this the government announced the expropriation of the village's land, which totalled 15,650 dunums.[64]

The case of the village of Kfar Berem, which was occupied on the same day as Ikrit, is very similar. After being evacuated to the village of Jish in the same way and on the same pretext, the villagers eventually appealed to the Supreme Court in 1953.[65] At the beginning of September, the court ordered the authorities to state what reasons there were to prevent the villagers from returning to their homes. The reaction was extremely violent. In a great display of force, the infantry and air force attacked the village on September 16, 1953, bombing and shelling until it was completely destroyed. Even before this took place, the government had announced the expropriation of Kfar Berem's land, which amounted to 11,700 dunums.[66]

Both Ikrit and Kfar Berem were to become thorns in the side of the Israeli government; they remained active problems both inside and outside Israel. Metropolitan Georgios Hakim, head of the Greek Catholic community in Israel, brought the incidents to the attention of the Vatican and many other Christian institutions outside Israel, asking for intervention on behalf of the villagers and pressure on the Israeli authorities to allow the people to return to their homes.[67] The government's reaction was to make exhaustive efforts to settle the two cases by paying compensation and persuading the villagers to give up their villages. What little success was achieved came through the help of Metropolitan Hakim. Changing his position, he persuaded some of the Ikrit villagers to give up their rights to the village and accept compensation.[68] He himself accepted compensation for the property of the village church.[69]

The majority of the population in both communities, however, insisted on returning home, refusing any alternative solutions. As recently as the summer of 1972, the whole question flared up again. The two communities had gone to the villages to repair the churches but then refused to leave. In this they had the support of Metropolitan Hakim's successor, Metropolitan Joseph Raya. The police had to intervene and take the villagers away. The case was reviewed by the government, which again expressed its opposition to the villagers' return, fearing to set a precedent.[70] This decision only increased the tension. Early in August 1972 a large number of Jews went from Tel Aviv to the two villages to demonstrate solidarity.[71] This was followed by a meeting between a delegation of Jewish writers and Prime Minister Golda Meir at which the writers stated their objection to the government decision.[72] Then some two thousand people marched with Metropolitan Raya in the streets of Jerusalem.[73] Popular feeling was further aroused when government claims that most of the villagers had received compensation for their property proved false; in fact, compensation had been paid for only 916 of Ikrit's 15,650 dunums. The villagers of Kfar Berem refused to accept any compensation worth mentioning.[74] The case of the two villages is still unsettled. When the security zones regulations ceased to be effective at the end of 1972, the Israeli authorities declared Ikrit and Kfar Berem closed areas according to the defense regulations.

Yet another incident resulting from the enforcement of the security zones regulations involved the village of Khasas in Upper Galilee, near the Israeli-Syrian border. In 1949 the villagers were driven from their village to Mount Canaan and from there to Wadi Hamma near Tiberias. In 1952 they appealed to the Supreme Court to be allowed to return home. The court decided in their favor, but the army immediately served them with orders to depart, as required by the security zones regulations. When the case came up a second time, the court decided that it could not interfere with or annul the "evacuation orders," since the powers of the authorities issuing such orders were "absolute" where "security matters" were concerned.[75]

The fourth link in the chain of expropriation laws is known as the Emergency Regulations (Cultivation of Waste Lands) Ordinance, 5709—1949. These had originally been drafted by the provisional Israeli government in mid-October 1948.[76] The official claim was that these articles were necessary as a result of the war because of the "lands being abandoned by their owners and cultivators and left untilled, plantations being neglected and water resources remaining unexploited." In calling for an extension of these regulations, the minister of agriculture said that "the interest of the state demands that . . . agricultural production be maintained and expanded as much as possible."[77] He went on:

> Jewish farm organizations and all their branches are cooperating with us on this project, they are consulted at every step and will be in the future. . . . So far we have been able to cultivate and sow more than half a million dunums of tilled land. The problem we shall soon be facing, especially after the liberation of the Negev and the transfer to the state of huge areas of land left by its former owners, will be making use of an additional million dunums.[78]

Thus the minister of agriculture was enabled to "assume control of the land in order to ensure its cultivation" in cases where "he is not satisfied that the owner has begun, or is about to begin or will continue to cultivate the land" (Article 4).

In practice, these regulations contributed to further expropriation. By them the authorities had the power to legitimize the forceful seizure of Arab land by the kibbutzim and Jewish settlements, through the minister of agriculture's ability, according to Article 24, to approve all or any incidents of land seizure resulting in the cultivation of fallow land, even where land was taken without permission and before the articles were drawn up.

Another way in which these articles helped land expropriation was in coordination with the military government's power to declare any area closed or a security zone. The minister of defense, or the military governor, would declare an area closed or a security zone, whereupon entry without written permit became a serious security offense. At the same time, for "security reasons," permits could not be issued to the owners of the land to get to it and farm it. The land soon became "uncultivated," and was immediately declared "uncultivated land" by the minister of agriculture. At this point, "in order to ensure that it is cultivated," he could have such land farmed either by "laborers in his own employ" or by "handing it over to someone else to farm." Invariably, the "other party" was a neighboring Jewish settlement. Shafa Amr provides just one example of expropriation by this method: about twenty-five thousand dunums of land was taken over, some of it owned by Jews who had neglected to farm it.[79]

According to the original version of the articles, the minister of agriculture could not keep such land for more than two years and eleven months; but the period was later extended for as long as the state of emergency exists.[80] And thus most of the land became state property.

In addition to these, there was a fifth law permitting the confiscation of Arab land and property, especially urban property. This was the Law for the Requisitioning of Property in Times of Emergency, 5710—1949.[81] It originally stemmed from the need for housing new Jewish immigrants and for vacant buildings for use as government offices.

Article 3 of the law enables the government to appoint a "competent authority" with the power to "order the seizure of property or the use of property as housing" whenever it deems such orders necessary for "the protection of the country, public security, safeguarding essential supplies and services, or for settling immigrants, veterans or disabled soldiers."

In its original form the law states that "requisitioned property . . . cannot be retained for more than three years." But before its expiration the period was extended to six years.[82] Before the six years were up, another modification of the law extended the period to August 1, 1958.[83] Any land the government considers necessary for national security reasons and retains beyond that date is treated as expropriated property.

These five land expropriation laws form a self-sufficient entity representing the first phase in the confiscation of Arab land in Israel by the Israeli government. The wording of the laws mentions the "transfer," "use," and "seizure" of property but never its "ownership." Indeed, much of the expropriated land officially still belonged to its original owners, regardless of the fact that they were prevented from using it. One final step was necessary, namely, the official transfer of ownership to the state of Israel and its various official bodies. To accomplish this, the Land Acquisition (Validation of Acts and Compensation) Law, 5713—1953, was passed.[84]

This law is the epitome of its five predecessors. Briefly, it empowers the minister of finance to transfer expropriated land to the possession of the state of Israel through the development authority. Obviously, in making this law, the government wanted to settle the question of land seizure and remove any legal complications arising from it. In proposing the bill to the Knesset, the minister of finance stated quite openly that its purpose was:

> to legalize certain actions taken during the war and after it. . . . When the government began to take over absentee property for security reasons or for necessary development projects, other expanses of land were seized for the same purpose, essentially in agricultural areas where the rights of ownership were not sufficiently clearly defined. There are reasons connected with national security and necessary projects that make it impossible to return these lands to their owners.[85]

The true aim of this speech was to approve the seizure of Arab land by the kibbutzim during the war and after.[86] The law in fact gave the authorities the power to legalize any seizure of property. Article 2 stipulates that by certifying that a certain property was not in the possession of its owners on April 1, 1952, and between May 14, 1948, and that date "it was used or assigned for purposes of essential development, [Jewish] settlement or security" and "if it is still needed for any of these purposes," the minister of finance could turn the property over to the development authority. Regardless of the truth of the certificate's contents, as long as it was signed by the minister it was sufficient to transfer ownership. In June 1955, Shmuel Mikunis (of the Communist Party) proposed an amendment allowing an owner whose land had been unjustly seized to request annulment of the certificate by the Supreme Court if he could prove that its contents were false. But the Knesset rejected the amendment.[87] The law also provided for the payment of compensation to former property owners, within defined limits. It soon became clear, however, that this compensation merely served as a cover for the seizure of Arab property at the lowest possible prices.

Opposition to the land acquisition law was strong, both inside and outside the Knesset, and its expression more extreme than in 1950 when the absentee's property law was passed. Many Jews in the Knesset objected to the extensive powers it granted the authorities while compensation to the victims was minimal.[88] Others likened it to the laws resulting in the confiscation of Jewish property in Spain during the Middle Ages and to the Nazi laws. Dr. Israel Carlebach, founder of *Maariv* and its first editor, described the circumstances leading to the passage of the land acquisition law and its true implications in the form of a dialogue with his daughter:

> This land was Arab land in the old days which you can't remember. The fields and villages were theirs. But you don't see many of these now—there are only flourishing Jewish colonies where they

used to be . . . because a great miracle happened to us. One day
those Arabs fled before us and we took their land and farmed it.
And the old owners went to other countries and settled there.

But here and there you do sometimes see some Arab villages.
These are the villages of the few who remained among us. . . .
they have become citizens in our state. . . .

"Where are the fields?" you will ask.

There are none, my dear.

"What happened to the fields?"

We simply took them.

"But how? How can one take land belonging to someone else,
someone living among us and cultivating that land and living off
it?"

There is nothing difficult about that. All you need is force.
Once you have the power, you can, for example, say: "These
fields are a 'closed area,' and stop anyone from getting to them
without a permit. And you only give out permits to your friends,
to people living in the kibbutzim nearby whose eyes have feasted
on that land. You don't give permits to the Arabs who own the
land. It is really very simple.

"But is there no law? Are there no courts in Israel?"

Of course there are. But they only held up matters very
briefly. The Arabs did go to our courts and asked for their land
back from those who stole it. And the judges decided that yes,
the Arabs are the legal owners of the fields they have tilled for
generations, and even the police saw no reason why they should
not sow the land and harvest it. . . .

"Well then, if that is the decision of the judges . . . we are a
law-abiding nation."

No, my dear, it is not quite like that. If the law decides against
the thief, and the thief is very powerful, then he makes another
law supporting his view.

"How?"

All those who took part in the robbery gather in the Knesset.
And who hasn't? The land was taken . . . by the departments of
government, by Mapai and Mapam and the religious parties—all of
them. They say: "We are used to this land and we don't want the
courts to disturb us and stop us farming it. Come, let us make a
law that will make it impossible for anyone to take this land from
us."

"But how? How can you make a law contradicting another
law?"

They simply decided that as far as this land is concerned there is no law, that in this matter there is no law or court, and that the owners of this land cannot appeal to the courts.

"Very well, but where does this get them? There must be a record somewhere that this land belongs to the Arabs, there are deeds. . . ."

Yes, there is a record, but what of it? Into the law they wrote that the documents must be corrected and the names of the Arab owners crossed out and replaced by the names of the Jewish owners. . . . The Arab owners are obliged to confirm that the land had been taken from them legally. The Arabs obviously are not eager to cooperate with the competent authority and do not rush to its offices in crowds to "arrange matters."

"If the Arabs refuse to cooperate or sign, then the whole plan is a failure."

No. The law is not so naive as to be swayed by the [wishes] of the Arabs. It changes the rights to their property without involving them in the process. It even grants the Arab owners compensation without their receiving it. . . . I am not joking . . . it is all very possible. . . . For one thing it is the Arab who has to establish his ownership of the land rather than the Jew who has taken it from him. . . . Even when he can prove it, it does not help him much, since there is no court to study his case—the decision lies with the official in charge of granting compensation. And even if this official recognizes that an Arab once owned the land, he cannot give him full compensation. For example, if compensation is requested in the form of cash, according to the law it can only be given for the value of the land as it stood three years ago on January 1, 1950. . . . [The law] acts as if the peasant who is paid twenty pounds for a dunum of land, which was a fair price three years ago, can hope to find a third, or a fourth or even a fifth of a dunum for this price today.

"Let him refuse the money then, that's all."

Wait, my dear, we are a wise and clever nation, and this too has been thought out. Refusing the money would not help him either. The money is deposited with the court . . . and there it remains. But whether the Arab land owner receives the money or not does not concern us . . . since it does not affect the "legal" transfer of his land to us.

"But why would he need money anyway?" you may ask. "As a farmer, what he needs is land."

You are right. And the law has taken care of this also. In

special cases, the law recognizes that farmers have a right to land: for example, when the expropriated land is, first, under cultivation, second, a main source of livelihood, third, the owner has no other land to live off. . . . The owner of the land has to establish that he has no source of income . . . that for six years he has been starving . . . that he is on the point of dying of hunger . . . in which case . . .

"In which case one of the Jewish kibbutzim which have seized tens of thousands of dunums will return him enough land to live off?"

No, in which case, we offer him some other land, which he may rent but never own! There is no legal obligation to offer him as much land as was taken from him, "part" is enough. There is no need even to satisfy him, it is enough to make an offer. . . . They are offering them land that they cannot possibly accept . . . they are offering land that once belonged to fellow Arabs who fled beyond the borders. Of course the Arabs say: "This is not your land to offer." And so they refuse it. But that does not concern us or the law. We are only bound to make the offer. If they refuse it, the loss is theirs. . . .[89]

Yet in spite of all the objections, and the fact that this law was no more than a feeble pretext for robbing the Arabs of their land, the government persisted in carrying it out to the last detail. Indeed it is one of the very few laws that has not been amended or modified since it was passed.

In the entire history of land expropriation laws only one was successfully opposed. In 1960 the Israeli government proposed a bill for concentrating all agricultural land, whose aim was as follows:

The state, the development authority and Keren Keymeth Leisrael are the legal owners of hundreds of thousands of dunums in Galilee, the Triangle, and Wadi Ara. There are more than 250,000 dunums divided into small plots which are swallowed up among the plots owned by Arabs. In this form it is impossible to make use of the land for settlement or development. We need government intervention to concentrate this land and the proposed bill would enable the state and the development authority to merge the plots they own into larger areas which could then be settled or developed or improved according to the needs of the nation.[90]

In its new form, the land could, of course, be used for establishing additional Jewish settlements.

In order to concentrate this land, the government proposed to the Knesset that the minister of agriculture be given the power to declare a given area "a land concentration area" with the authority to exchange plots of land under the pretext of grouping state-owned land into one area and land owned by others into another. If the state does not own sufficient land, the minister of agriculture would be authorized to offer compensation for privately owned land, with the approval of a committee appointed by the minister.

There is no doubt that, had the Knesset approved this bill, it would have opened the door to further expropriation of Arab land and the payment of compensation with the excuse that the state did not have "enough land" to exchange for it. With a wealth of experience in having their land confiscated, the Arabs understood the implications of this law and rallied against it. One action was the vote by thirteen local Arab councils condemning the bill. Three protest meetings were held by the Organization of Arab Farmers (a small organization under the influence of Mapam and the Popular Front), the most important of which was a conference in Acre on February 5, 1961, attended by representatives from forty-three Arab villages. Strikes and demonstrations were also announced in villages such as Ailbun, Tayba, Kfar Yasif, and Rama.

This wave of protest and intense opposition on the part of the Arab population led to the omission of the bill from the Knesset's agenda. It was one of the rare occasions on which the Arab population, through organized popular action, was able to defeat a government proposal against it.

But despite the failure of the land concentration bill, by the late 1950s the Israeli government had taken the basic steps for seizing the largest possible area of Arab land. The next phase was the final absorption of this land after settling the few remaining problems attached to it.

5

"Liberating" the Land

The second phase of the government's measures affecting Arab land inside Israel coincided with the general change in Israel's policy toward its Arab subjects, which began in the middle of 1959. Opposition to government action with respect to Arab land had heightened, especially when it became obvious that the policy was having an extremely negative effect on relations with the Arabs in Israel. Indeed at times it seemed to be more detrimental than the security policy and the military government. Among the Arabs there was almost unanimous opposition to the security and land measures, especially during the decade 1948-58 when talk of "military rule" and "land expropriation" was on every tongue. Realizing that in order to win the friendship of the Arabs, eliminate the causes of their discontent, and maintain peace, compromise on the land problem was necessary. The government tied in its change in land policy with the easing of security and military restrictions. But while the measures announced for the military government promised a turn for the better, the new land policy, though moderately worded, was in practice much more severe. It was no more than the completion of the first phase, its aim being the establishment of the land expropriation measures as final, so that the seizure of Arab land became permanent.

The real objectives of the policy were patently clear in Ben-Gurion's announcement in 1959 of a modification in the government's attitude toward the Arabs. After mentioning the changes in security measures, he went on to other measures that the government viewed as essential to its security policy. Briefly, the government had decided to stop what it termed "the illegal seizure of public and absentee land. At the same time, the use of uncultivated land and the reclamation of rocky ground would be encouraged in order to create a reserve of land for the development of Galilee by additional [Jewish] agricultural settlements into which new immigrants would be absorbed. The new settlements in Galilee would be important from the point of view of security also." In furtherance of this the government intended to take steps which would remove sources of danger. These steps were:

(a) the speedy settlement of [Arab] refugees and absentees inside Israel, in their present places of residence or other suitable locations to be determined in consultation with the security departments; (b) the speedy establishment of Jewish settlements in Galilee which would in future lead to a reduction of the area under enforced military surveillance; (c) the preparation of the ground for the establishment of security settlements along the axis of the Wadi Ara road in the Triangle, this being the communications lifeline between northern and central Israel; (d) the passage of a law for the settlement of the Bedouins and their transfer to permanent homes in the Negev; (e) the speedy solution of the problem of compensation to be paid to the present absentees for their land, which would aid in their early resettlement; (f) the encouragement by the state of Arab migration to the cities of mixed population, to live there permanently with the help of the government.[1]

To summarize all these twists and turns, the expropriated Arab land was to be absorbed for the establishment of more Jewish settlements. Jewish settlement would be generally encouraged and increased, especially in regions like Galilee, which are predominantly Arab. At the same time a long-term policy of encouraging Arabs to leave their villages and the principal centers of Arab population for the large cities would be employed. This was a change from the past, but it would mean the dispersal and absorption of closely knit social groups. With the breakup of Arab rural society, there would be less need for strict security measures. The Israeli government has been making concentrated efforts to realize these objectives since the beginning of the 1960s.

The most significant of the new measures was step (b): the plan to increase the Jewish presence in Galilee. At first this was called the "Project for the Judaization of Galilee," but it was soon renamed "Project for the Development of Galilee," the hint of racism in the first title being "incompatible" with Israeli taste. But despite the change in name, the Israeli government did not deny the plan's purpose, even if strengthening the Jewish presence occurred at the expense of the Arab population. This was not simply a question of gaining additional settlements, always regarded as an important achievement. A genuine Jewish presence would be essential to counter any future demands for the return of Galilee, or part of it, to the Arabs. The areas that had been designated as part of the Palestinian state in the United Nations Partition Plan of 1947 were felt to be especially vulnerable.

Israeli intentions in Galilee were no secret but openly discussed and published on the front pages of the newspapers. The publicity seems to have been organized with the support of the Israeli security departments to win over all those not convinced of the usefulness of the project. Those who favored the plan had many reasons, including the fact that "throughout the region between Nazareth and the Lebanese border, the [Jewish] settlers form a minority of the population . . . making it a potentially dangerous stretch of land . . . between Israel's Arabs and the enemy. This has led to social and security problems also, with the Jewish minority feeling cut off in the midst of a hostile Arab majority. And these Jews feel more threatened than the Arabs among a general Jewish majority." [2] Another reason offered was that "the claim has been repeatedly made that Galilee was not intended as part of Israel according to the Partition Plan, and this continues to feed the hope that a plebiscite will be held in the area, which is after all Arab and not Jewish." Thus "the problem of Galilee is a Jewish problem . . . it is an Arab empire within our borders . . . and those who believe with the government that military rule alone will liberate [Galilee] are simply mistaken."[3]

Shimon Peres, deputy minister of defense, summed up the situation by saying: "The areas in Israel that are still unsettled, or only settled in a certain manner, are and will continue to be a subject for special attention beyond Israel's settlement policy. The Arab countries which covet areas inhabited by Jews will be all the more greedy for the completely uninhabited regions and parts where there are no Jews."[4]

The idea of Judaization seems to have been the brainchild of Joseph Nahmani, one of the originators of "redemption of the land" and head of Keren Keymeth from 1935 until his death in 1965. He had been disturbed that Arabs had remained after the establishment of Israel, especially in "his area"—Galilee. He had been unable to redeem any significant areas of land in Galilee before the creation of Israel and so decided to carry out his plans with the help of the government.

In January 1953, Nahmani sent a memorandum to the minister of defense, Ben-Gurion, which began:

> Though Western Galilee has now been occupied, it still has not been freed of its Arab population, as happened in other parts of the country. There still are fifty-one villages and the city of Nazareth whose inhabitants have not left—in all, there are 84,002 Arabs, not counting Acre, controlling 929,549 dunums of land . . . most of them farmers, who make up 45 percent of the Arab minority in the country. They are living in a self-contained area stretching right up to the borders of Arab Lebanon. The Arab minority centered here presents a continual threat to the security of the nation. . . . Its presence adds to the burdens of the government and will create problems when the permanent borders are finally defined. The very existence of a unified Arab group in this part of the country is an invitation to the Arab states to press their claims to the area. . . . When the time comes, it will play the part played by the Germans in Czechoslovakia at the beginning of World War II. . . . At the very least, it can

become the nucleus of Arab nationalism, influenced by the nationalist movements in the neighboring countries, and undermining the stability of our state.

For these reasons, Nahmani considered it "essential to break up this concentration of Arabs through Jewish settlements. . . . As for the Jewish settlements to be created in the Arab areas and on the borders of Lebanon, it may be more prudent not to send immigrants newly arrived from Arab countries to live in them." These would, in time, find much in common with the Arabs. It would be better to send specially trained members of the youth movement.

Nahmani points to another possible threat to the success of his plan, namely the presence of large numbers of Arab refugees in the area and of Arabs no longer owning property who were pressuring the government to give them land. In his view, "the government will not be able to withstand such pressures . . . and will have to satisfy any justified demands." In the public interest, Nahmani stresses the importance of

creating faits accomplis which will make it impossible for the government, for all its good intentions, to give up any of the uncultivated land for the Arabs to live on. The safest way to accomplish this would be to hand over all abandoned or government-owned land [in the area] to the Keren Keymeth. The Arabs will not be able to ask for land from the Keren Keymeth knowing, as they do, that it is a Jewish nationalist company whose lands are reserved for Jewish settlement alone, nor will they be able to demand from the government land that it does not own.[5]

Nahmani had to wait a long time for a reply; almost three years passed before Ben-Gurion responded. Meanwhile he addressed himself to other quarters. In December 1955 he wrote a letter to the president of the state of Israel, Yitzhak Ben Zvi, who was an old friend from pre–World War I days. After describing the unsatisfactory situation in Galilee he complained that Ben-Gurion "did not even consider it necessary to acknowledge receipt of his memorandum" and asked Ben Zvi to intervene on his behalf especially as Ben-Gurion "was not particularly sympathetic to Keren Keymeth." This letter had no more success than the memorandum, so Nahmani turned to Joseph Weitz, one of the leading officials of Keren Keymeth, sending him letter after letter through 1956 in an attempt to persuade him to adopt his plan.[6]

In contrast to Nahmani and Ben Zvi, who seemed ineffectual, Joseph Weitz had worked toward the redemption of the land and the establishment of Jewish settlements for more than forty-four years. During this period of service he had gained influence and high office and was respected "for his ability to eat up two ministers at one sitting," as a colleague put it, if they dared interfere in his province. As soon as he was convinced of the logic of Nahmani's plan, he began his own campaign. In his memoirs, Weitz describes a meeting with Ben-Gurion, at the end of August 1958, during which he proposed the settlement of Galilee. Two weeks later he made the same proposal to Levi Eshkol, minister of finance. By the end of 1958 he had met with various influential people, from the minister of agriculture to the leaders of Mapai, to convince them of the project's worth.[7] Two years later he became the first head of the Israeli Lands Administration, which was to encourage Jewish settlement. At the end of October 1962, Weitz addressed a memorandum to Ben-Gurion, pointing out the threat presented by the Arab majority in Galilee and suggesting the reinforcement of Jewish settlement there. At first, Ben-Gurion expressed approval of this suggestion, though he later disassociated himself from it, in the form described by Weitz.[8] Not the least discouraged by Ben-Gurion's attitude, Weitz seized the first opportunity after Ben-Gurion's resignation to explain his project to Levi Eshkol, the new prime minister, in August 1963. Less than six weeks later he was informed by Eshkol that the government had unanimously approved the project.[9]

The Israeli government had, in fact, already taken some steps toward Judaizing the Galilee area.

On the eve of the Sinai war in 1956, Arab nationalist feelings ran high, so much so that the government was forced to take prompt and decisive action. As the Arab center in the north, Nazareth was a headquarters for the roused nationalists and for this reason was chosen by the government to suffer the first "blow." After lengthy and careful research, the decision was made to "graft" a Jewish town onto Arab Nazareth, its main, indeed its only, purpose being to "break up" [quotation marks in the original] the concentration of Arabs in the city and the surrounding area, and eventually to create a Jewish majority in the population.[10]

As a first step, the announcement was made that some twelve hundred dunums of city land northeast of Nazareth had been expropriated. This was the entire land area remaining for any future expansion of the city. The land was confiscated on the pretext that it was needed for building government offices, in accordance with the 1943 Land (Acquisition for Public Purposes) Ordinance.[11] An appeal by the holders of the land was rejected by the Supreme Court which recognized building government offices as a "public purpose."

Once the land was taken, however, it was used for the construction of housing for new Jewish immigrants and for a chocolate factory and spinning and weaving industries nearby to provide work.[12] The Arab workers in Nazareth meanwhile had to commute daily to Haifa and other distant Jewish towns to look for work. Soon the authorities gave the new town the name of Upper Nazareth, and it eventually became the capital of Israel's northern district. Regional offices were moved to Upper Nazareth, including those that had been in Arab Nazareth, to add to the importance of the Jewish town and to increase its population. The original plan seems to have been to increase the population of Upper Nazareth until it outnumbered Arab Nazareth, at which point the two towns would be unified and a Jewish mayor appointed, as in Jerusalem. Indeed Mordecai Allon, chairman of the local council in Upper Nazareth, more than once declared his willingness to fill the position.[13] Eventually the idea of a Jewish mayor was abandoned, the government preferring an Arab like Seifeddin Zu'bi who would go to any lengths to cooperate. An Arab mayor would also be an asset from the point of view of Zionist propaganda abroad.

The construction of Upper Nazareth was not, at first, part

of the Judaization of Galilee, though it was incorporated in the project later. It provided the model, however, for the construction of similar Jewish settlements in Arab areas of Galilee.

After the creation of Upper Nazareth, work was begun on Maalot—another Jewish town in western Galilee, in the vicinity of Tarshiha—and a number of small Jewish settlements were established in various parts of Galilee and the Triangle. Then toward the end of 1961 the authorities announced the expropriation of some 5100 dunums of land belonging to the villages of Deir al Asad, Bi'na, and Nahf (in the center of Galilee on the main Acre–Safad road) for the purpose of building the town of Carmiel. Preparation for this expropriation had begun five years earlier, when the land—which contained the finest stone quarries in Israel—was declared a closed area.

The expropriation of this land was opposed with an intensity rarely encountered before, except in the case of Ikrit and Kfar Berem. The protest was quite effective in the long run, since after Carmiel there were no more expropriations on such a scale. The villagers first pleaded with the government to reconsider its decision to seize their finest agricultural land and in its stead offered a stretch of land in the same area, which would be suitable for the construction of a town. The government persisted in taking the land, assuring the villagers that it would compensate the owners with rich land in the same region. The falsity of this promise was uncovered when the Knesset finance committee studied the case, after it was brought before the Knesset by Moshe Sneh (Communist Party) and Yusef Khamis (Mapam) at the request of the villagers.[14] In its draft report, the minority on the committee stated that "the committee is not convinced that there is no alternative to the expropriation of the agricultural land belonging to the three villages. There is no justification for this land seizure, not only because the government has no means of compensating the owners with comparable land [there is no land of this quality in the area] but because there is no need for the land for the establishment of the town, since the planning authority has no intention of constructing any buildings on the site."[15] After lodging their complaint with the Knesset, the villagers called a protest meeting for late March 1962, but the military governor of Galilee declared the three villages a closed area for the day; no one could reach the villages and the meeting was cancelled.[16] The same tactic was used to foil a second protest meeting planned for mid-January 1964.[17] Meanwhile the three villages had appealed to the Supreme Court which issued a temporary restraining order in mid-February 1963. The villagers retracted their appeal, however, because two of the court's panel of three judges, in whom the villagers had "no confidence," refused to stand down.[18]

The story of Carmiel did not end there. When the first stage of construction was finished and Jewish settlers began to move in, some of the Arabs in the neighboring villages asked for permission to move into the town too, but they were refused. When the minister of housing, Joseph Almogi, was questioned in the Knesset, he refused to say whether Arabs were forbidden to live in Carmiel, and despite pressing demands for an explanation, limited himself to the comment that "Carmiel was not built in order to solve the problems of the people in the surrounding area."[19] The official position of the government angered many Jews, who felt that the Arabs were being discriminated against. In the middle of February 1965, some four hundred people went from Tel Aviv to the closed area near Carmiel and remained for several hours, demonstrating their disagreement with the government and protesting "discrimination against a section of the citizens of the country." Representatives of the group went to the nearby police station to inform the police of their presence in the area without permits, inviting them to make arrests. No one was arrested by the police that day, but as soon as the excitement died down, those who were considered the instigators were arrested and brought before a military tribunal.[20]

The last noteworthy incident involving Carmiel and its Arab neighbors took place in January and February 1972. An Arab contractor from the village of Deir al Asad announced his readiness to invest capital in industries for Carmiel in which both Jews and Arabs would be employed. The offer divided the townspeople but those who objected to it finally won and the scheme was turned down.[21] Carmiel wants neither Arab residents nor Arab funds. This attitude does not, however, prevent the city from allowing Arab laborers to work on construction sites for new housing, pave the road, or work as gardeners.

Despite all these efforts, the Judaization of Galilee has not been successful to any significant degree. In 1970, after more than ten years' work, the Arabs in the northern sector (the districts of Acre, Nazareth, Tiberias, and Safad) still constituted almost half the population—four times the usual proportion of Arabs to Jews in Israel. In the district of Acre, at the beginning of 1970, there were more Arabs—112,767— than Jews—67,479.[22] The situation will probably remain unchanged for many years to come, in view of the difficulty of establishing Jewish settlements there.

While the Zionist settlement foundations were occupied with the Judaization project, officials at the ministry of justice, the Israeli Lands Administration, and the surveys department of the ministry of labor were engaged in a related effort to prevent the Arabs from "seizing" public land or absentee property.

The notion of preventing Arabs from seizing land belonging to the state fits in with the Zionist concept of land redemption. The problem originally arose when the expropriation of rich Arab land in the plains left only hilly, rocky ground for the Arab peasants to work and improve in order to ensure some means of livelihood at a time when the land at their disposal had greatly diminished and their numbers were increasing year by year. Toward the end of the 1950s large-scale land expropriations had for the most part been accomplished and the government was searching for new categories of land to redeem. It realized that most of the land the Arabs had been developing for subsistence farming lay in areas that had not been surveyed, where the rights to the land had not been permanently defined. During the British Mandate only about one-quarter, or 5 million dunums, of Israel's 20 million dunums of land had been surveyed.[23] According to the Ottoman land laws and the laws of the British Mandate, which were still in effect in Israel, in the event of a land survey, the Arab farmers had the right to ask that the land they were farming be registered in their names. In other words, the Arab farmers could "seize" land that should have been considered "state property" in the first place. To avert this danger, the government rushed through the Prescription Law, 5718—1958.[24]

In order to understand clearly the provisions of the Prescription Law and the way they were enforced, it is necessary to look briefly at some of the articles of the 1858 Ottoman Land Law and the Mandate Land (Settlement of Title) Ordinance of 1928. These two laws stipulate that when a survey of property rights is made, anyone who can establish that he or she has used and cultivated a piece of land for ten consecutive years (the "prescription period") can ask that the land be registered in his or her name on the records of the land registration department, thereby becoming its legal owner. The surveys consisted of detailed records of every plot of land with clear descriptions of its area and boundaries. Any plot that had been farmed for ten years or more was registered in the name of the farmer; otherwise it was considered public land. The British found it convenient to apply this law in solving land-ownership problems, but the Israeli government felt it necessary to improve on it. By increasing the prescribed period to more than ten years under the new Prescription Law, it seriously affected the rights of the Arab farmers.

In the original draft of the law, the prescribed period had been fifty years, which meant that an Arab claiming ownership had to establish that he and the previous owners of a piece of land had cultivated it for fifty consecutive years. When this draft was published, the Arabs saw it as tantamount to a takeover of all the land that remained to them, since it is difficult to find proof of all the transactions involving a piece of land for half a century and to determine its state before World War I. No consideration was to be given to the great efforts expended by Arab farmers to develop and improve it in the intervening years. Protest meetings were held and delegations and memoranda sent to the minister of justice, the prime minister, and the Knesset. One of the memoranda submitted to the Constitution, Law, and Justice Committee contained the following:

> There are many Arab peasants, who over a long period of time, and as a result of great efforts, have developed large areas of land. This land is not registered in their names because there had been no official survey of the area during the British Mandate. In the event of a land survey at the present time, those making use of the land are justified in asking that it be registered in their name, since they have in most cases been cultivating it for more than ten years, and can easily prove it. . . . The extension of the "pre- scribed" period to fifty years would be gravely prejudicial to the legitimate rights of the Arab peasants. . . . We regard this law as yet another effort by the authorities to dispossess the Arabs of their land.[25]

Following a flood of complaints from the Arab population and, apparently, because of the difficulty of proving control for fifty consecutive years, the prescriptive period was ex- tended only from ten to fifteen years. But an additional pro- vision was written into the law whereby: "in the case of a person who came into possession of any land after . . . March 1, 1943, the five years beginning on the day of the coming into force of this law [April 6, 1958] shall not be taken into account in calculating that period." Thus, for those who started to cultivate a piece of land after March 1, 1943, the period is in fact twenty years, or twice what it had been under Ottoman and British law.

It was difficult at first to understand why this provision was introduced, but two subsequent events disclosed the real motives behind it. The first was the announcement before March 1, 1963—before twenty years had passed since March 1, 1943—that all land not yet surveyed was subject to survey.[26] This prevented the fulfillment of the twenty years' requirement. The decision to survey the land in a certain area is a simple matter which does not normally merit a special announcement in the *Official Gazette* by the head of the land registration department. The formality of the announcement, however, has a magic legal effect, in that it brings the passage of time to a halt and protects the "rights" of the state of Israel to the land involved. To put it more simply, the Israeli courts could as a result of this step determine the ownership of any land inside Israel on the basis of its circumstances in 1943, regardless of the improvements made by those farming it after that date.

The second event occurred during the hearing of a case brought by an Arab from Galilee who claimed ownership to a certain piece of land. At one point the government representative produced an aerial photograph of the area in question with the number forty-five written on it, explaining that the Israeli government possessed such photographs taken by the British Air Force in 1944 and early 1945 of the whole of Palestine. In the aerial photograph the land in question did not appear to be cultivated and would therefore be turned over to the state of Israel. The survey official accepted the photograph as concrete proof and made his decision accordingly. This decision was upheld by the Supreme Court on the grounds that: "the document before us seems to have been taken in 1945 and since no convincing proof to the contrary has been brought before us or the survey official, we accept it as it has been represented to us, as having been taken on the date that appears on it. . . ."[27]

Not only did the Prescription Law, interpreted in this way, undermine the rights of the Arabs to their land, but various other legal and administrative measures combined to deprive them of even more. The determination of ownership in accordance with the laws of the Mandate, later adopted by Israel, was a complicated process. After a preliminary survey and the preparation of detailed maps, all those claiming ownership to a plot of land have to submit to the survey official a written claim, with relevant documents, explaining how they came to own it. In the event of conflicting claims, the case is referred to the courts for a decision. From the beginning, the Israeli authorities relied on the series of aerial photographs in making their decisions. Land that appeared cultivated or covered with trees in the photographs was recognized as the property of the Arab claimant, whereas any land that looked fallow or neglected on the day the photographs were taken, regardless of the fact that its owners may have turned it into first-class farmland in the intervening years, was not admitted as property of the claimant. (Before the Prescription Law was passed and made to apply retroactively, it had been legal to claim land cultivated after 1945.) The Israeli interpretation of the Ottoman land law did not allow the constructing of a house on the land as "agricultural use" and the presence of a house on the aerial photographs did not therefore count as evidence in favor of the claimant.

Many of the properties claimed by Arabs contained stretches of rocky ground unsuitable for cultivation. The Israeli authorities would divide such properties, singling out the uncultivated land, in such a way as to enable the government to expropriate the greatest area possible. This was done by combining into single plots land that was mostly rocky and partly cultivated and then confiscating any plot that contained rocky land. In no instance did the Israeli government forgo any land it could claim, however barren or small. In some cases one thousandth or one ten-thousandth of an estate would be claimed even when it amounted to no more than a few square meters.

Eventually this insistence on owning every possible area was revealed as part of the government's plan to merge its fragmented properties into one through a series of exchanges. For example, the government would give up state land near a village in return for twice or three times as much land some distance away from the village. This would then be given to a Jewish settlement for cultivation or it would be used for the establishment of a new settlement. The authorities did not hesitate to employ all kinds of pressure and legal tricks. On many occasions when there was some doubt about the real owner of a piece of land, the government would produce

several claims from various quarters. The state would claim
the land on the grounds that it was not cultivated; the development authority would insist that it had a right to the land
since it had been expropriated for the authority's use; the
custodian of absentee property would claim the property as
originally belonging to an absent Palestinian refugee; and
sometimes the Keren Keymeth would join in, acknowledging
that the land had been the property of a refugee but claiming
that it had been bought from him or "his representatives."
The government did not, of course, care which of these four
agencies finally came into possession of the land as long as it
did not stay in the hands of the Arab farmer, while the Arab
claimant would frequently prefer to give up the land rather
than enter into long litigation incurring expenses greater than
its worth.[28]

The Israeli authorities exploited the survey to its utmost,
presenting thousands of claims and entering into hundreds of
court cases, despite the strong resistance offered by the Arab
peasants. In the decade or so following passage of the Prescription Law, by March 31, 1971, almost 10 million more
dunums, half the land area of Israel, had been surveyed. The
5 million dunums not yet surveyed lie mostly in the Negev—
far enough away from Arab farmers to be safe from
"seizure." In the north, where most of the Arab population
lives, only eight hundred thousand dunums remain to be surveyed (4 percent of the total area of Israel) and work on
them is proceeding with all possible speed.[29] The survey provided an opportunity for looting every conceivable plot of
land remaining in Arab hands. The government was acting on
the assumption that all the land in Israel is essentially public
land and that it is up to anyone claiming ownership to a
particular plot to prove his claim. Tens of thousands of
dunums were transformed from private Arab property to the
property of the state of Israel. Between 1960 and 1965 some
eight thousand cases relating to the land survey were brought
before the courts by various departments of the government.[30]

The Israeli authorities themselves implicitly acknowledged

the injustice of the land survey operation. In 1959, about one year after the passage of the Prescription Law, the Knesset passed a special law providing that any person whose land had been turned into state property as a result of the Prescription Law and whose land had been his "principal source of livelihood ... and of his relatives, and who has no other land sufficient for their livelihood" could ask to rent an equivalent piece of land for a period of no less than forty-nine years.[31] The generosity of the authorities in this particular did not change the essence of the situation. The land remained the property of the state and it was no great loss to relinquish the right to use it if further problems with the Arab farmers were thus avoided. The day would come when the land would cease to be "the source of livelihood" of the farmer and his family; it would then be state property. For their part, the Arab farmers rarely asked that their land be rented out to them, but continued to cultivate it as if nothing had happened, until they had to give it up to the Jewish settlers.

In conclusion, some of the contradictory measures taken by the Israeli authorities when the results of the survey did not favor them should be pointed out. During the Mandate much of the rural public land belonging to the village—especially the woods and land used for pasture or woodcutting or for future construction—was registered in the name of the High Commissioner on behalf of the villagers, since most villages had no local council to represent them. The Israeli authorities found it hard to see so much land, which would have been government property had the survey been conducted after the establishment of Israel, being used by Arab villages. A solution was found by declaring such land protected state forestland, which cannot be used or disposed of by anyone. By 1965 some thirty thousand dunums of land belonging to Sachnin, Tur'an, Kfar, Sam'i, Jatt, and Suaed Bedouins was declared state forestland. In 1969, 11,534 more dunums belonging to four Arab villages was added.[32]

Among the land seized by Israel from the Arabs was some

that was part of the Islamic *waqf*—property whose revenue goes to charitable purposes. There was some doubt on the part of the authorities as to how to deal with this property. Although it was placed in the keeping of the custodian for absentee property toward the end of 1948, he was not allowed to dispose of it. Meanwhile Ben-Gurion proclaimed that the government was studying "how to settle these matters according to the Islamic laws of the *waqf*, and current . . . circumstances in Israel."[33] But the current circumstances eventually took precedence over the laws of the *waqf*. When it became clear that the Palestinian refugees were not returning, the Israeli government formalized its position on the *waqf* in the provisions of the absentee's property law, which declared *waqf* property absentee property.

There was widespread opposition and criticism of this move among both Arabs and Jews. Not only was the decision considered illegal and unjust but also inexcusable, since *waqf* property is regarded as belonging to God and income from such property is devoted to charitable ends. In any case, God can hardly be classified as an absentee according to the absentee's property law.[34] Nor had the needy members of the Islamic community—for whose sake the *waqf* was endowed—disappeared from Israel; on the contrary there are thousands of them. The most natural action would have been to turn the *waqf* properties over to the leaders of the Islamic community to dispose of in accordance with religious laws, as the British had done during the Mandate. Indeed the Supreme Court of Israel expressed reservations and challenged the legality of the declaration.[35] But the government was not prevented by such criticism from proceeding with the takeover, and *waqf* property was put to the service of Zionist settlement like any other refugee property. "In 1951 an agreement was made between the custodian and the ministry of religions whereby the ministry . . . undertook to administer the property . . . and in 1954 and 1959, the custodian appointed the head of the Islamic and Druze department in the ministry of religions as his agent to administer part of the property in his charge [originally the mosques and the

cemeteries]." [36] As for the bulk of the *waqf* property—
amounting to tens of thousands of dunums of rich agricultural land in rural areas—the custodian "sold" it to the
development authority in 1953. [37] He had still not received
payment for it in 1967. Following this precedent, the custodian continued to sell any other *waqf* land that came into
his hands to the authority and considered the matter
closed. [38] There remained, however, the question of the fraction of *waqf* property that had been put into the care of the
ministry of religions. This consisted mainly of mosques,
cemeteries, and related buildings, many of them in Israeli
towns and villages with some Moslem population remaining.
(Mosques and cemeteries in villages destroyed by the Israelis
suffered the same fate as the rest of the village buildings.) In
some cities there were also residential buildings and stores
belonging to the *waqf*.

After insistent demands by the Islamic community that
such property be turned over to representatives of their faith,
the government agreed to transfer control of "the mosques,
cemeteries and holy places . . . to Islamic councils to be appointed by the minister of religions." [39] After such councils
had been appointed in Haifa, Jaffa, Lydda, and Ramle, the
custodian reserved to himself the right to administer some of
the properties—such as houses and stores which provided income. [40] When it became apparent that the holy places of
Islam could not be administered without funds, the government formed a committee of representatives of the minister
of finance and the minister of religions to dispense such
funds according to the recommendations of the Islamic
councils. [41]

These measures did not satisfy many Moslems in Israel,
especially because the funds were but a small fraction of the
income derived from *waqf* property and did not meet the
needs of the religious community. [42] Moreover, the members
of the Islamic councils were often chosen from among leading collaborators with the government ("a group of big shots
willing to put their thumb stamps to anything asked of
them," according to *Al Ittihad)* and did not handle the funds

in the most exemplary manner.[43] Meanwhile the government was most scrupulous about giving detailed information on how these modest sums were spent but refused to reveal the extent of the total income derived from the *waqf* properties it had seized.

Demands that the government relinquish the *waqf* properties continued until a bill to that effect was introduced in the Knesset in 1959.[44] Soon after this the Knesset was dissolved and preparations made for new elections, so no further action was taken. Seeing that the government was in no hurry to reopen the question after the elections in 1962, Mapam proposed a bill which was rejected after an announcement by the minister of religions that the government was about to settle the matter directly.[45] A year passed and nothing was done, so Mapam reintroduced its bill, this time with the Communist Party, and was again rejected.[46] Soon after this the government made its own proposal to release *waqf* property which was approved by the Knesset in February 1965.[47]

This amendment to the absentee's property law was acclaimed by the authorities far beyond its actual significance. Its provisions were that the government could appoint "board trustees" in no more than seven cities in Israel—Jaffa, Ramle, Lydda, Haifa, Acre, Nazareth, and Shafa Amr—which would be entrusted with the *waqf* properties within those cities.[48] These committees would be regarded as the legal owners of the *waqf* properties in that they were free of "any restriction, qualification, or other similar limitation prescribed by or under any law or document relating to the endowment." It was no accident that the committees were given so much power; the government soon began to manipulate the committees to its own advantage. In 1962 and 1963 the authorities had met with strong opposition from a large part of the Moslem population in Jaffa when they sold part of the Abdul Nabi cemetery in the north of Tel Aviv as a construction site for the Hilton Hotel. Eventually, in response to complaints, what must have seemed an excessive settlement had to be made.[49] In contrast the rest of the cemetery, as well as another cemetery, were sold with great ease

in 1971 after the Jaffa Board of Trustees approved the transaction.[50] The sites were used for housing Jewish residents of
Tel Aviv. A year later the same board negotiated with a company headed by Gharshun Peres—brother of the minister of
communications, Shimon Peres—about renting the mosque of
Hassan Bek for a shopping center.[51]

In short, the Israeli government acted no differently with
regard to *waqf* properties than it had in handling the rest of
the property of Arabs inside Israel. In both cases it aimed to
annex it permanently.

While settling the question of Arab property, the government also made many attempts to solve the problems of the
Bedouins during the second decade of the state of Israel. This
took the form of housing them within defined areas—step (d)
of the policy announced in 1959.

The state's relation to the Bedouins in Galilee and especially in the Negev involved more than a mere question of
housing, however, a fact the government seemed to disregard
in its ambivalent policies. Toward the end of 1948 officials
had made an agreement with a number of the tribes in the
Negev, some of which had fought on the side of the Israelis
during the war, that the Bedouins "would not attack the
[Israeli] security forces or interfere in political problems [be-
tween Israel and Arab neighbors] and the government would
recognize their rights and their ownership of the land they
lived on."[52] Subsequently, however, all the land of the
Bedouins who had been moved into reserved areas was expropriated on the grounds that the owners had "abandoned"
it.[53] Furthermore, the authorities refused to issue Israeli identity cards to the Bedouins, and at that time, anyone found
without such papers could be banished beyond the border.
Bedouins in large numbers were in fact expelled; it was not
until mid-1952 that they received identity cards.[54] Several of
the Bedouin tribes in Galilee were treated in a similar
fashion, including those among them who had collaborated
with Zionist military forces.[55]

This policy toward the Bedouins continued almost without

change until the late 1950s. More than any other group, the Negev Bedouins suffered the full and unrestrained harshness of military rule. Arabs in the north of Israel were better educated and therefore able to offer steady resistance to the military government, whether in organized demonstrations or in spontaneous outbursts. The Bedouins, on the other hand, usually had no alternative to submission, their leaders often collaborating with the Israeli authorities in return for support of their own positions.[56] Throughout this period tribes were moved from one location to another in the Negev, some relocating up to five times in one year.[57] In their absence, their properties were more vulnerable to seizure. Economically, they were worse off than other Arabs, especially during the frequent droughts in their region. Yet the Israeli authorities remained firm in restricting the Bedouins' movements, thus limiting their opportunities of finding work outside the Negev. Some form of government subsidy was provided in times of crisis.

When the change in Israeli policy toward the Arabs was proclaimed in 1959, it included the campaign to settle the Bedouins in specially designated areas, a project first proposed in 1948 on the grounds that "anyone adopting this form of living would become a good citizen, and those unwilling to do so would have to move to Sinai or Transjordan."[58] The official reason given in the early 1960s for settling the Bedouins was cultural—namely that some members of the government felt it a duty to bring the standard of Bedouin life up to that of the rest of the population. This could only be done by moving the Bedouins to permanent dwellings. Of course, other motives such as security and Jewish settlement played a very important part. As long as the Bedouins lived nomadic lives, there was no effective way the security forces could keep them under surveillance and control their movements. There was the added difficulty that the boundaries "recognized" by the Bedouins did not coincide with internationally recognized borders. For example, in the drought years the Negev Bedouins would send their flocks to Sinai or Jordan, where they would be tended by members of the tribe who lived there. Conversely, in the good years they would bring livestock from outside Israel, graze it for a few months for a fee, and then return it to its owners. These movements across the border also involved smuggling and, at times, intelligence. But Jewish settlement was probably the primary consideration, since the scattering of Bedouins over vast areas disproportionate to their numbers delayed Jewish settlement in the region. Furthermore many Bedouins were eventually housed in isolated areas, with no evidence of a development plan, suggesting that the neighboring land was being reserved for systematic Zionist settlement. With the prospect of large stretches of the Negev being vacated by the Bedouins, under the new policy, the call to settle them became more urgent so that Jewish expansion could begin. This operation would also enable the government to seize additional land, in exchange for services to the new Bedouin communities or with the excuse that the Bedouins were now living at an inconvenient distance from their properties.

However, despite countless proclamations, the Israeli government did not seem altogether in earnest about this project; the necessary funds had not even been reserved. There was no hurry to make preliminary studies. Approval for the project had been given in mid-1959, but it was not until the end of 1960 that deliberations began and they continued inconclusively until mid-1964. Moshe Dayan, who was in charge of the project as minister of agriculture, changed his mind on the subject, as usual, from one session to the next.[59] And yet Premier Levi Eshkol had stated in July 1963 that "the commission has completed its deliberations on the designation of sites for the construction of Bedouin communities and its findings will be presented to the government for study and approval."[60]

Whatever the reasons for the uncertainty at high levels, efforts to achieve Bedouin settlement were made by various bodies. Most of the action was taken in behalf of the Bedouins in Galilee. No doubt this was closely linked to the Judaization project, in that it made possible the vacating of comparatively large areas of land. The means by which the

Bedouins were "persuaded" to move to sites chosen by the government were excessively harsh and went beyond the usual limits.

The first tribe to be chosen as a candidate for "civilization" was the Suaed Bedouins who lived in northern Israel between the Galilee villages of Nahf, Rama, Deir Hanna, and Sachnin. This tribe had in fact voluntarily accepted the modern way of life and most members had built houses for themselves in the area. Relations with the authorities had never been good, however. Immediately after the occupation of Palestine, an unsuccessful attempt was made to drive the Suaed off their land. During the early 1950s the land was declared absentee property in order to prevent them from using it but they were not to be stopped.[61] In 1956 the military government declared the land closed for use by the Israeli army for maneuvers. The tribe ignored orders to leave the land and wholesale restrictions were imposed.[62]

Pressure was again put upon the Suaed in 1962. Their elementary school was closed on the grounds "that it was lacking in the minimum safety requirements and thus a hazard to the lives and safety of teachers and pupils."[63] The army had planned military maneuvers in the vicinity of the school, so the two hundred children attending it had to interrupt their studies. However, public pressure later forced the government to reopen the school. In 1964 the government campaign against the Suaed and another tribe, the Na'im Bedouins living near Shafa Amr, became more harsh. "About forty-five houses and huts, and even wells the Bedouins had dug decades previously to store drinking water for themselves and their cattle, were blown up."[64] This took place between June and September of 1964, the government having decided to speed up Jewish settlement in the area.[65] But the Arabs still refused to leave.

From 1961 onward, the authorities had been declaring some of the new houses built by the Suaed "closed areas," which meant that a person going into his or her own house without a permit could be arrested and brought before a military court for having broken the emergency regulations.

Other harassment included charges that the new houses had been built on "public land" without licenses and on sites that had not been set aside for construction. In September 1964, most of the houses belonging to the Na'im tribe were blown up, in the expectation that the coming winter would force them to accept the government's housing plan. It was said that once the houses were demolished "the officials at the Israeli Lands Administration who handle Bedouin affairs need do nothing but sit in their offices and wait for representatives of the tribe to bring word that they agreed to the proposals of the administration to resettle them."[66] But the Na'im sent no representatives; instead, they pitched their tents next to the ruins of their houses and continued to live where they had always lived. If there was an element of innate obstinacy in their reaction, the Na'im also had a very real cause for apprehension of the government's attempt to gain large areas of Bedouin land at low cost. It is not surprising that they resisted vehemently.

The resettlement of the Bedouins was not entirely without positive aspects. In 1965, for example, a village called Basmet Tab'un was built for the Zubaidat, Sa'dieh, and Hilf Bedouins next to Tab'un on the main Haifa–Nazareth road. A similar village was built in Bir Maksur, near Shafa Amr, for the Hujairat Bedouins. The fact that many of the tribesmen were serving as volunteers in the Israeli army helped to bring this about. The Knesset Finance Committee had agreed in September 1965 to the establishment of three settlements for the Negev Bedouins in Tel Sheba, Shuval, and Ksifeh.[67] In 1967, Tel Sheba was built near Beersheba; then in 1972 foundation stones were laid near Shuval.[68] Construction also began in May 1972 on a village in Wadi Hammam, near Tiberias, for Arab refugees in the area. Most of these came from Ghabisiya and Khasas in northern Galilee, which they had been forced to leave in 1948 even though some had fought against "the Syrian invaders."[69]

Despite these achievements, there is a long way to go before the problem of Bedouin land is solved. Only a fraction of the Bedouins have been involved in these initial settlements; the circumstances of the rest are unchanged. The government is not unaware of this and, according to the most recent information available, ten more villages are planned to house the remaining Bedouins in Galilee. It is hoped that this will stop them from spreading over larger areas and prevent "illegal land seizures," especially since the destruction of Bedouin houses has proved useless; they simply rebuild elsewhere.[70]

Finally, the Israeli government wished to solve the problem of compensation for expropriated land—step (e). From the first seizures of Arab land, the government had announced its readiness to pay compensation. It continues to do so to this day and does not neglect an opportunity for demonstrating the progress it has made in this.

The authorities' eagerness and persistence in paying the rightful owners compensation is indeed remarkable. Although most of the expropriated land has been annexed and used for Zionist settlement and the boundaries so changed that it would be difficult to set the clock back without eliminating the Zionist presence in Palestine, the government uses every possible means to induce the owners of expropriated land to accept compensation. Yet a large number of Arabs adamantly refuse to accept such payment and to sign legal documents giving up their rights to their land and to their country, preferring to leave things as they are until some solution is found for the Palestine problem. No doubt this insistence on paying arises from the Israeli fear that the whole question may some day flare up again. It would be advantageous, in such a situation, to be able to produce documents relinquishing as much of the land as possible and showing that "suitable compensation" was, at any rate, paid for it. One of the classic features of Zionism is the conviction that a national home can be bought in Palestine for a few dozen or a few hundred million pounds.

Israel has been taking over Arab land within its borders since 1948, but the decision to pay compensation was not made until 1953 on the passage of the Land Acquisition

(Validation of Acts and Compensation) Law, 5713—1953. A glance at this law will show that it was intended as a legalization of expropriation through the payment of nominal "compensation." Article 5 states that the Israeli government will pay compensation for the expropriated land in Israeli currency according to its value on January 1, 1950, although the law had come into effect in 1953. In its draft form, the bill had set the date of the partition of Palestine, November 29, 1947, for the valuation of the land. Certificates of expropriation were made out during 1953 and 1954, and although the Israeli pound had suffered a palpable devaluation, the government continued to offer compensation at the 1950 rates as if there had been no change.

It was not that the government was unaware of the rise in the price of land, of course. This very question came up during the first meeting held to implement the law, at the end of May 1954. Some officials at the conference were of the opinion that the amount of the compensations should be increased, and Moshe Sharett said outright that compensation according to the land acquisition law represented "a scandalous robbery, since the Israeli pound is worth only one-fifth of its former value."[71] No modifications were made, however, and during the period 1954-1970, with the exception of the 1966/1967 financial year, the Israeli government paid compensation of £22,056,000 and 43,540 dunums for 166,733 dunums, half the land expropriated under this law.[72] Assuming that the land given as compensation was equal in value to that expropriated, the rate paid was £180 per dunum.[73] For a day laborer in construction this amount represented only ten days' work and for an elementary school teacher, one-third of a month's salary. Meanwhile, the market price of one dunum of land was hundreds and sometimes thousands of pounds.

In 1959, on the recommendation of the finance committee, the government had formed five people's committees in different parts of Israel "to advise the Development Authority on the amount of compensation to be paid to owners of expropriated land." This was intended to help settle the compensation problem as swiftly as possible. However, the minister of finance soon ordered these committees dissolved, apparently because "their recommendations . . . would raise the price of the land taken, to three and four times what it had been in 1950."[74]

These guidelines for paying compensation were applied to all other land expropriated under Israeli law, notably the absentee's property law. Having rejected all requests for modification of the law and having refused to return expropriated property—at least to "absentees" living in Israel or their heirs—the government magnanimously declared its willingness to pay compensation.[75] The government's offer is still open today.

Simultaneously with the settlement of compensation, the government tried to solve the problem of Arab refugees and deportees inside Israel who had left their villages, or been forced out of them, during the 1948 War and after. According to one official estimate, by 1957 there were about twenty thousand such refugees (3,500 families).[76] In the early 1960s they were

> living mostly . . . in shanty towns on the outskirts of the villages [they had been moved to] and were regarded as transients. A very few rich refugees managed to buy some land in the villages they were now living in and built new homes, or else rented houses. In some cases their own villages were being partly inhabited by newcomers. Most of the land suitable for agriculture was annexed by established Jewish colonies to round out their property or else given to new settlements. Again this is not true for all the land. The great majority of these refugees asked to return to their villages. Despite their poverty, they refuse to sell their right to their property. They refuse to become part of some other village and persist in their stance. . . .[77]

Until 1952 these refugees received aid from the United Nations, but when the international organization realized that they were "property owners" in Israel, its support was cut off. The Israeli government ignored the problem the first ten years; then in 1958 a special project for rehousing refugees was announced. Special units would be built and a fund set aside for grants and loans. At the end of 1962 an official body for housing refugees was set up, but its activities were discontinued after three meetings when it became apparent that each ministry in the government was handling the problem in its own field.[78]

After this description of the expropriation laws and their use, the question of how much land Israel seized from the Arabs living within its borders becomes rhetorical. It would be a hard question to answer with respect to the property of Palestinian refugees living outside Israel and even more difficult for the Arabs in Israel. Information on the subject is neither comprehensive nor exact, and—apart from the half-truths published by various Israeli circles, both official and unofficial—the available facts at times seem contradictory.

Among the sources is *Village Statistics 1945*, published by the Mandate government. This consists of an index of all the villages in Palestine, with the land belonging to each divided into qualities of soil and fertility and distinctions between Arab, Jewish, and other property. There are some reservations about the accuracy of this work.[79] After the establishment of Israel a census was made (in 1949-50) of all the agricultural land within Israel belonging to Arabs. A summarized version was later published, but it is very general and thus not very reliable.[80] To complicate matters further this summary mentions land "in the possession of" rather than "owned by" Arabs, and one cannot assume that the terms are synonymous. During 1953-54, 450 certificates of expropriation were published in the *Official Gazette* in accordance with the provisions of the 1953 Land Acquisition Law. Taking up 330 pages, these documents refer to 1,225,174 dunums of land, forming part of the property of 291 Arab villages.[81] About two-thirds of the land cited in the certificates reportedly belongs to Palestinian refugees outside Israel. Obviously the certificates do not give complete information, since some of the villages lost all their land—corresponding exactly to the entry in *Village Statistics 1945*—while others had only a few dunums expropriated. The rest of their land was apparently already considered the property of the custodian for absentee property (see Appendix, Table 5). Also, many of the properties are so intertwined that it is difficult to distinguish between land belonging to refugees and that belonging to Arabs in Israel. Another survey of agricultural land was made in 1962, but it did not include the Arab areas south of Jerusalem and the land belonging to the Bedouins of the Negev.[82] A field study would be all that is necessary to arrive at some reasonable findings. But despite the conflicting evidence and the gaps in the information, it is still possible to form a picture of the loss of land suffered by many of the Arab villages. The total loss suffered by 78 (out of 104) Arab villages between 1945 and 1962 amounts to 704,809 dunums, or 65 percent of their land. Assuming that the same proportion applies for the land expropriated from the rest of the Arab villages in Israel, even a cautious estimate puts the total land area lost through expropriation during those years at about 930,000 dunums. This does not include the land of the Arab refugees and deportees living in Israel or the land of the Bedouins.

The land belonging to the Bedouins is the most difficult to assess, especially in the Negev, since the existing information is contradictory. In Galilee, the property of the Bedouins—some 19,000 dunums—forms a small part of Arab-owned land, according to the 1949-50 census. In the Negev, until very recently available information indicated that all the land expropriated from the Bedouins between 1953 and 1954, under the land acquisition law, amounted to about 250,000 dunums.[83] The Bedouins retained an equal area of land, which they still held in 1958-59.[84] Thus the total area belonging to the Bedouins was 500,000 dunums, a figure which is supported by the 1949-50 census. However, Shmuel Toledano, the prime minister's advisor on Arab affairs, recently stated that the area in conflict between the government and the Bedouins was 1 million dunums, not a quarter of a million.[85]

Apparently, even the responsible Israeli authorities are uncertain of the exact area of the land expropriated. For example, in its 1961 annual report, the Israeli Lands Administration estimated the land taken under the Land Acquisition Law at some 380,000 dunums. Yet the 1963 annual report mentions an area of 250,000 dunums and yet another report, 350,000 dunums—despite the fact that the very same authorities ordered the expropriation and thus presumably had the relevant files and documents.[86] Assuming that the last estimate is the true one, the total area of land expropriated under the expropriation laws—including 418,000 dunums under the absentee property law and 205,000 dunums under the Prescription Law—totaled 948,000 dunums.[87] If the land expropriated under the Prescription Law after 1962 or 1964 were added, the total area taken from the Arabs in Israel since 1948 would be more than 1 million dunums.

Eventually, the expropriated land was used to further dozens of Jewish agricultural settlements. With the exclusive use by Jews of land from which Arabs had been cleared, most, if not all, the aspirations of colonialist Zionist imperialism—"to redeem and liberate the land of *Eretz Israel*"—were realized. All that remained was to foster these settlements until they gained full strength before searching for new fields of activity. But it soon became apparent that redemption of the land was not a single operation but a continual process requiring more and more action against the Arabs (and against the Jewish settlers when the need arose), even at the risk of exposing the unjustifiably racist nature of such action.

There was a disturbing feature about the new settlements that forced the government to take special measures to safeguard its accomplishments in recovering the land. When immigrants, most of them Oriental Jews, were flocking into the country immediately after the establishment of Israel, the Zionist foundations were forced to make some changes in the classic settlement plan. The main difference in the new settlements—the *moshavim*—was a measure of freedom for the individual settler in managing his or her personal affairs, in contrast with the collective ideology of the old kibbutzim. In most instances, individual settlers would be given a share of land and water which they could use for their own personal profit, if they wished. The Zionist foundations made every effort to provide financial support for these settlements until they discovered signs of an unpleasant development the Israeli authorities had always firmly opposed: some of the new settlers were renting their share of land to fellow settlers and moving to the cities to work.

This in itself would not have troubled the government, nor would such drastic steps have been taken to stamp out the practice, had not a further danger been found. Some of the new settlers were hiring Arab farm laborers, who were willing and available in almost every part of Israel, to farm their land. Others were renting out their whole share in return for a lump sum, leaving the Arabs the choice of how to best use the land. Still others formed partnerships with their Arab laborers under terms that allowed the workers to use the land for unlimited periods of time. It goes without saying that the sole motive behind these arrangements was financial gain. The Oriental Jews, especially, were not very impressed with Zionist abstractions, of Ashkenazi origin, about redeeming the land and the "conquest of labor." Meanwhile all the agreements between settlers and Arab laborers invariably proved profitable to the settlers, whether because they paid low wages or because they were receiving a share of the harvest without incurring any expenses, while they earned a living elsewhere.

The Zionist institutions did their best to suppress these developments. Their concern was not so much with the exploitation of Arab labor as with the fact that these arrangements were allowing the Arabs to return to the land, undermining the supreme efforts made by the Zionists. The anxiety on this subject spread to other circles not usually concerned with such matters. In February 1965, for example, Knesset member Shlomo Gross (Agudat Israel) asked the minister of agriculture for a statement on the plans of his ministry to counter this practice.[88] The various Israeli newspapers had already reported the subject. Four months later, in June 1965, Knesset member Shneur Abramov of the right-wing Gahal Party, requested the inclusion of this question on the Knesset agenda. Gahal, throughout its history, has had no deep sympathy with this kind of settlement because of the "socialist" tinge it had acquired. It was with a touch of irony that the minister of agriculture thanked Abramov for his concern for "the nation's well-being" and promised that the government would take action on the matter.[89]

One Israeli journalist—Habib Kanan—had anticipated the employment of Arab labor by the settlers and had said very early:

> We must remember that the problem of Arab refugees has not yet been solved. Hundreds of thousands of eyes are watching from beyond the border to see what is happening to the land that the Palestinian Arabs have lost. . . . it is useless to try and hide from the world the fact that it has been taken over for Jewish settlement, but in order to maintain Jewish title to the land it is not enough to proclaim it Jewish property; for all practical purposes, the real right to the land lies with whoever cultivates it. . . .
>
> When a Jewish farmer hands over the work on his land to Arab peasants, he is supporting one of the important claims of Israel's enemies, namely, that the Jews in Israel do not have deep roots in the land they claim as their fatherland. They have the support of facts when they point to the Jews as city dwellers whose only interest is the exploitation of Arab labor. Nor would it be difficult to describe the Jews as a negative element turning back the social clock several decades to the time when the landowning effendis lived in the cities while the peasants did the farming on their land.[90]

The action promised by the minister of agriculture was in fact taken. On August 1, 1967, the Knesset once more approved a special law to prevent Jewish settlers from renting out their land to Arabs.[91] Those breaking the law would be deprived of their right to use the land.[92] The government did not enforce the law very strictly, preferring persuasion and pressure to court action. But at the same time, a committee was appointed to keep a record of transgressions; in 267 instances, only three involved kibbutzim and the rest, moshavim.[93] In some cases "the settlers were renting land to Arabs who had lived on it before the [1948] war . . . so that the Arabs were in fact returning to their land albeit by a circuitous route."[94] With such "grave" instances of "law infringement," the authorities began to sue the settlers and take their land from them.[95] Meanwhile the National Religious Party's press was cheering on the government in its protection of Zionist settlement from the "harm" of Arab labor.[96]

But apparently, none of these steps was sufficient. Recently the government has proposed a bill to modify the agricultural settlement law to include all kinds of settlements and "stop the introduction of aliens into the framework [of Zionist settlement] by using alien manpower to farm the land" except with special permission. Obviously the existing law "did not solve ... the problem in its entirety."[97] With this the Israeli government took the final step toward permanently keeping the Arabs off their land. Having had their land expropriated and turned over to the Jewish settlers, the Arabs are now prevented from working on their land even as day laborers.

III
The
Strong-
Arm
Policy

"Knesset member [Faris] Hamdan has mentioned some pieces of glass and furniture. I assume that he is not speaking of ivory objects and pianos destroyed during the search. No doubt a few glasses and a chair or two were broken at the time of the search, and I shall not grieve over them. I think it only proper that this incident not be included under acts of violence."

—Pinhas Lavan, deputy minister of defense,
responding to a complaint that the army had been
violent during a search in the village of Tira,
Knesset Debates, Aug. 5, 1953, p. 2149.

6

From
Deir Yassin
to
Kfar Kassim

In realizing its aim of founding a Jewish state in Palestine, the Zionist movement did not hesitate to use force. The option of resorting to force has always been present in Zionist thinking; if it was first contemplated only theoretically, it was soon employed on a practical level. As early as the beginning of this century, there had been an armed organization—Hashomer—founded by the Zionist settlers. After the British occupation of Palestine in the early 1920s, the Jewish settlers formed the quasi-military Haganah, from which I.Z.L. separated a decade later. I.Z.L., in its turn, dissolved in the early 1940s when the most extreme and violent Jewish organization, Lehi, was formed. In the early 1940s Haganah also trained special mobile striking units called the Palmach. Finally, in 1948, Haganah had become the Israeli army and the authorities ordered all other organizations to disband and join that army.

The professed objective of these organizations—or at least of Haganah, the largest—was to protect the lives and property of Jewish settlers. Their long-range aim, however, was to subdue the Palestinian Arabs and ensure their silence during the colonization of Palestine. Their first opportunity for full-scale action came during the Arab Revolt of 1936-39, when the Arabs demanded independence from the British. Throughout the revolt the Haganah cooperated closely with the British forces, in order to crush the uprising and strengthen its own ranks while winning the support of the British.[1] I.Z.L. was working toward the same end by undertaking terrorist raids against the Arabs—spraying bullets indiscriminately with the intent of killing as many as possible, planting time bombs in places frequented by Arabs, and setting off cars loaded with explosives in Arab marketplaces.[2]

Having had a taste of force during the revolt, the Zionist organizations, and later Israel, continued to think and act in terms of force and even bloodshed where the Palestinian Arabs, and Arabs generally, were concerned. Thousands died as a result. Violence did not become a daily practice but was adopted when political circumstances demanded it. For example, after the revolt and during the early years of World War II, Zionist military action died down, although some groups were collaborating with the British forces. During the latter part of the war, however, I.Z.L. and Lehi, later joined by Haganah, took up operations against the British, attempting to induce them to agree to Zionist plans for establishing a Jewish state in Palestine. They were active from 1944 until the British left in 1948, engaging in undisguised acts of terrorism: taking and killing hostages, planning and carrying out assassinations, dynamiting police posts, bridges, and civilian buildings, raiding banks, and attacking army posts and military installations.

Even after the partition of Palestine in 1947, the creation of Israel in 1948, and the departure of the British, Zionist terrorism continued in an attempt to induce the Arabs living in the country to leave their homes. Although Zionist leaders attributed terrorist acts to the two "offshoot" organizations —I.Z.L. and Lehi—over which they had no influence, during the 1948 War terrorist activity very clearly shifted from I.Z.L. and Lehi to the Haganah and later to the Israeli army. Although I.Z.L. and Lehi were responsible for the massacre at Deir Yasin on April 9, 1948, which left some 250 Arabs dead, the massacres of Lydda and Ramle during the summer and several massacres before and after that were the work of the Haganah.[3] There is no doubt that the Israeli army embraced the "tradition" of violence established by I.Z.L. and Lehi and put it to effective use during the 1948 War, with the result that tens of thousands of Palestinian Arabs were driven from their homes and their county occupied.

The astonishing thing about the Zionist strong-arm policy is that the Israeli army continued to resort to violent methods even after Israel's recognition as a state, using methods more suitable to gangsters than to the regular army of a self-respecting nation. There was a period of relative calm along the Israeli-Arab borders in the early 1950s, after truce agreements had been signed. The Israeli government decided, however, that the infiltration of Palestinian refugees into Israel constituted a threat to the peace and security of the country, and a special commando unit of the Israeli army, called Unit 101, was created to deal with the problem. Unit 101 operated inside neighboring Arab countries.[4] There were frequent terrorist raids into Jordan, Egypt, and Syria between 1953 and 1956, usually in the form of shelling refugee camps—often in daylight when they were most crowded—or dynamiting houses, schools, public buildings, and police posts or attacking army barracks and military installations.[5] In this way Israel hoped to inspire "awe" and pressure the Arab countries into preventing Palestinian refugees from infiltrating across the borders.

Even during the period of relative quiet between the Suez War in 1956 and the June War of 1967, there were acts of aggression against the Arab countries and incidents of terrorism against Arab civilians—for example, the raid on the village of Samuu' in the West Bank in 1966, during which many villagers were killed.

But Israel's policy of force accompanied by terrorist operations reached its height during the June War and the period immediately following. New Arab territories, several times the size of Israel, were occupied and more than a million Arabs came under Israeli rule. Many groups in the occupied territories proclaimed their opposition to Israel and many of the inhabitants joined resistance organizations. The Israeli government used every possible means to suppress this resistance, from wholesale arrests to torturing and killing detainees in prison camps, taking relatives of resistance members hostage, blowing up houses, imposing penalties on whole communities, driving people from their land, seizing their property, and banishing them across the borders. Nor did countermeasures stop at the borders. As in the 1953-56 period, raids were made into the neighboring Arab countries, but on a larger and more intensified scale. Since 1967 there have been numerous attacks, by land and air, on civilian targets; refugee camps, villages, and factories have been hit, in some cases with napalm.

It is clear that the use of force, with the resulting crimes, sabotage, and murders, formed an important element in Israeli policy toward the Arabs. Furthermore, this was not limited to the Arabs in Palestine during the British Mandate, or to the neighboring Arab countries; the Arabs continuing to live inside Israel also experienced their share of violence.

On October 29, 1956, on the eve of the British, French, and Israeli attack on Egypt, Israeli forces perpetrated a massacre in the Arab village of Kfar Kassim, near Petah Tikvah in the Triangle, killing forty-nine Arabs. The cause of this slaughter was the breaking of a curfew by the victims, who were unaware that it had been imposed on their own and neighboring villages. The massacre was carried out by the Frontier Guard, which had been formed in the early 1950s to protect Israel's borders. A description of the events at Kfar Kassim follows, as recorded by the Israeli military court:

> On the eve of the Sinai War ... a battalion attached to the Central Area Command was ordered to prepare itself to defend a section of the Israeli-Jordanian frontier. [With this end in view] ... a unit of the Frontier Guard was attached to the said battalion and the commander of this Frontier Guard unit, Major Shmuel Melinki, was placed under the orders of the battalion commander, Brigadier Yshishkar Shadmi. In the morning of 29 October 1956, the Commander of the Central Area, Major General Zvi Tsur informed Brigadier Shadmi and the other battalion commanders, of the policy it had been decided to adopt toward the Arab population.

The area commander went on to emphasize to the battalion commanders that the safeguarding of the operation in the south [the Suez campaign] required that the area coterminous with Jordan be kept absolutely quiet.

... Brigadier Shadmi requested that he be empowered to impose a night curfew in the villages of the minorities in the area under his command in order to: a) facilitate the movements of his forces, and b) prevent the population being exposed to injury by the reserve troops. These arguments convinced the area commander, who empowered Brigadier Shadmi to impose a curfew. . . .

On the same day Brigadier Shadmi summoned Major Melinki to his headquarters, informed him of the duties of the unit under his command, and gave him instructions about the execution of these duties. One of the duties of this Frontier Guard unit was to impose the curfew . . . in the villages of Kfar Kassim, Kfar Barra, Jaljulya, Tira, Tayba, Qalansuwa, Bir al Sikka, and Ibtin during the night. The two commanders agreed that the curfew should be enforced between 5 P.M. and 6 A.M.

The battalion commander [Shadmi] also told the unit commander [Melinki] that the curfew must be extremely strict and that strong measures must be taken to enforce it. It would not be enough to arrest those who broke it—they must be shot. In explanation he said, "A dead man [or according to other evidence "a few dead men"] is better than the complications of detention."

When Melinki asked what was to happen to a man returning from his work outside the village, without knowing about the curfew, who might well meet the Frontier Guard units at the entrance to the village, Shadmi replied: "I don't want any sentimentality" and "That's just too bad for him."

Shadmi gave his orders to Melinki verbally, while they were alone, and Melinki wrote the following words in his diary during the interview: "Curfew imposed from evening till morning (1700-0600). Strict policy."[6]

Similarly, the order drafted by Melinki and handed to the reserve forces attached to his group, shortly before the curfew was imposed, contained the following words under the heading "Method": "No inhabitant shall be allowed to leave his home during the curfew. Anyone leaving his home shall be shot; there shall be no arrests."[7]

Armed with these instructions, Major Melinki returned to his headquarters, where with the help of his officers, he prepared a series of orders for his forces. During this meeting,

> he informed the assembled officers that the war had begun, that their units were now under the command of the Israeli Defense Army, and that their task was to impose the curfew in the minority villages from 1700 to 0600, after informing the mukhtars to this effect at 16.30. With regard to the observation of the curfew, Melinki emphasised that it was forbidden to harm inhabitants who stayed in their homes, but that anyone found outside his home [or, according to other witnesses, anyone leaving his home, or anyone breaking the curfew] should be shot dead. He added that there were to be no arrests, and that if a number of people were killed in the night [according to other witnesses: it was desirable that a number of people be killed as] this would facilitate the imposition of the curfew during succeeding nights.
>
> . . . While he was outlining this series of orders, Major Melinki allowed the officers to ask him questions. Lieutenant Frankenthal asked him, "What do we do with the dead?" [or, according to other witnesses "with the wounded?"]. Melinki replied, "Take no notice of them" [or, according to other evidence, "There will not be any wounded."]. Arieh Menches, a section leader, then asked, "What about women and children?" to which Melinki replied, "No sentimentality" [according to another witness, "They are to be treated like anyone else; the curfew covers them too."]. Menches then asked a second question: "What about people returning from their work?" Here Alexandroni tried to intervene but Melinki silenced him and answered: "They are to be treated like anyone else" [according to another witness, he added, "It will be just too bad for them, as the commander said."].[8]

In the minutes of the meeting, which were taken down and signed by Melinki a short time after he signed the orders, the following appears: "As from today, at 1700 hours, curfew shall be imposed in the minority villages until 0600 hours, and all who disobey this order will be shot dead."[9]

After this psychological preparation, and the instructions given to the policemen-soldiers to "shoot to kill all who broke the curfew," the unit went out to the village of Kfar

Kassim to start its work. There Lieutenant Gabriel Dahan divided his unit into sections of three or four men each (including their leader) armed with submachine guns, rifles, and automatic rifles, and posted each section in a place overlooking one of the quarters of the village, at the entrance to the village, and at its end. He made the leaders of each section responsible for the enforcement of the curfew and authorized them to shoot according to his previous instructions, which he repeated.

On the same day at 16.30 hours, a Frontier Guard sergeant informed the mukhtar of the village that a curfew was to be imposed from 5 P.M. to 6 A.M. the following morning and warned him that it would be strictly enforced and would involve danger of death, telling him to inform the village. The mukhtar, Wadi Ahmad Sarsur, informed the sergeant that "there were four hundred villagers who worked outside the village, some of them in the neighborhood or in nearby places, while the remainder were in more distant places, like Petah Tikvah, Lydda, Jaffa and elsewhere, so that he could not inform them all of the curfew in time. After an argument the sergeant promised the mukhtar that he would let all men returning from work pass on his own responsibility and that of the government. The mukhtar, assisted by his relations, announced the imposition of the curfew in the center and to the north and the south of the village, saying that everyone inside the village must enter his home before 5 P.M."[10]

In other words, the curfew, of which the mukhtar was informed at 4:30 P.M., came into force half an hour later when dozens of the villagers were in different places of work, so that they could not possibly know of the curfew. And a bitter fate awaited them when they returned to the village. In the first hour of the curfew, between 5 and 6 P.M., the men of the Israeli Frontier Guard killed forty-seven Arab citizens in Kfar Kassim. The killing was carried out in cold blood and for no reason. Of the forty-seven, forty-three were killed at the western entrance to the village, one in the center, and three to the north; several other villagers were wounded.[11]

The forty-three killed at the western entrance included

seven boys and girls and nine women of all ages—one sixty-six years old. Most of them were inhabitants of Kfar Kassim, returning from their work outside the village, nearly all by the main road, a few on foot, the majority on bicycles or in mule carts or lorries. In most cases the villagers were met by sections of the Frontier Guard who ordered the passengers to get down from their transport. When it was clear that they were residents of Kfar Kassim returning from their work, the order to fire was given, and shots were immediately fired at short range from automatic weapons and rifles, "and of every group of returning workers, some were killed and others wounded; very few succeeded in escaping unhurt. The proportion of those killed increased, until, of the last group, which consisted of fourteen women, a boy and four men, all were killed except one girl, who was seriously wounded."

The killing might have gone on like this but Dahan who had personally taken part in the killing and who had seen what was going on as he went round the village in his jeep, informed the command several times over the radio of the number killed. Opinions differ as to the figure he gave in his reports, but all agree that in his first report he said "one less" [one killed], and in the next two reports "fifteen less" and "many less; it is difficult to count them." The last two reports, which followed each other in quick succession, were ... passed on to Melinki who was at Jaljulya. When he was informed that there were "fifteen less" in Kfar Kassim, Melinki gave orders, which he was unable to transmit to Dahan before the report of "many less" arrived, for the firing to stop and for more moderate procedures to be adopted in the whole area. . . . This order finally ended the bloodshed at Kfar Kassim.[12]

This is an outline of the principal events in Kfar Kassim, but the details are no less important as reported in the files of the Israeli military court:

The first to be shot at the western entrance to the village were four quarrymen returning on bicycles from the places where they worked near Petah Tikva and Ras al Ayin. A short time after the curfew began these four workmen came round the bend in the road pushing their bicycles. When they had gone some ten to fifteen meters ... they were shot from behind at close range or from the left. Two of the four were killed outright. The third was wounded in the thigh and the forearm, while the fourth, Abdullah Samir Badir, escaped by throwing himself to the ground. The bicycle of the wounded man fell on him and covered his body, and he managed to lie motionless throughout the bloody incidents that took place around him. Eventually he crawled into an olive grove and lay under an olive tree until morning. Abdullah was shot at again when he rolled from the road to the sidewalk, whereupon he sighed and pretended to be dead. After the two subsequent massacres, which took place beside him, he hid himself among a flock of sheep, whose shepherd had been killed, and escaped into the village with the flock.

A short time after the above incident, a two-wheeled cart drawn by a mule arrived at the bend. Sitting in it were Ismail Mahmud Badir ... and his little daughter, aged eight, who were coming back from Petah Tikva in the cart, with three people, one of whom came from Kfar Barra, walking beside or behind the cart, carrying vegetables. One of these was a boy of fourteen, Muhammad Abdul Rahim Issa. At this moment Dahan arrived at the bend in the jeep with the mobile squad ... on a tour of inspection. Dahan ordered his men to get out of the jeep.... He then told Ismail to get out of the cart and stand in a row with the other two men [who had been walking beside the cart] at the side of the road. Dahan then ordered the boy Muhammad to get into the cart, and sent him off to the village with the weeping girl. Dahan ordered the three men to be shot, shooting them with the Auzi he was carrying. The three men fell under the rain of bullets and the firing continued after they had fallen. Two of them ... were killed, while Ismail was seriously wounded, with several bullets in his hips and thigh—he survived only because the Frontier Guards believed him dead.

A short time after this killing a shepherd and his twelve-year-old son came back from the pasture with their flock. They approached the bend ... the shepherd throwing stones at sheep that had strayed to turn them back onto the road. Two or three soldiers, standing by the bend, opened fire at close range on the shepherd and his son and killed them. . . .[13]

A man in a lorry was killed, then a four-wheeled cart carrying two men arrived at the bend. Near the bend, a soldier stopped the

cart, ordered the two men to get down and to stand beside it in
the road. . . . Immediately after the arrival of this cart, several
groups of workers started arriving, riding bicycles with lighted
lamps. The soldier ordered them all to lay their bicycles beside
the cart and stand in a row with the two men. . . . There were
thirteen men in this row, and when one of them . . . tried to stand
at the end of the row, the soldier shouted at him: "Dog, stand in
the middle of the row." He thereupon moved to the middle.

When no more bicycle lamps were visible on the horizon, the
same soldier asked the men standing in the row where they came
from. They all answered that they were from Kfar Kassim,
whereupon the soldier took a step backwards and shouted to the
soldiers lying opposite the row: "Mow them down." All the men
in the row fell under the hail of bullets that followed, except for
[one] who escaped by jumping over the wall. The soldiers
continued firing at any of the fallen men who showed any signs
of life. When it was clear that they were all dead, or almost so,
the soldiers cleared the road of the bodies, piling them on the side
of the road. Of these thirteen men, six were killed, while four
were seriously injured. . . .[14]

A short time after the killing of the cyclists, a lorry with its
lights on approached the bend. Ten to fifteen meters before the
bend it was stopped by a soldier, who ordered the driver and
passengers [eighteen persons] to get out and stand in a single
group to the left of the road, in front of the vehicle. The soldier
then asked them where they came from, and when they said they
were from Kfar Kassim, he ordered two of his men, who were
lying beside the road between this group of workers and the
bend, to open fire. They killed ten of the nineteen. . . .

[A survivor] Raja [Hamdan Daud] said in his evidence that at
five o'clock, his little son Riyadh came with the boy Jamal and
told him that there was a curfew in the village and that his
mother had said that he must hurry home. . . . Nineteen people
got into the lorry including the driver . . . and set out for the
village. The people in this lorry, unlike most of the other people
returning to the village, knew of the curfew, but they did not see
that this prevented them from returning to the village. On the
contrary . . . they tried to get back to their homes as soon as
possible because of the curfew. Indeed, it was Raja who persuaded the driver, who had no license to carry passengers, to take
them because he thought that it would be safer to go by lorry

rather than on foot during the curfew. After the lorry had been stopped, and Raja and his companions had got out, his little son shouted: "Father, take me down." This was why Raja went back and took his son down from the back of the lorry, and rejoined the group on the road.

Raja held out his identity card to the soldier and was about to ask him why they had been detained, But at that moment the soldier gave the order to fire, and a hail of bullets mowed down the workmen. When Raja jumped over the wall, the Bren gun was fired at the wall, and this is perhaps how some of the workmen escaped. But Raja's son, Riyadh, aged eight, and his friend Jamal, aged eleven, were among those killed.[15]

Two more men in a lorry were killed, and then a third lorry arrived, carrying four men and fourteen women, aged twelve to sixty-six years, on their way to Kfar Kassim. The lorry went on past the bend without stopping, whereupon a soldier who was still at the site of the previous incident ran behind it shouting "Stop!" The lorry had already passed the bend and was making for the school road; the soldier crossed the space between the two roads and again shouted "Stop! Stop!" At the same time he called to two or three other soldiers who were standing in the space between the two roads to follow him, which they did.

The lorry stopped in the road that passes near the school, whereupon the first soldier ordered the driver and the passengers to get out. The driver hooked the steps on to the back of the lorry, and said to the women: "Get out, sisters, and have your identity cards ready." The women had already seen the dead bodies of people from their village as the lorry turned the bend, and started imploring the soldier in command to let them stay in the bus. But he took no notice of the identity cards or of the women's entreaties, and insisted on their getting out. As soon as the fourteen women and four men had got down from the lorry he ordered the other soldiers, who had by then joined him, to fire. They obeyed and continued firing until seventeen of the total of eighteen persons were killed. The sole survivor was a girl of fourteen, Hannah Suleiman Amer, who was seriously wounded in the head and leg and appeared to be dead. . . .

Two of the girls who were killed were twelve years old, and two others fourteen.[16]

The government took great pains to remove all traces of

the crime in Kfar Kassim and to hide the truth from the Jewish population, despite the fact that certain circles spread news of the massacre throughout the Arab sectors, apparently to "encourage" the Arabs to leave. A three-member committee headed by Benjamin Zohar, a district court judge in Haifa, was appointed to investigate the incident. The two other members, in whom the authorities had great confidence, were Abba Hoshi, mayor of Haifa and head of the Arab department in the ruling Mapai party, and Aharon Hotar Yshay, who had once been a lawyer for the Haganah. When the committee had concluded its investigation, some ten days after the massacre, Prime Minister Ben-Gurion issued a brief press release in which he referred to the fact that some people in the Triangle had been "injured" by the Frontier Guards and stated the government's determination to bring the matter before the courts and to pay compensation.

This did not stop rumors about the extent of the crime from spreading. Tawfiq Tubi made his way to Kfar Kassim as soon as news of the crime reached him in order to see for himself what had happened. On his return he gave his information to Uri Avneri, the editor of the periodical *Haolam Hazeh*, which devoted a special issue to it. The story was taken up by the press, there was a great uproar, and a wide range of Jewish groups expressed concern. The poet Nathan Alterman, a close friend of Ben-Gurion's, was moved to publish a poem censuring the deed and calling for a trial of all those responsible, with detailed disclosures of what had taken place.[17] A special session of the Knesset was held, lasting twelve minutes, during which Ben-Gurion spoke of the "shocking incident in the villages of the Triangle," and cited his appointment of the fact-finding committee as soon as he had heard of the event—three days after it occurred. He added that the government had paid compensation ranging between one thousand and £5000 to the families of the dead, but clearly that "no sum of money could compensate for the loss of human life."[18] At the end of the session, all members present stood in mourning for the dead.

Following the recommendations of the committee, eleven

officers and soldiers of the Frontier Guard were brought to trial for "carrying out illegal orders."

> The trial was lengthy; judgment was finally given on 16 October 1958, two years after the incident.
>
> The court found Major Melinki and Lieutenant Dahan guilty of killing forty-three citizens and sentenced the former to seventeen years imprisonment and the latter to fifteen years. The third accused, Sergeant Shalom Ofer, who perpetrated most of these terrible killings, was found guilty, with Dahan, of killing forty-one citizens, and was sentenced to fifteen years imprisonment. The accused Private Makhlouf Hreish and Private Eliahu Abraham were found guilty of killing twenty-two citizens, while Corporal Gabriel Olial, Private Albert Fahimi, and Private Edmond Nahmani were found guilty of killing seventeen citizens. All these five were sentenced to eight years imprisonment and deprived of their ranks. The remaining three accused, including two young Druze volunteers, were acquitted.

These light sentences (premeditated murder incurs a sentence of life imprisonment or twenty years) astounded many Jews as well as Arabs and gave rise to deep fears that similar incidents might occur in the future. On the other hand, there were many in Israel who thought that the trial of the killers, and even their arrest, seemed a grave injustice. They argued that these men were performing their duty and were therefore in no way responsible for their deeds. An extensive campaign for the release of the killers was launched as soon as it was known that they would be brought to trial. This was intensified after the sentencing. The Israeli press was clearly involved in this campaign.

> With two or three exceptions, the press has been party to a conspiracy of silence, throwing a veil over the incident. It wrote of condemned men instead of killers; instead of a killing or a crime in Kfar Kassim it wrote of a "misfortune" and a "mistake" and a "regrettable incident." When it mentioned the victims of the calamity, it was difficult to tell whom it meant, the dead or the killers. When the sentences were handed down, a cowardly campaign against the judge was begun. . . .[19]

What was remarkable about the official Israeli attitude was
that various authorities made efforts to lighten the killers'
sentences. An appeal was brought before the Supreme Military Court, which rendered a judgment that the sentences
were harsh and should be reduced. Thus Melinki's sentence
was reduced to fourteen years, Dahan's to ten years, and
Ofer's to nine years. The chief of staff then proposed to
reduce Melinki's sentence to ten years, Dahan and Ofer's to
eight years, and the rest of the killers' to four years each. The
president of the state followed suit; he granted a "partial
pardon" to Melinki and Dahan and reduced their sentences to
five years each.[20] Finally it was the turn of the "Committee
for the Release of Prisoners," which ordered the remission of
a third of the prison sentences of all those convicted. Thus,
the last man was released at the beginning of 1960—about
three and a half years after the massacre. They reportedly did
not spend the time in prison but were held in a sanatorium in
Jerusalem.

Moreover, in September 1960 the municipality of Ramle
engaged Gabriel Dahan, convicted of killing forty-three Arabs
in one hour, as officer for Arab affairs. Melinki, ten years
after the event, felt no embarrassment about boasting of his
services to Israel in the field of security, both before and
after the massacre.[21]

But the Kfar Kassim affair would not go away. Particular
concern was aroused by the part played by Brigadier Yshish-
kar Shadmi, the man under whose command Melinki's unit
had operated. Shadmi was not originally brought to trial and
the part he played became known only after the military
court had rendered its judgment. During the trial, public
indignation was aroused by certain comments Brigadier Shadmi had made during his briefing concerning the imposition of
the curfew, particularly his replies to the officer who asked
what was to happen to people returning from work: "I don't
want any sentimentality" and "Allah have mercy on them."
In its judgment, the military court (presided over by Dr.
Benjamin Halevy, president of the district court in Jerusalem,
who was on loan to the army for the trial) stated indispu-

tably that Shadmi was responsible to a greater degree than any of the others.[22] This put the Israeli authorities in an embarrassing situation. They were forced to bring Shadmi to trial, with the knowledge that in self-defense he would reveal the instructions he must have received from his immediate superiors, including Major General Zvi Tsur, commander of the Central Area, and Moshe Dayan, army chief of staff. The military court found the following in assessing Shadmi's role in the massacre of Kfar Kassim:

> The defendant Melinki, when he gave his orders to his unit, was not acting on his own initiative or according to his own judgment. He was obeying orders. It was not he who initiated the imposition of the curfew—either as a curfew or as regards the manner of its enforcement. He only passed on the order he had received from his responsible commander, Brigadier Shadmi. . . . There can be no doubt that the order given by Melinki was only one link in a chain of firm orders given in detail by the brigade commander. The orders given by Melinki were the direct result of the placing of a Frontier Guard unit under the orders of the brigade of the Israel Defense Army commanded by Brigadier Shadmi and of the assignment to that unit of a task in accordance with the wishes of the brigade commander and with the direct order he gave in connection with the curfew and the way in which it was to be carried out.
>
> Shadmi not only entrusted Melinki with the "task"; he also informed him of the "method" by which the curfew was to be enforced. The method . . . was defined, as stipulated by the brigade commander, as one of "stringent severity" and "decisive policy," the enforcement of the curfew by firing rather than by arrests. We are satisfied that the "method" prepared by Melinki before the bloody incidents at Kfar Kassim, as a summary of the orders of the brigade commander and for the purpose of including it in the orders to be given to the units ("No villager shall leave his home during the hours of curfew"; "Anyone leaving his home will be killed"; "There will be no arrests") was a true reflection of the order given by the brigade commander. There was no misunderstanding by Melinki as to how the curfew was to be enforced, as decided by the brigade commander, and the harsh distinction made in the order given by the unit commander, Melinki, between villagers in their homes, who were to come to

no harm, and persons out of doors, to whom the principle of shooting was to be applicable in its full severity, derived from the order given by the brigade commander, Shadmi. The unit commander's statement that, "It would be better that several people should be killed" was derived directly from the statement of the brigade commander to the effect that "It is better to get rid of some in this way" (his words being accompanied by a gesture with his hand as described by Melinki) "than to have the complications of arrests." . . . Our conclusion is that the method of enforcing the curfew, as decided by Melinki in his orders (before the questions and answers), corresponded in all important aspects with the methods of enforcing the curfew stipulated in the order given by the brigade commander. It was Brigadier Shadmi who initiated and ordered, in a manner that could not be disobeyed, the enforcement of the illegal instructions; it was he who ordered the shooting of citizens as a way of enforcing the curfew, and Melinki, in submitting to the orders of his commander, was only transmitting these instructions to his subordinates."[23]

This is a very clear indictment of Shadmi, and when it was published it aroused various demands that he be brought to trial. Opposing the trial was a group led by officials of Shadmi's own party, Achdut Haavoda, who warned of the consequences of such action. A week after the court decision, an article appeared in the party's daily newspaper signed by a "Hebrew prisoner," the nom de plume of Knesset member Moshe Carmel, one of Achdut Haavoda's leaders and then minister of transportation.

It is essential that we should ask whether the ultimate responsibility was Shadmi's and his alone. A brigadier commanding a brigade in the Israel Defense Army who is charged with the task of supervising an area of operations does not act in accordance with his own personal opinions; he is restricted to a framework of plans, orders, and instructions drawn up somewhere and imposed on him by the authority of a higher command. And inasmuch as the court has disclosed the facts to the people at large, the people have the right to know, and insist on knowing, what orders and instructions were given to Brigadier Shadmi by those responsible for him, in accordance with which orders he acted, and then gave his own more detailed orders in the light of conditions as he saw them and in the field in which he had experience, and also from whom he received his orders.

If it is indeed found that the orders given by Brigadier Shadmi, whether oral or written, were a cause of the tragedy that took place, the following question must be asked: Were these orders *incompatible* or *compatible* [italics in the original] with the orders he received? It is on this basis that the problem must be considered.[24]

The warning behind these words is clear. If Shadmi were brought to trial it would lead to the exposure of the role of his superiors, who no doubt briefed him and gave him the instructions which led to the massacre. But the authorities soon found a way out. Shadmi was hurried into court, but there was a change in the formation of the court. Justice Halevy had stepped down. The second court tried Shadmi rapidly, found him guilty of a "technical error," and sentenced him to a reprimand and a fine of one Israeli piaster. (Since then "Shadmi's piaster" has become proverbial among the Arabs in Israel.) And so the curtain was lowered on the massacre at Kfar Kassim.

Every year the families of Kfar Kassim, and with them many of the Arabs in Israel, try to hold memorial ceremonies for the dead in the village cemetery. The authorities have, on occasion, declared the village a closed area on the anniversary of the massacre, preventing anyone outside the village from entering on that day.[25]

The massacre at Kfar Kassim is not the only occasion on which Israeli forces killed, or caused the death of, Arabs living inside Israel, but it is a powerful illustration of the strong-arm policy the Israeli government pursued. Acts of aggression, terrorism, and murder by the Israeli "security forces" have been frequent since the establishment of the state. The aim at Kfar Kassim was the same as that at Deir Yasin, to induce the Arabs remaining in Israel to emigrate to the neighboring Arab countries. This time, however, the Israeli authorities were not so successful.

Naturally, not all the incidents of this nature have been

recorded, but the available evidence is enough to give an accurate picture. At the end of July 1948, after conducting a search in the village of Elot near Nazareth, the Israeli army arrested forty-six young men and took them away. On August 3 several of these men were found dead in the hills near the village. On the same day fourteen of those arrested were killed in an olive grove, in full view of the villagers.[26] On October 30, 1948, four Arabs were killed in the village of Jish after an army search. In November 1951 Meir Vilner complained in the Knesset of the harsh treatment the Arabs were suffering in the Triangle, citing information that at least five persons had been killed in the area just a short time before.[27] Toward the end of January 1952, one of the Arabs held at the Acre police station was found to have "died in his sleep."[28] Three days later, "while being interrogated," an Arab "jumped" to his death from a second-floor window of the Haifa police headquarters.[29] In June 1952 two Arabs from the village of Ara were killed when the army opened fire on a group of villagers who were trying to meet relatives at the border, which is near the village.[30] In the middle of September 1961 five young Arabs were killed by the Frontier Guard on the southern border of Israel while attempting to flee to the Gaza strip.[31] This incident led to unprecedented angry demonstrations by the Arabs in Nazareth, Shafa Amr, Haifa, Acre, and many of the Arab villages, and a display of the corpses of the dead in effigy.[32] The Frontier Guard had become "expert" at killing Palestinian refugees who were moved to cross into Israel. After the 1967 War it was used to keep order in the occupied territories. It is second only to Unit 101 and the paratroopers of the Israeli army in crimes committed against Arabs. During the Kfar Kassim trial, which was public, a clear picture emerged of the criminal way in which the Guard treats the Arabs.

With the deliberate cold-blooded killings at Kfar Kassim the policy of employing force against the Arabs had reached a peak, however. There were few incidents of this kind thereafter, the most notable being a demonstration at Shafa Amr in November 1959, during which the police opened fire on workers who had gathered to demand transportation to Haifa and their places of work. One of the workers was killed and the demonstration forcibly dispersed.[32]

With the decrease of incidents in which Arabs were killed, a new style of terrorism began. Bombs were suddenly discovered in public places in Arab cities and villages, reportedly placed by "persons unknown." The wave of bomb scares lasted from 1956 through 1958. In those two years bombs were found near schools in Tayba, Nazareth, the villages of Ein Mahil and Jish, Baqa al Gharbiya, Kfar Kassim, Ramle, and Tur'an, near a church at Shafa Amr, in a children's playground in Baqa al Gharbiya, and in the village of Sandaleh. A bomb exploded in August 1957 in Umm al Fahm, wounding four children, and in 1956 a bomb exploded in Sandaleh, causing the deaths of fourteen schoolchildren who had found it and were playing with it.[33]

The position of the Israeli authorities toward the bombings is interesting, as are the explanations offered. Replying to questioning in the Knesset, Bikhur Shitrit, minister of police, said that "in every one of these incidents it was found that the explosives had been in place for a long time, in most cases since the days of the [1948] War. In some instances the material was the same as that used by the Arab armies [during their attack on Israel]."[34] Shitrit added that "in 1956 the police handled 648 incidents of this kind and in the first eleven months of 1957, 295 additional cases were recorded." But the minister failed to explain why the schoolchildren did not find these bombs until eight years after they had been planted and why more than nine hundred bombs had suddenly been found within this two-year period —and those only in areas inhabited by Arabs.

The Arabs in Israel also had to put up with problems stemming from the fact that for some reason the Israeli army favors certain populated Arab districts for its maneuvers. To the present day two large areas, one in central Galilee and the other in the Triangle, have been reserved for operations of this kind, in spite of the fact that these areas are very densely settled. Over the years there have been numerous protests and requests to remove the maneuvers from the midst of the civilian population, but the authorities persist in carrying them out, even though they frequently result in casualties or damage to property. For example, two Suaed Bedouin boys in Galilee were killed and four wounded when the army was in their area at the end of July 1957. In February 1958 a schoolboy in the village of Sakhnin was killed by a stray bullet from nearby army maneuvers. In September 1958 another boy was killed in identical circumstances in the village of Deir Hanna. A number of maneuvers took place between November 1961 and July 1962 and between April 1963 and April 1964, near the villages of Umm al Fahm and Umm al Qutuf in the Triangle and near the Suaed Bedouins in Galilee, during which a number of people were wounded and Arab property damaged.[35] In late January 1970 two villagers from Sakhnin were wounded when they happened upon a mine left behind by the army.[36] In the middle of June 1971 a woman from the village of Mu'awiya was hit during army maneuvers nearby.[37]

After repeated requests that their houses and places of work be protected from such hazards, the Arabs were promised that the army would transfer its operations to uninhabited parts of the Negev. The authorities eventually announced that such a transfer would be impossible, however, and that instead of limiting the areas used by the army, they actually intended to extend them.[38] During the months of May and June 1971, the minister of defense issued orders that an area near the village of Tayba, totaling some three thousand dunums, be reserved for maneuvers.[39]

The final incident in the whole episode took place in August 1972 when the villagers of Barta'a "rebelled" and forcibly stopped some army tractors that were preparing ground near the village. A delegation from the village met with Moshe Dayan and asked that the maneuvers be held elsewhere. Their request was granted.

The incidents recorded above are in no way a complete list. Nor do they cover other forms of coercion, such as curfews imposed on whole villages for "breach of peace" and the forcible dispersion of demonstrations, including the shooting of demonstrators. The causes of such demonstrations—demands for employment, complaints against forcible seizure of Arab property, complaints against long detention and harsh sentences disproportionate with the crimes—in themselves form a further list of grievances.

The violence that has been a feature of Israeli policy toward the Arabs has continued to the present day. Whatever the hidden motives for such a position, there is no doubt that the incidents described, in conjunction with the military government and security measures, helped to bring the Arabs in Israel under complete control of the government.

IV
Strangers
in
Their
Own
Land

"To this day, there is no clear, open policy regarding the Arabs in this country. The present policy will neither drive a majority of the Arabs to decide in favor of emigration to some other country, nor will it facilitate a quick acceptance of the Arabs in Israel and encourage their integration into Israeli society."

—Yigal Allon,
Curtain of Sand (Tel Aviv, 1960), p. 324

"I believe that as Jews we have followed a policy toward the Arab minority that is a disgrace to the Jewish people."

—Yaacov Hazan,
Maariv, January 1, 1965

7
Political and Societal Circumstances

An intrinsic feature of Israeli politics is the large number of parties and factions. This was deeply rooted in the political life of the Jewish settlers in Palestine and in the World Zionist movement, which originated in numerous political clubs and organizations. One result of this system has been the relative ease with which new political parties are established or separate from existing parties. Another is the spirit of avid competition and sharp dispute among the various groups in their pursuit of the people's vote.

The provisional government, the first to be formed in Israel, consisted of a coalition of the major political parties; the Provisional State Council, a temporary parliament, represented every political group in existence at the time. The first general elections were held early in 1949; twenty-one factions participated and twelve gained seats in the Knesset.[1] Israeli elections have continued like this up to the present time. During the following six elections, more than one hundred slates appeared on the ballot sheets, seventy-seven of which won seats—an average of twelve a Knesset.[2] As a result, no single party or faction has ever had a clear enough majority to form a government on its own. Israel's governments have always been coalition governments.

During the British Mandate this multiparty situation encompassed only the Jewish minority. After the creation of Israel, most of the settlers and their leaders were so accustomed to thinking in terms of the Jewish community alone that they were at a loss as to how to act with regard to the

political rights of the Arab minority. The fact that most
Arabs were peasants or Bedouins, with little or no experience
of political activity or organization, only added to the
problem. What political leadership there had been among the
Arabs moved outside Israel after 1948. Meanwhile, the
situation inside Israel called for a general election early in
1949, even before the fighting had ended or the ceasefire
agreements had been signed. The Israeli authorities were thus
forced to define their position on the Arabs. Despite some
feeling against Arab involvement in Israeli politics, they were
allowed to participate in the first elections.

In preparation for this election the Israeli government
itself, as represented by Mapai, was the most politically active
group among the Arab population. It sponsored two Arab
lists, one of which won two seats in the Knesset. Next in
influence among the Arabs was Mapai's principal opponent,
the Israeli Communist Party, one of whose successful candidates was an Arab. Third came Mapam, with one Arab list,
but it failed to obtain any seats.[3] The rest of the Zionist
parties, "which all but overwhelmed the Arab voters" with
their promises, did not go so far as to sponsor Arab lists or to
add Arab names to the lists of their own candidates but
contented themselves with making energetic attempts to
sway the Arab voters, who "viewed the elections with no
great enthusiasm."[4] There was lively competition, each party
hoping to keep the Arab "representation" exclusively within
its own ranks. With some very slight modifications, the
inclusion of Arab lists attached to different political parties
became the practice in the following elections. In the second
election (1951), Mapam introduced a minor change by
always having one Arab candidate rather than a list.

Through this sole method of political representation seven
or eight Arabs have been elected to the Knesset in every
general election except the first, when there were only three
(see Appendix, Table 6). The Arabs members were firmly
bound to the parties patronizing them, though the assumption
was that they represented the interests of the Arab voters. Arab
nationalist organizations, when they existed, were carefully

kept out of the picture. Thus were the Arabs introduced into Israel's political life. Many, even most, gladly accepted their part in the performance, firmly believing that they were exercising their civil rights and bringing their influence to bear on the government. In practice the system worked differently. A former advisor to the prime minister on Arab affairs described it as a "struggle carried on by Jews in the name of the Arabs, for the benefit of the Jews."[5]

Mapai has always set the standard for political activity among the Arabs, while the other parties merely reacted to Mapai's enterprise. Even in the early 1930s the Party of the Workers of the Land of Israel, to call it by its official name, was the leading political party among the settlers. It maintained this position after the establishment of Israel, never holding less than a third of the seats in the Knesset, and thus continuing to be the most important party in the formation of Israel's governments. (In 1968 it joined forces with Achdut Haavoda to form the Israeli Labor Party and has been known by that name since then.) Four of the most important posts—prime minister, minister of defense, foreign minister, and minister of finance—have always been held by Mapai party members or their protégés. Because of its size and prestige, Mapai has played a significant role in the struggle between the Zionist movement and the Arabs, in Palestine and elsewhere, during the last forty years.

Although Mapai considers itself part of the social-democratic stream, it is not entirely clear what position it holds on the Arab nationalist movement generally and on Palestinian Arab nationalism in particular. There has rarely been an official party statement on Arab nationalism. As for the Arabs in Palestine, Mapai limited itself to the proclamation that they were "inhabitants of the land of Israel" and had the right to live in the Jewish state. Later the Arabs were referred to as "citizens of Israel." The internal political situation immediately after Israel's creation, however, did not allow Mapai to remain so vague. As the most prominent party among the Jews, it could hardly resist the challenge to hold a comparable position among the Arabs. By gaining the support of the Arab population and by demonstrating that Arabs and Jews can live peacefully under Zionist rule, Mapai could also have some positive effect on the Arab-Israeli struggle over the long run. Mapai had always claimed that there is no basic conflict between the interests of Arabs and Zionists in Palestine but that the differences were the fabrication of a conservative Arab leadership which abhors Zionism.

Mapai's decision to become politically active among the Arabs was undertaken with some hesitation. There was nothing in its history or ideology to attract the Arabs or win their support. For a start, the party did not even accept Arabs as ranking members, on the grounds that no Arab could be a loyal member of a Zionist party.[6] The party's "experts" on Arab affairs soon suggested solutions, however, for these and other difficulties. Arab participation would be in the form of special lists drawn up before each election on the basis of residence and religious sect from among the party's Arab hangers-on. The party machine would undertake financial and influential support of these lists, thus "freeing" them from having to set up their own political apparatus. The allegiance of the successful candidates to the party and their support for the party's position would thus be guaranteed.

There has been no change in Mapai's basic methods. The Arab lists have had the same religious and regional qualifications in every election. In 1949 the Nazareth Democratic List won two seats, one occupied by Seifeddin Zu'bi, a Moslem, and the other by Amin Jarjura, a Christian.[7] By the second general election, in 1951, the Triangle had become part of Israel as a result of the 1949 Armistice Agreement between Israel and Jordan and the situation in Galilee had stabilized. It therefore seemed only proper to send Arab representatives of these regions to the Knesset. In the meantime, the Israeli government had begun an attempt to isolate the Druze sect from the rest of the Arab population and to treat it as a separate "nation." Independent Druze representation thus became necessary. Mapai took all these changes into consideration and entered three Arab lists in the election. The

Nazareth Democratic List, appearing under a new name—
Democratic List of the Arabs of Israel—won three seats,
occupied by Zu'bi, Jabr Ma'di, a Druze from Yarka in
Galilee, and Masad Qassis, a Christian from Mi'lya in the same
region. Of the other two lists, Progress and Labor elected
Saleh Khneifes, a Druze from Shafa Amr in Galilee, and
Agriculture and Development, Faris Hamdan, a Moslem from
Baqa al Gharbiya. These lists were kept unchanged for the
third general election in 1955. The Democratic List of the
Arabs in Israel then won two instead of three seats, Ma'di
occupying Zu'bi's seat (Zu'bi having resigned); Progress and
Labor gained an additional seat, occupied by a Moslem from
Shafa Amr, Saleh Saleem; Saleh Khneifes retained his seat.

Then in the fourth general election, in 1959, Mapai
replaced all its former candidates and made some changes in
the names and formation of its lists, though still pushing
three lists. Cooperation and Brotherhood won two seats,
Progress and Growth two, and Agriculture and Development
had one successful candidate. Before the fifth election in
1961, Mapai reduced its Arab lists to two and the Arab
Knesset members attached to Mapai were reduced from five
to four. The party took care thereafter that these were
always two Moslems, one Christian, and one Druze.

Before the 1969 election, a further change was made that
revealed that the Arab candidates have little say in the party
and in the composition of the lists. "I do not believe that we
count for anything in this," Zu'bi said; "we are bound by the
decisions made at party headquarters."[8] In its electioneering
Mapai had emphasized local and religious differences among
the Arabs, thus restricting the possibility of a regional
leadership. On the other hand, not choice but the force of
circumstances had led to Mapai's political involvement with
the Arabs. When this later proved to be useful, it was difficult
to turn back, as Yehoshua Palmon, a former advisor on Arab
affairs, relates:

> With the creation of the state of Israel, the Arab intellectuals
> refrained from all political activity or contact with the Israeli

government, so that the latter had to encourage every other initiative. Thus it was that the Arab candidates and the Arab lists in the first Knesset election did not represent the choice of the Arab community. Three precedents were then established: the Arab intellectuals relinquished their natural role in politics; the Arab members of the Knesset were not in fact chosen by the Arab community; and the Arab members of the Knesset and the Arab lists were not independent agents. . . . It is also true that the Israeli parties are not prepared to give up this state of affairs.[9]

How did Mapai choose its Arab representatives? Judging from their careers, some seem to have been susceptible to a promise of personal gain, whatever the party in power; the rest belonged to prominent families and the local establishment and had shown a willingness to cooperate with the party. The "big two" of the Arab lists, whose services the party could not do without, as it discovered more than once, were Seifeddin Zu'bi and Jabr Ma'di, both of whom, on their own admission, had been Haganah intelligence agents. Zu'bi had been awarded Israel's Freedom Fighters' Medal "for his part in protecting the settlements and organizing defense action in the meadows [surrounding Nazareth] and at the risk of his life, neutralizing armed attacks against Jewish settlements."[10] His first contacts with Zionist organizations began in the late 1930s when he sold a piece of land he owned to the Keren Keymeth. He then became a broker for the company, buying Arab land on its behalf. Eventually he made the acquaintance of the head of Keren Keymeth in Haifa and through him was introduced to Abba Hoshi. From then it was easy to continue cooperating with the Zionists and he became the most important collaborator with the military government in Nazareth after the fall of the city in 1948.

Jabr Ma'di had worked for Israeli intelligence at a monthly salary of forty pounds and had helped the Israeli forces in 1948 in the occupation of a number of Druze villages in Galilee. [11] As a result he was nominated for the Israel Independence Medal, but the award was postponed after some Israeli groups suggested that Sheikh Ma'di was a double agent, working for the Israelis and for the Arab liberation army. Two other Knesset members, Labib Abu Ruken (1959-61) and Saleh Khneifes (1951-59), were nominated for the award for similar actions.[12] Khneifes had also helped the Israeli forces during the occupation of Acre in 1948.[13] In contrast, Elias Nakhleh, elected to the Knesset in 1959 and a candidate of the General Zionist Party in the previous election, believed that "Mapai chose me because of my family's good name."[14] And Faris Hamdan (1951-59) described why he agreed to become a Knesset member on an Arab list allied to the party in 1951: "Mapai is the most powerful party in the country, and the base on which the government rests. It alone can help us. Obviously the weak have to lean on the strong, and so we decided to go along with the government and benefit from the association."[15]

Unfortunately, "going along with the government" did not reap great advantages for the members or their constituents. From the information available it appears that the Arab Mapai members won only the slightest material benefits. For example, a member might be appointed to the board of a company marketing Arab agricultural products, or he might be allowed a deferment in the payment of his taxes, or he might be granted a license to carry arms.[16] He might be allowed to rent a few hundred dunums of farmland from the absentee properties, which he could in turn rent out to Arab farmers for a fee.[17] The only one who seems to have received significant help was Hamdan. The ministry of industry and commerce invested hundreds of thousands of pounds to help him finance a canning factory in Baqa al Gharbiya. Because of bad management, the enterprise eventually went bankrupt.[18] How Arab constituents fared will be discussed later.

The moral support given the Arab members by the party was as meager as the material benefits. Mapai regarded its Arab Knesset members as mere hangers-on, whose duty it was to vote the party line and support it during the formation of a government. They were never consulted about the composition of the government nor given ministerial or high offices until very recently, and then only in response to the initiative of other parties. It is symptomatic that Ben-Gurion, the party leader, did not find time to meet the members of the Arab lists until 1958. When he was finally introduced to them, the meeting was intended, in part, to dispel the bad impression created by Ben-Gurion's rejection of his identity card because it was printed in Arabic as well as in Hebrew.[19] There was a second meeting at the end of 1958, and when Ben-Gurion announced the changes planned in the military government for 1959 he said they had been arrived at after consultations with the Arab members. This was a way of boosting their prestige, since in fact Ben-Gurion had been pressured into making the changes by the other parties in the government coalition.[20]

When they did attend Knesset sessions the Arab members limited their activity to making generalized speeches about problems experienced by the Arabs and humbly asking the authorities to find some solutions. If they ever touched on foreign affairs, it was to call on the Arab nations to make peace with Israel. Their position allowed them to fill the limited role of intermediary between individual Arabs and various departments of government and to dispense patronage in their own districts. Diab Ebeed has described his service to fellow Arabs during the five years (1961–65) he was a member.[21] He mentions 2,000 letters he addressed to different branches of government, which led to the settlement of 3,233 cases, 214 of which dealt with general problems regarding Arab villages and local councils. He was able to arrange 723 meetings between Israeli Arabs and relatives living in the Arab countries and 1,319 loans to individual Arabs. He helped resolve 368 problems between Arabs and the ministry of education and smooth 594 individual difficulties with government departments. Through him 15 families were reunited with relatives who were living as refugees outside Israel. Commenting on this list of achievements, a *Haaretz* reporter noted:

> Knesset member Ebeed, whose vote gave the government the necessary majority to defeat the bill abolishing military govern-

ment, makes no mention of any bill he has challenged or proposed. All his activity, and the source of his pride, lies within the narrow scope of influencing the appointment of a school-teacher, or having him transferred from a distant school to one nearer his home; or arranging meetings at the Mandelbaum Gate in Jerusalem between Arab citizens and their relatives living in Jordan; or speeding the grant of a loan. In a democratic society, an ordinary citizen may expect to attain such things without having to appeal to a member of parliament.[22]

Unfortunately, the examples listed represent the upper limit of Ebeed's political achievement. Once when asked his opinion on peace between Israel and the Arabs, Ebeed replied that "peace has nothing to do with us but with high-level politics . . . and that is not my business."[23]

The other Arab Knesset members are no different from Ebeed; they too abstain from "high-level" politics, but each uses his influence in his own district and among his own acquaintances. Indeed, they bring to mind the fictional "Fashid," the Arab as Herzl imagined him in the future Zionist state, accepting his fate and behaving exactly as the Zionist society expects him to behave.[24] This seems to be the first of Herzl's prophecies to have come true in Israel; it may well be the only one.

To this day the Arab lists capture a considerable proportion of the Arab vote—about 40 percent—though the number tends to decrease in each election (see Appendix, Table 7). It is not only the illusory prospect of material benefits and services that is persuasive, Mapai also uses all its power to promote the Arab candidates.[25] Most important, the military government apparatus has been brought into action, as described in Chapter 1. Even now, the military government's diminished power is used to harass the numerous Arab groups supporting the new Communist list (see Appendix, Table 8).[26]

Another source of influence exploited by Mapai is the advisor to the prime minister on Arab affairs and his assistants. Indeed, though they are public officials, they behave as if they were part of Mapai's organization. One described the advisor on Arab affairs once as being "not so much an advisor as someone who carries out other people's advice. . . . He is an executive and it is possible that he may even guide some departments of government at times. He has considerable contact with the military government, though it is not clear who instructs whom in that relationship. . . . It does not look as if the prime minister seeks much advice from his consultant on Arab affairs."[27] At the request of the Labor Party, the office prepared a study prior to the seventh Knesset election in 1968 on the best way to capture the Arab vote. The Gahal rightists, who were part of the government coalition, were outraged. At a general session of the Knesset they demanded an investigation into the matter but were refused.[28] The advisor for Arab affairs was in no way deterred and attended a meeting of the heads of the Arab divisions in the Labor Party at the end of January 1973 in order to study tactics to be used in the coming elections.[29]

The Arab department in the Histadrut is another important source of help for Mapai's Arab lists during elections. Even before Arabs were accepted as members of the federation, the Arab department was responsible for educational work among Arab workers, and it has taken charge of distributing information. It published the only daily Arabic-language paper, *Al Yaum*, which remained in circulation from September 1948 until the end of May 1968.[30] In July 1960, *Al Yaum*, the Histadrut, and the government agreed that the government would cover half the newspaper's expenses and pay any debts outstanding from previous years.[31] Although it was practically an official newspaper, *Al Yaum* was in fact a reduced version of *Davar*, with the special function of making Mapai's positions known to the Arab public. When necessary it attacked other Israeli parties, including Mapai's partners in the government coalition. Considering the amount of support it received, *Al Yaum* never had a large circulation—it rose from 1,500 copies a day in 1948 to 5,000 in 1962, of which some 1,800 copies went to regular subscribers, mostly Arab schoolteachers whose subscriptions were deducted automatically from their salaries.[32] Finally, its growing deficit, combined with poor circulation (a result of its blind support of any official government position), forced its closing.[33]

In its eagerness to supply the Arab public with a daily paper, the Israeli government started a new paper five months later, *Al Anba'*, published in Jerusalem. This too was subsidized and controlled by the government.[34] But those in charge had learned from their experience with *Al Yaum* and modified *Al Anba's* tone, making it acceptable not only to the Arabs in Israel but also to those living in the territories occupied in 1967.[35] A former head of the Arabic section of the Israeli broadcasting service was appointed editor.

Periodically, Mapai would also try to reach the Arabs "ideologically." In 1962, for example, a call was made for "Arab-Israeli Awareness." Enthusiasm over this did not last, however, and nothing more was done until August 1964, when a Conference of Intellectuals was held in Haifa. It included most of Mapai's Arab supporters and was supposedly to study "the ideological arguments opposing the aims of the Arab revolution."[36] These turned out to be a denial of the right of the Arab refugees to return to their homeland, on the grounds that it is impossible "to demand an increase in the population of the country by 40 percent with people officially considered enemies," and criticism of the Arabs in Israel "for not proving their unqualified loyalty to the country . . . and its well being, and for harboring the hope, in some cases, that there will be a change in the political balance of the area."[37]

Two years later, in June 1966 Mapai announced the creation of an Arab Committee for Israel, presided over by Rustum Bastuni, who described his aims as follows:

First, at the regional level, to clarify Arab-Israeli relations inside Israel . . . since the Arab problem in Israel is essentially a Jewish one, and a question, above all, of the attitude of the Jewish populace. Second, through the United Nations, to try and contact the Arab missions to the U.N. in order to explain the position of the Arabs in Israel regarding the existing conflict between Israel and the Arab countries, and their position on the Palestine

Liberation Organization. Third, on an international level, to settle the Israeli-Arab struggle by direct negotiations between all sides . . . bringing the influence of world opinion to bear on the Arab governments [to agree to] begin direct negotiations.[38]

Again, the party's eagerness did not lead to anything worth mentioning. So the search for an "ideology" for the Arabs in Israel continues, and it appears to have gone astray in the more difficult search for an "ideology" for the Arabs in the territories occupied in 1967.

This pattern of Mapai activity dominated from the creation of the state until 1968-69, when Mapai merged with Achdut Haavoda to form the Israeli Labor Party. Just before the seventh Knesset elections the Labor Party and Mapam formed the Mapam–Labor Party alignment. The new alliances resulted in some changes in these parties' work among the Arabs, changes that were reflected in the Arab support they received.

Most other parties followed in Mapai's footsteps in their attempts to win the support of the Arabs and capture a share of their vote. Foremost among these was Mapam, the United Workers' Party, which takes a unique, sometimes even bizarre, position regarding the Palestine problem and the Arabs. The party's background may offer some explanation. Shortly after the emergence of Mapai in the early twenties, Mapam's elders first appeared in Palestine as a kind of scouting movement that soon turned to settlement. By the late twenties the movement was founding its own kibbutzim in different parts of Palestine, as part of a larger association called Hashomer Hatzair (Young Guardians). Hashomer Hatzair soon acquired some characteristics that distinguished it from the numerous other kibbutz associations. In its search for an ideology it embraced a Marxist interpretation of Zionism expounded by Ber Borochov. As a result, Hashomer Hatzair (and later Mapam) found itself adopting contradictory positions, which exposed it to criticisms from both Marxists and Zionists.

Of most interest is Hashomer Hatzair's call, in the days of the British Mandate, for the establishment of a binational Arab-Jewish state in Palestine. It was a controversial policy, involving the party in lengthy debates within its own ranks and with other World Zionist groups. After the creation of Israel, however, there was no further mention of binationalism because "those who supported the policy felt that, since the state of Israel has been established in part of a divided Palestine, it must necessarily be Jewish. At the same time, they strongly feel that the Jewish state must give the Arabs living within its borders complete equality, that it must recognize them as a minority group, with all the rights and obligations that such recognition entails."[39] In the spirit of this declaration Hashomer Hatzair, more than any other Zionist party, welcomed contact with the Arabs in Israel.

Meanwhile, there had been internal changes. In 1948 Hashomer Hatzair had merged with a workers' group, which had split from Mapai in 1946, to form the Mapam Party. The leaders of the workers group (later known as Achdut Haavoda) had been members of the Haganah and Palmach. It opposed Hashomer Hatzair's earlier attitude to the Arabs and prevented Mapam from adopting it. The new party used Mapai's methods in the first Knesset election, sponsoring one Arab list. This was not an easy decision to make because the two groups differed on the question of accepting Arabs as party members. It failed to win any seats for its Arab candidates in the first election, but in the second one Arab candidate, Rustum Bastuni, won a seat.[40] Thereafter, Mapam made sure that one of its Knesset members was an Arab: Yusef Khamis in the third, fourth, and fifth Knessets, and Abdul Aziz Au'bi in the sixth and seventh. In 1954 Achdut Haavoda broke off from Mapam to form its own independent party, and Mapam accepted Arabs as party members, with equal rights and responsibilities, at least officially. Mapam continues to be the only Zionist party to accept Arabs. Before the split between Mapam and Achdut Haavoda, a small leftist faction, led by Moshe Sneh, also left Mapam, eventually joining the Israeli Communist Party.[41] Rustum Bastuni left with Sneh's group, then later joined Mapai, for which he worked a considerable length of time, before finally emigrating from Israel.[42]

The main difference between Mapam and the other Zionist parties active among the Arabs was that it went beyond material advantages and tried to win the Arabs ideologically, hoping to convert them to socialist Zionism. It set about its work earnestly, forming cells among the Arabs quite early, and in 1951 began to publish a weekly newspaper in Arabic, *Al Mirsad* (The Observation Post), which is still in circulation. In the mid-1950s it founded an Arab Pioneer Youth Movement to deal with some of the problems of Arab youth and soon after it helped form a union of Arab farmers to encourage Arab agriculture.[43] The two organizations remained marginal. In 1958, Mapam took a hand in a cultural monthly in Arabic, *Al Fajr* (The Dawn), which was published successfully for several years. That same year it also founded the Arab Book Society, which printed and distributed many works by the great Arab writers living outside Israel at a time when the importation of Arabic books into Israel was forbidden.[44] The financial possibilities of the entreprise spurred the commercial houses to follow suit. Further, in a period when it was difficult for Arab workers to find work in Israel, the party kibbutzim employed them in large numbers. Whenever Mapam was part of the government coalition, the departments under the control of Mapam members made an effort to settle numerous difficulties relating to the Arabs. One also senses that Arab members of Mapam, in contrast to those affiliated with the other Zionist parties, retained some measure of "independence" as far as their opinions and nationalist sentiments were concerned.

For all this, Mapam made no substantial progress among the Arabs; its impact was limited and the number of votes it won decreased from election to election (see Table 7). The reason for this failure lies in the party's misguided attempts to supplant the two major forces active among the Arabs, Mapai and the Communists. Having neither the means of Mapai nor the zeal of the Communist Party in defending the

Arabs, locally and abroad, Mapam was bound to fail. This is typical of the contradictory character of the party, a result of its desire to conciliate all sides at once. For example, the party's Hebrew daily paper, *Al Hamishmar*, bears the slogan "For Zionism, Socialism, and the Brotherhood of Peoples," while *Al Mirsad* declares that it is for "Social and National Liberation, and the Brotherhood of Peoples." The subtle difference goes beyond the front page and is reflected in the columns of the two papers, whose positions vary on a great number of issues. The young Arab whose support Mapam is eager to attract is usually able to read both languages. With such evidence of the party's ambivalence before him, he stays away. Mapam's support for national liberation movements has not convinced its Arab members of the sincerity of its attitude toward Arab nationalism either, and its proclaimed belief in the right of nations to self-determination is not compatible with its position on the Palestine question. Meanwhile, its opposition to the expropriation of Arab land does not prevent it from building its kibbutzim on just this land.[45] When called upon to join in the formation of a government, Mapam has accepted, ostensibly "to fight on the inside" by taking part in the determination of Israel's domestic and foreign policy. In practice, it has called for moderation (for fear of "provoking" the military government), thus proving its inability to effect any meaningful change in Israeli policy, whether inside or outside government. All this has inevitably lowered the party's prestige in the eyes of the Arab population.

After twenty years of independent political activity, in 1968 Mapam shared a slate in the seventh Knesset election with the Israeli Labor Party. This hampered its work among the Arabs, and the Mapam–Labor Party alignment won fewer votes than each party's individual total in the previous election (see Table 7). However, Mapam won what it considered a victory for its Arab policy by including the name of its Arab candidate, Abdul Aziz Zu'bi, on the joint slate list, on a par with the Jewish candidates. It then announced that after the elections it would push the appointment of Zu'bi as deputy to one of its ministers. The Arab candidates on Mapai's list were angered, regarding the appointment as a reward to Mapam's Arabs for undermining the Arabs in Mapai. They felt a member of their party should take precedence to be the first appointed to such a post. Mapai's Seifeddin Zu'bi, a cousin of Abdul Aziz Zu'bi, expressed his appreciation of Mapam because it "does not abandon its members or throw them to the dogs," adding that "the Arabs in Israel are right to criticize us, since [some in the Labor Party] show little respect for the Arab Knesset members: they interfere with us, insult us, and play games with us."[46] As a result of the uproar, the Labor Party granted its Arab supporters' request and Seifeddin Zu'bi was elected deputy chairman of the Knesset when the new session began in 1969. Mapam's desire to appoint an Arab as deputy minister was not realized until two years later when Abdul Aziz Zu'bi became deputy minister of health in May 1971. Shortly afterward Jabr Ma'di was appointed deputy minister of communications; Elias Nakhleh replaced Seifeddin Zu'bi on his resignation.

Undoubtedly it was thanks to Mapam that the move to appoint Arabs to higher posts was first made, a debt Abdul Aziz Zu'bi acknowledged on taking office.[47] Zu'bi differed from his Arab colleagues in the Knesset in that he worked loyally within Mapam and gradually came to occupy various posts in the party machine.[48] He had been an employee in the office of the custodian of absentee property in Nazareth when he joined the party in 1955. He left this in 1958 to work on *Al Mirsad* and *Al Fajr*. He later became head of the Arab Book Society and has continued to work in the party in one capacity or another. Mapam does not seem overly concerned about achieving positive results for the party or for its Arab supporters from the appointment of Arabs to ministerial posts. Nor does it appear concerned about the limited extent of the power or achievements of the new appointees.[49] Zu'bi, on the other hand, saw his appointment as

a step toward complete equality for the Arab population and their integration into the state on a firmer basis. Increased Arab participation in national affairs will have political significance both at home and abroad. Of course, there will always be those who say that I was appointed so that tourists can be told, "Look, we have an Arab as deputy minister," but it is an indication of Israel's good faith and its aim to cooperate in a climate of mutual respect with the neighboring Arab countries, as an independent nation among equals, once peace is achieved.[50]

Mapam seemed unaware that, despite its support of appointing Arabs to high positions, it was part of an Israeli government that not only consistently ignored the rights of the Palestinians but forbade them any political activity at all. This is but another example of Mapam's contradictory position.

The rest of the Zionist parties followed Mapai and Mapam's lead in trying to court Arab voters and almost any party entering the lists could find some Arab support. But while Mapai and Mapam had created special divisions to direct political activity among the Arabs on a regular basis, the efforts of the other parties were no more than a seasonal enthusiasm, reaching its height on the eve of the elections.

The General Zionist Party looked upon itself as part of the Zionist right, claiming that it would eventually supplant Mapai as the ruling party. Before the third Knesset election in 1955 the General Zionists, who were then part of the government coalition, approached some Arab small-property owners who had suffered from Israel's early economic policies and assisted them in assembling an Arab list headed by Elias Nakhlen. The fact that the minister of the interior at the time, Itzhak Rokah, was a member of the General Zionist Party did much to help the undertaking. (As shall be seen, it was not unusual for the Israeli parties to benefit at election time when a party member happened to be minister of the interior.) Despite this advantage, however, the Arab list sponsored by the General Zionists did not win a single seat, and the party did not repeat the experiment.[51] The Progressive Party also added a few Arab names to its list of candidates, in its weak slots, in the 1959 election. None were successful. In

1960 the General Zionists and the Progressives joined to form the Liberal Party, which did little to win over the Arabs in the 1961 election. They were even less enterprising in 1965 and 1969 after an alliance (which became known as Gahal) with Herut. Apart from a limited amount of superficial propaganda, no effort was made to gain any of the Arab factions' support, mostly because of Herut's extremist attitude to the Arabs.[52]

A latecomer on the Arab scene was Achdut Haavoda. In the first election after its secession from Mapam, in 1955, the party made no serious bid for the Arab vote. By 1959, however, as part of the government coalition and with one of its members—Israel Bar-Yehuda—as minister of interior, its campaign among the Arabs was intense. Departing from the other parties' custom, despite the opposition of the military government, Achdut Haavoda pushed the establishment of an Arab party linked to itself, called the Arab Labor Party. It began publishing an Arabic weekly, Al 'Amal (Labor) and also helped prepare an Arab list, which took part in the elections on its own. None of its candidates were elected. Further modifications were introduced in the 1961 election when the party included a few Arab candidates in its own list in some of the safer places. Again, none were elected. In 1964, in order to demonstrate its good faith, the party induced one of its Jewish Knesset members, Yitzhak Ben-Aharon, to resign and put Saleem Khalil Jabbara (from Tira in the Triangle) in his place. Jabbara remained in the Knesset until the end of the session in 1965. By the 1965 (and 1969) elections, Achdut Haavoda had joined with Mapai and took part in the election on an alignment slate. In 1968 the two parties were formally united as the Israeli Labor Party, which allied itself to Mapam on a Mapam–Labor slate for the 1969 election. With this political shuffling all Achdut Haavoda's independent work among the Arabs ceased, and it eventually merged its activities with those of Mapai.

Despite all these alliances, the Zionists were far from united; nor was their political work among the Arabs a concerted effort. At the time of the 1965 Mapai–Achdut Haavoda alignment, a small faction protested Mapai's tendencies by disassociating itself. Under the leadership of Ben-Gurion (in opposition for the first time), Moshe Dayan, and Shimon Peres, it entered a separate slate in the elections, calling itself Rafi, the Party of the Workers of Israel. Not content with campaigning among the Jews, Rafi assembled an Arab list, the "List of Peace," rallying around it all the Arab collaborators "who admired" the military government for its effective "maintenance of security." Though it had several thousand Arab votes (see Table 7), these were not enough to win a seat.[53] In the 1969 election, Rafi again campaigned energetically among the Arabs but courted and won a fair portion of votes for itself, instead of sponsoring an Arab list.

It is interesting to note how far the Zionist parties and their leaders were prepared to go in wooing the Arab electorate. In the 1965 campaign, for example, Rafi launched an intensive attack against its rivals, especially Mapai, denouncing them equally in front of Jewish and Arab audiences. At an election meeting in Tira attended by some three thousand people, Moshe Dayan described the official Israeli policy of integrating the Arabs into the nation as follows: "This is going too far. It shall not be. It is unnecessary." He added, for the benefit of his Arab listeners: "I recognize emphatically that, as Arabs, you have your own language, your own history and culture and traditions. I see no harm in your having relations with the other nations of the Middle East. Listen to their broadcasting stations, read their newspapers. You can produce your own writers and poets, and stop anyone else writing your papers for you. Write them for yourselves. ..."[54] At the beginning of his speech Dayan had cautioned his audience not to be deceived or pressured into selling their votes for money. Ironically, Dayan's colleagues on the Rafi list, and to some extent Dayan himself, were responsible for the official policy he had criticized and for the corruption he warned against.

Last among the Zionist parties to try to influence the Arab vote was a group of religious parties—the National Religious Party, Agudat Israel, and Workers of Agudat Israel. Given their beliefs and feelings about Israel's existence, the religious parties did no serious campaigning among the Arab voters. Their aim was to spread Jewish religious customs into every facet of Israel's public and private life and their concerns were with such things as keeping the sabbath, enforcing the dietary laws, and increasing the number of Jewish religious schools, none of which were of any interest to the Arab electorate. Instead they trusted in the persuasiveness of material benefits and offered money. The National Religious Party had a slight advantage in that it could also exploit the post of minister of interior, which it had held since the early 1960s, and thus capture a number of Arab votes at every election. The usual method was to promise to support local Arab groups with funds and influence.[55] The election results show (see table) that the religious parties were able to secure a respectable proportion of the Arab votes.

Finally there was the Haolam Hazeh list, headed by Uri Avneri (editor of a weekly paper, *Haolam Hazeh*), which was known for its pro-Arab stance on many local questions. *Haolam Hazeh* first appeared in the 1965 elections when it won 2 percent of the total vote in the Arab districts. In the 1969 election, it managed to secure only 1.2 percent, a decline attributed to Avneri's closeness to the Israeli establishment. During his years in the Knesset, he had slowly changed his tone when addressing Jews, while maintaining his original style with the Arabs.[56] This double standard (which also led to the resignation of the editors of the Arabic version of Avneri's paper) put off a number of Arab supporters.[57]

The Zionist parties soon had a rival for influence among the Arabs in the Israeli Communist Party, the only non-Zionist party legally active in Israel since 1948.

The Communist Party has played an important role in the political history of Israel's Arabs. It has attracted large sectors of the Arab population, becoming second in importance after Mapai and in some areas the most popular party (see Appendix, Table 8). Even before the creation of Israel there had been a Communist group among the Arabs known as the

League for National Liberation, which joined the Jewish Communists in 1948 to form the Israeli Communist Party.[58] After Israeli occupation, several well-known Arab Communist leaders, such as Tawfiq Tubi, Emil Habibi, and Emil Toma, quickly resumed their activities. In general, the Communists did not waste much time. For example, on September 2, 1948, Shmuel Mikunis, a member of the Provisional State Council, was asking the minister of interior why there had been a delay in granting Tawfiq Tubi a license to publish a newspaper. Application had been made 4 August 1948.[59] Again, in January 1949 the records show Mikunis asking the minister of defense and the minister of interior to explain the military governor's refusal to allow him to enter the city of Acre to attend an election meeting held by the Arabs and protesting this violation of his party's right to campaign.[60] All this was before the first general election, in which four Communists were voted into the Knesset. Of these, Tawfiq Tubi won the party a considerable proportion of the Arab vote by opposing the government's Arab policy and trying to protect Arab rights.

To some extent, the Israeli government's own policies consolidated the position of the Communists among the Arabs. As the military government became more oppressive and the expropriation of Arab land more extensive, the Arabs' means of livelihood diminished and they felt hemmed in on all sides. Campaigning against these policies among both Arabs and Jews, the Communist Party was soon leading the Arab opposition to domestic policy. The Arabs did not pay much attention to foreign policy until the mid-fifties. When the government seemed to be tying the country to United States policy in the Cold War and withdrawing from the socialist camp and the Soviet bloc's support of the Arab nations, the Communist Party and the Arabs found themselves on the same side. The Communists focus on both fronts by protecting Arab interests on the local level and by advertising Soviet aid to the Arab countries. They have also appealed to Arab nationalism, going so far in their twelfth party congress in 1958 as to champion "the right of the Arabs of Israel to self-determina-

tion, even to the extent of seceding." Together with broad-
casts from neighboring Arab countries, the party has helped
to spread nationalist sentiment among Arab youth and they
have reciprocated with support and votes.[61] It is no accident
that on the eve of an election nationalist slogans appear more
frequently in the Communist press.

In 1954 the party gained some ground among the Jews
when Moshe Sneh's leftist group broke with Mapam and
joined them. Just before the 1965 elections, however, the
party split into two factions, an Arab one led by Tubi,
Habibi, and Vilner and a Zionist faction led by Sneh,
Mikunis, and Esther Wilenska.[62] The first group called itself
the new Communist list—Rakah—and took part in the elections independently, winning 20,691 Arab votes as opposed
to 511 for Maki, the second group. Four years later Rakah
won 29,871 Arab votes and Maki, 744 (Table 7).

Unlike the other Israeli parties, the Communists had
neither power nor financial resources with which to lure the
Arab electorate (except for a few dozen scholarships which
have been offered to Arab students since the early sixties,
permitting them to finish their college education in countries
of the socialist bloc). On the contrary, the party has often
had to appeal to Arabs and Jews for donations to finance
election campaigns and support regular activities. It found
nothing incongruous in this; on the contrary, in addition to
Arab sympathy for its views, the party sought to increase its
Arab membership, especially among the young. From 1948
onward, the Communist Party was continually active, setting
up branches in every Arab group it was able to reach. In time
it had more cells, with more far-reaching influence, than any
other party. A relatively wide network of party newspapers
and magazines published in Arabic helped. The oldest of
these is *Al Ittihad*, which was first published in 1944, and
became the party's most important publication in Arabic.
Since 1952, it has been published twice a week. A literary
and cultural monthly, *Al Jadid*, was first issued in 1953; a
youth-oriented magazine, *Al Ghad* appeared in 1954; and the
party's ideological organ, *Al Darb* has been published since

1951. The new Communist list—Rakah—has been publishing a Hebrew weekly, *Zo Haderekh*, since 1965, while the Maki group has taken over the party's daily Hebrew paper, *Kol Haam*, converting it to a weekly. To supplement these publications the party frequently distributes posters and pamphlets explaining various policies. The Communist press has kept an almost complete record of the experiences of the Arabs in Israel and is widely read by the Arab population.[63] Many Arab poets and writers living in Israel, such as Mahmoud Darwish, Samih Qasim, Tawfiq Ziyad, and Salem Gibran, first appeared in print on its pages.

On the practical side, the Communist members of the Knesset, especially the Arabs among them, have shown great interest in any problem or case involving Arabs; they address hundreds of questions to the different ministers and officials, introduce dozens of bills (few of which are passed) designed to improve the circumstances of the Arabs, and take active part in any debate on matters relating to them. The presence of Tawfiq Tubi in the Knesset since its creation (when he was twenty-seven) and his continuous efforts to protect Arab interests are a shining proof of the close relationship between the party and a large number of Arab voters.[64]

The Arab population's support of the Communist Party, however, is not constant. Election results vary in accordance with the two factors motivating support for the party: sympathy with the Communist position on foreign affairs and Arab nationalism and rejection of the Israeli authorities. For example, support grew as Soviet ties with such Arab countries as Egypt and Syria were strengthened in the mid-fifties. When Communists and nationalists in the Arab countries were airing their differences in 1959, however, only three Communists were elected to the Knesset, in contrast to six in 1955. When the external conflicts were settled, the Israeli Communists regained their popularity: five won Knesset seats in 1961.

The second factor's influence is reflected in the fact that election results from the different Arab settlements (Table 8) show that the Communists gain a much larger proportion of

the Arab vote in Knesset elections than they do in the
local ones. For example, in eleven Arab communities in the
1969 Knesset election they won more than twice the votes
cast for them in the local elections. The same was true in six
communities in 1965. This discrepancy has been attributed
to the fact that a pro-Communist Arab vote in Knesset elections is a kind of protest vote, whereas in the local elections
Arab votes are cast according to personal advantage or family
loyalty, which do not necessarily coincide with support of
the Communists.[65] The absence of any serious opposition
parties and the impossibility of forming an independent Arab
party are additional factors.

Since 1959, Israeli election results have shown a general
increase in Arab support for the Communist Party (Table 8).
This is true for all classes of Arab society, regardless of their
"cultural" differences, although there are variations in the
voting patterns of Bedouins, rural Arabs, and city dwellers—
the Communists getting least support from the Bedouins and
most from Arabs in the cities. This is not surprising considering the varying levels of education and political awareness.
Similarly, the government's ability to exert pressure on the
population varies, the Bedouins and inhabitants of small villages being the most easily restrained from supporting the
Communists. A contributing factor to the general rise in pro-
Communist votes is the increase in the proportion of young
Arab voters (the minimum voting age is eighteen), whose
nationalist feelings draw them to the Communists.

The Israeli authorities were quick to recognize the role
played by the Communist Party and tried to limit its activities by enforcing the military government restrictions against
its Arab members. Travel permits were withheld and orders
given for house arrests and administrative detentions. The
authorities have been careful to keep their interference within bounds, disrupting the Communist Party's work without
banning it entirely. The reason for such moderation is probably the desire to maintain relations with the countries of the
Soviet bloc, where many Jews still live, and also to leave
some room for protest among discontented Arab youth, in-

stead of forcing them underground. The Communist Party, on the other hand, has been meticulous about keeping within the letter and spirit of Israeli law. For example, whenever a member or supporter is charged with "disturbing the peace," the party immediately denounces the deed and disassociates itself from the perpetrator, announcing that it will expel him or her from the party (whether or not they follow through). This practice has been so successful that the party is considered by many as the Communist faction of the Israeli establishment. The most recent of its conciliatory gestures was support of a 1969 government bill (perhaps the first instance of unqualified Communist support of a government bill) to finance electoral campaigns with public funds. In due course, the Israeli Communists received their share of the public funds (£360,000).[66]

One thing all Israeli parties have had in common has been the desire to prevent the formation of an independent Arab organization at any cost. So far their efforts have met with remarkable success, for although the Arabs have tried to form their own political party, the attempt has been doomed from the beginning.[67]

In the first years after 1948, very few Arabs were thinking along these lines. For one thing, the Arab population was handicapped by its lack of political experience, and for another the Israeli government dealt firmly with all Arab activists. Any group interested in politics or wanting to express its views had no way of doing so except by joining a party. "Independent" Arab political activity was limited to occasional protest meetings and conferences condemning the government's Arab policy or to joining some Arab or Jewish political group and forming committees to draw up recommendations on particular issues. Since the 1950s, Arab political activity has been concentrated among nationalist elements and the Communist Party, especially after the two had drawn closer to each other politically. From time to time the Arabs received support from minor Jewish groups.

After the disturbances of May 1, 1958, in Nazareth and

Umm al Fahm and a number of unprecedented measures against the Arabs generally, registering protest through mass meetings, as the Arabs had been doing, suddenly ceased to be valid. It seemed necessary to organize a permanent body that would voice Arab criticism and oppose specific government measures when the need arose. After consultations between opposition groups, both nationalist and Communist, an invitation was issued in the name of Yammi Yammi, chairman of the local council in Kfar Yasif, and Taher Fahum of Nazareth, to a public meeting in Acre on July 6, 1958; a similar meeting was scheduled in Nazareth the same day. Some 120 people attended the meetings, and about forty others, including two Arab priests, were put under house arrest by the military governors to prevent them from attending.[68] The outcome was the formation of the Arab Front, which changed its name to the Popular Front when the district commissioner refused to recognize or register the organization, citing an Ottoman law dating to 1909 which forbids the registration of any "nationalist-sounding" association.

As the name suggests, the (Arab) Popular Front was simply a group of Arabs, nationalist and communist, whose objective was to deal with the internal problems of the Arabs in Israel. The aims of the Front, as laid down in its constitution, were to abolish the military government, to end the expropriation of Arab land, to effect the return of expropriated property to its owners, to abolish racial discrimination, to introduce the use of Arabic in all government departments, and to work toward the return of all refugees to their homes.[69] After only six months' activity, at the end of 1958, there were branches in Nazareth, Acre, Haifa, Tayba, Kfar Yasif, and Yafa al Nasra.[70] The government fiercely opposed the Front, imposing restrictions on many of its leaders and supporters, especially after Ben-Gurion's declaration that the

> founding of the Arab Front under this name is the first attempt to exploit the political cover of the Communist Party, with all its influence, on certain elements among the Arabs in the country. This attempt has come about after a decision taken by the Arab half of the Communist Party about a year ago, without the

knowledge of the Jewish members, that they would openly side with Arab movements hostile to Israel.[71]

Adding a statement of his own view of the Front, Ben-Gurion said that "in their original plan, the Arab activists in the Communist Party were to lead those initiating an Arab movement for 'national liberation' [quotation marks in the original], but to disguise their intention they included a few personalities who were not members of the Communist Party."[72] No wonder the Israeli authorities warded off danger by containing the Front.

Luck was on the authorities' side and they were saved considerable trouble by the increasing tension between nationalists and communists in the Arab world outside Israel, which split the Popular Front, paralyzing its activities. When the Communist Party decided to back its fellow Communists in the Arab countries, the non-Communist members of the Front asked the party to keep its activities within the framework of Israeli domestic problems and to refrain from attacking the nationalists. This request was rejected and what was known as the "nationalist wing" withdrew from the Front. The Front became merely an association linking the Communist Party to a small group of Arabs; its position had been shaken and its activities declined.[73] Apart from a conference on refugees and land, held on July 4, nothing worth recording was achieved in 1959. Even so, the authorities tried to disrupt the conference by arresting and sending into exile about twenty of its leading members.[74] Officially, the Front continues to exist, but its presence is felt only on the eve of elections, when it sometimes campaigns on behalf of the Communist Party.

Shortly after leaving the Popular Front, the nationalist group, led by Mansour Kardosh and Habib Qahwaji, announced its intention to undertake independent political work and founded *Usrat al Ard* (Family of the Earth), signifying the attachment of Palestinian Arabs to their land and affirming their right to their country. It published its own weekly newspaper, *Al Ard* (The Earth), and the group itself

became known as Al Ard. Al Ard was hindered in beginning
its practical work by a delay in the official response to its
application for a license to publish a newspaper. Under strong
pressure from the Communist Party and its supporters in the
Popular Front, Al Ard decided to publish each weekly issue
under the editorship of a different member of the group, on
the assumption that this procedure did not require a license.
To help the public recognize the source of the publication,
the word Al Ard was incorporated into the names of the
different issues, such as *This Earth, Call of the Earth*, and so
on. The tone of the paper was severely critical of Israeli
policies and of the Zionist movement generally. It openly
called on the Arabs in Israel to handle their own affairs,
leaving no room for doubt that Al Ard was an Arab nationalist group.

The official reaction was to regard this as open provocation, especially since the call to Arabs in Israel to organize,
apart from its nationalist aspect, was a denial of the most
venerated principle of Israel's official policy. Retaliation was
prompt. At the end of January 1960, the advisor on Arab
affairs, Shmuel Divon, held a press conference at Sokolow
(Journalists) House in Tel Aviv, in which he warned against
"this Nasserite group which is inciting the Arabs," whose
publication had been described by Cairo radio as "gladdening
the hearts of all Arabs."[75] The press conference was taken as
the signal for attacks on the group. The police closed down
the newspaper and confiscated its latest issues (only thirteen
had been published). Six of the editors were taken to court
on charges of publishing a paper without a license. Al Ard
supporters had their travel permits withdrawn by the military
governor.[76] At the same time, the Communist Party publicly
denounced Al Ard because its paper had called for a boycott
of the November 1959 election. Finally, the governor of the
northern region announced his inability to grant the group a
license to publish because the editor did not fulfill the requirements of the Israeli Press Ordinance.

Al Ard's attempt to form an independent organization and
a publication occupied it totally throughout its existence.

Except for participation by its supporters in protest meetings and the organization of lectures and study groups, and so on, its work was generally limited to trying to break through the restrictions that hemmed it in and to obtain some kind of legal standing in Israel so that it could work openly among the Arabs. All its efforts were to prove unsuccessful but were a unique experience with Israeli democracy.

After its initial defeat, Al Ard began to reorganize by establishing a commercial printing and publishing firm called the Al Ard Company Ltd. This was to be a source of funds for political work. At first the registrar of companies refused to register it, on the grounds, according to the government's judicial advisor, that its work "undermined the security of the nation and the public interest." When the matter was brought before the Supreme Court, it ruled that keeping the nation's security was not the business of the registrar of companies, and he was ordered to register the company.[77] When the judicial advisor to the government appealed the ruling before a panel of five judges, it was upheld, and Al Ard Ltd. was finally registered.[78] Shares were sold to founders and supporters but otherwise restricted lest they fall into unreliable hands and be abused.

The group's next undertaking was to apply, again, for a license to publish a weekly paper. It took more than a year before every condition set by the Press Ordinance was fulfilled, at which point the district commissioner refused the license, citing the emergency regulations, which allowed him "in his discretion and without assigning any reason therefore," to grant or refuse any permit.[79] Again the group appealed to the Supreme Court but without success. The court ruled that the powers of the district commissioner were absolute in such matters, and that "we cannot overrule the decision of the competent authority . . . even if we might have, individually or as a group, decided differently had the matter been up to us."[80]

The denial of the license was a heavy blow. Without a paper, Al Ard could not reach the masses and its work was crippled. In retaliation, the group prepared a memorandum

on the conditions of the Arabs in Israel, explaining most of
their grievances. Copies were sent to the Secretary General of
the United Nations, to a large number of newspapers and
internationally known personalities, as well as to foreign em-
bassies in Israel, members of the Knesset, and various Israeli
institutions. The report was received with great interest outside Israel, especially by some groups in the Arab nations,
which reacted as if they had discovered for the first time that
there were Arabs in Israel. The ensuing uproar incensed the
Israeli government, and Levi Eshkol was known to be consulting with his advisor on Arab affairs and with the security
service on how to counter Al Ard.[81] Meanwhile, various
groups in Israel made anonymous threats against the group
and its supporters. The appeal to international bodies was
considered vicious, although this was neither the first nor the
last time that Arabs in Israel had sent memoranda with their
grievances to various international associations. The authorities had apparently decided to wipe out Al Ard. The group's
decision to register as a political party, however, temporarily
stayed the government's hand.

As a political party Al Ard would be able to work openly
and express its views without depending on a newspaper,
since it could call political meetings and publish manifestos.
Thus in the middle of July 1964 the formation of the Al Ard
movement was announced. For the first time its objectives
were clearly stated and the authorities officially apprised of
them. Among the articles of association was the following:

> To find a just solution for the Palestine question, considering it a
> whole and indivisible unit, in accordance with the wishes of the
> Palestinian Arab people; a solution which meets its interests and
> desires, restores it to its political existence, ensures its full legal
> rights, and regards it as the first possessor of the right to decide
> its own fate for itself, within the framework of the supreme
> wishes of the Arab nation.

Another article stated that the group intended to "support
the movement of liberation, unity, and socialism in the Arab
world, by all legal means, while considering this movement as

a decisive force in the Arab world, for which reason Israel should regard it in a positive manner."

Leaders of the movement had more than once stated the need for an Arab party and the objectives of such a party, even before the list of aims had been drawn up. For example, Mansour Kardosh, secretary of the movement, felt there was an urgent need for an Arab party which would

> foster a sense of national pride [among the Arabs in Israel] ... and firmly insist on the right to complete equality for all citizens, which would insist on the recognition of the rights of the refugees who wish to return ... so that the country could follow a policy of positive neutrality and peaceful coexistence between the two active camps.[82]

Kardosh also said that "the Arab party would cooperate with Jewish progressive and democratic movements for their mutual benefit."[83] Another leader of Al Ard, Saleh Baransi, stated:

> We have worked ... side by side with other progressive and democratic forces in order to win for the Arabs their rights and equality. We still feel that the world must hear the voice of our masses ... crying against oppression, discrimination, military rule, land robbery, and demolition of houses, when we do nothing to impose on the rights of others to live in peace.[84]

Al Ard made a special point of the need for establishing a Palestinian Arab state. "It is true that the Arabs in Israel are not a nation, but they form part of a great nation," Al Ard stated. "The Arabs of this country were and still are part of the Palestinian Arab people, which is indivisibly part of the Arab world ... their right to establish a Palestinian Arab state has been forcibly taken from them."[85] If the Jews had a right to an independent state, "the people of Palestine also have a right to an independent state ... we live within cease-fire lines ... there is no reason to decide that every Arab living in this area is an Israeli ... the present borders did not fall from the sky, they can be modified here and there."[86] If it should come about that a Palestinian Arab state is established, and if with the passing of time Israel demonstrates that it has abandoned its expansionist greed, "it could then live peacefully as an organic part of the Middle East and as a member of a federation which would include Israel and the united Arab nations." [87] This point, more than anything else, eventually drove the authorities to eliminate the movement.

The authorities viewed Al Ard's wish to be registered as a political party as an act of extreme provocation. Two days after notice of the movement's formation had been received, the district commissioner of Haifa said that after studying its objectives "and other material that has been furnished to me . . . I declare that the Al Ard movement . . . has been formed with the intent of violating the security and the very existence of the state of Israel." [88] It was therefore illegal and if it continued, the necessary measures would be taken against it. The media campaign against Al Ard was intensifying.

Once more Al Ard appealed to the Supreme Court, which departed from its usual position and agreed to a political debate over the aims of the movement. It concluded that the article concerning the Palestinian people was "an absolute and utter condemnation of the existence of the state of Israel in general, and of its existence within its present borders in particular." [89] As for the article about "liberation, unity, and socialism" in the Arab world, the court considered it as supporting the "hostile attitudes [of the Arab world] toward Israel and the elimination of Israel by force." [90] The court therefore upheld the district commissioner's decision not to recognize or register the movement. Two days after the court's ruling, three of Al Ard's leaders were arrested on suspicion, according to the police, of having broken the security regulations. Apparently "some agents of Lebanese and Egyptian intelligence recently captured in Israel had stated under cross-examination that they were instructed to contact these men." [91] At any rate, the arrested men were soon released without charges and put under house arrest. The minister of defense then used his powers under the emergency regulations and declared "the people known as the Al Ard movement or the Al Ard group, whatever its name may be, and the persons associated with the Al Ard Company Ltd., or who acted for the shareholders of the said company, or any part of them, an illegal association."[92] This declaration resulted in the termination of the movement and the banning of its activities. All its assets were seized and anyone attempting to continue its work was subject to ten years in prison.

Al Ard seemed to have arrived at a dead end. Few missed it on the political scene.[93] The Communist Party was an exception, stating formally that

> the courts were not established to pass judgment on the legality of any political movement . . . and to represent the courts as the judicial custodian of political movements must be regarded as a debasement of the essential separation of the legislative, judicial, and executive powers. To deny the Al Ard group its right to engage in legitimate political activity is not simply a blow aimed at one movement but an attack on democratic freedoms in the country under the bogus pretext of "security"—a situation we emphatically condemn.[94]

Writing under the nom de plume Juheina, Communist Knesset member Emil Habibi stated, after the attacks on Al Ard:

> We hope that the Al Ard group will draw the correct inferences from the new revolutionary developments [in the Arab world] and in the whole national liberation movement. All revolutionaries are now demanding total emancipation and socialism, they are advancing along one front, in one direction, toward one party . . . and in our country this party is the Communist Party.[95]

Al Ard was being invited to return to the fold and work with the Communist Party within the (Arab) Popular Front. But this invitation was not accepted.

There is one final chapter in the story of Al Ard. In 1965, the Knesset elections were set for early November and members of Al Ard resolved to try to win at least one seat. If one of their members could resume political activity through the immunity of office, they would have made a breakthrough. The requirements for nominating any electoral list were relatively easy: 750 signatures from voters backing the list and five thousand Israeli pounds to be deposited with the Central

Elections Committee. Fulfilling these conditions, Al Ard announced that it would take part in the elections under the Socialist list, with ten candidates, all members and supporters of Al Ard. Official reaction was the same as in the past. Before the formal registration of the list, an order from the military governor banished four of the candidates as "instigators of activities hostile to the nation."[96] They were sent into exile in Arad, Beisan, Tiberias, and Safad, four towns with no Arab population, until some time after the elections. Simultaneously, orders of compulsory residence were meted out to many of the activists in the movement.

Despite this, the list was assembled and its confirmation requested from the Central Elections Committee. The authorities' next move did not become clear until much later when numerous letters began to arrive at the committee asking that the writer's signature be withdrawn from the Socialist list. The letters turned out to be identical in form, indicating some kind of official interference.[97] Since the committee's members are from parties represented in the previous Knesset, it is interested in limiting the number of rival lists. It decided against the Socialist list with the approval of its chairman, Judge Moshe Landau, who was on the Supreme Court panel that had banned the Al Ard movement. The reason for this decision, according to Judge Landau, was that the sponsors of the Socialist list "condemned the existence of Israel and were a threat to its security."[98] When Al Ard appealed to the Supreme Court, the court upheld the decision of the committee.[99] Al Ard thereupon abandoned its efforts to attain legitimacy within the Israeli system.[100]

The dissolution of Al Ard did not stop the campaign against the movement and any of its surviving pockets. Among these were some sports clubs in the villages of the Triangle, which were supposedly encouraged by Al Ard. These associations were formed by young Arabs mainly as a way of finding some independent solution to their problems, since the responsible Israeli departments seemed to ignore them.[101] The authorities regarded them as centers of nationalist gatherings and therefore "security risks," as well as a challenge to the Histadrut's monopoly on organizing clubs; they put pressure on club members to close them.[102] For example, the military governor declared the village of Kfar Kara in the Triangle a closed area merely to prevent an athletic festival from taking place, since it was to be attended by sports club members.[103] Such measures usually had the desired effect but in two cases, Tayba and Tira, club members continued their activities, ignoring punitive residential restrictions and orders to close.[104] The Tayba club was then declared an illegal association and put out of action.[105] In Tira, all official pressure proved useless, until late in 1968, when one of the club's members was found to belong to Al Fatah. The minister of defense then declared the club illegal and ordered it closed.[106]

Unable to break through the restrictions that bound it, Al Ard did not leave a memorable record of achievement. At times the group may have miscalculated the vehemence of its tone and the frankness of its attitude, antagonizing all political parties; to have Mapai as an enemy was dangerous. Indeed to protect its own interests Mapai opposed any organization wishing to work among the Arabs. It was, for example, continually harassing Mapam's Arab members.[107] There is an essential difference, however, between a faction enjoying support from influential quarters in the government and Al Ard, with its few supporters and negligible influence. On the other hand, it is difficult to see how Al Ard could have acted differently, considering its principles. One of its obvious mistakes was to trust in Israeli justice and democracy; another was to underestimate the Zionist concept of "security," and how widely it could be interpreted when convenient.[108]

The Al Ard experiment did not pass without leaving some mark both on the Israeli regime and on a section of the Arab community, however. The fact of its existence and the repercussions resulting from its elimination were among the factors that led to a more liberal Arab policy in the mid-sixties, aimed at containing the impact of Al Ard and preventing similar movements in the future.[109] Further, young Arabs did not forget Al Ard, and five years after its elimination a study of Israeli Arab support of guerrilla action showed that "the

personal histories of a fair number of those who had some
kind of connection [with the guerrillas] . . . reveal some relationship with the Al Ard movement before the Six Day
War."[110] These Arabs had come to believe that obeying the
law and trusting in justice and democracy in Israel were not
the best way to deal with the Israeli regime—and it seems
difficult to contradict them.

The government's disapproval of independent Arab organizations did not include Arab university student associations.
The first of these, in 1959, was the Arab Students' Committee at the Hebrew University in Jerusalem, which advised
Arab students on educational and social problems. As the
number of Arab students increased at the universities of
Haifa and Tel Aviv, similar committees were set up on those
campuses, although the Jerusalem committee continued to be
the most effective. Inevitably, the students' committees also
turned to politics—attending protest meetings against the military government and land expropriations, prodding the
authorities on certain unresolved difficulties, supporting the
Al Ard movement, and voting for the Communist Party in
elections.[111] Despite this, on no occasion did the Israeli
authorities oppose the formation of a committee or try to
eliminate it by force. They went no further than to apply the
usual pressures exerted against those disapproved of by the
government, although several leaders were charged with security violations. In contrast, the student committees were not
content to organize university students but extended their
activity beyond the campus, trying, unsuccessfully, to organize Arab high school students and then Arab academics,
successfully.[112] On December 1, 1971, the Arab Students'
Committees of Hebrew University and Tel Aviv University
jointly formed a Union of Arab Academics, with the aim of
improving teaching conditions and academic standards for
the educated Arab.[113]

In the early stages this union was exposed to a great deal
of criticism and defamation. The founders were described as
"behaving like spoilt and disturbed children, demanding for

themselves all the rights and freedoms of the Jews in this country."[114] They were said to be "orphans of Al Ard, orphans of the only party adhering to outside policy."[115] But the authorities did not interfere with the union and even requested that the conditions complained of be corrected.[116] And yet, judging from past policy, the Union of Arab Academics qualified for immediate liquidation, since it was fundamentally "nationalist," like the Arab Front, and included a number of former members of Al Ard. Its continued existence indicates a change in official policy, after 1967, regarding Arab organizations. When, for example, the prime minister's deputy advisor on Arab affairs, Uri Standel, objected to the union, his opinion was disregarded, and when he handed in his resignation in protest it was accepted.

Not content with restricting political activity among the Arabs, the Israeli government turned its attention to religious divisions. By feeding and reinforcing confessional loyalties until they eclipsed national feelings, the government hoped to consolidate its own political position. Of course, this was not a definite policy, publicly proclaimed, but rather a gradual process. The authorities first decided to appoint religious leaders, under the guise of guaranteeing religious services to all sects, and later exploited these appointments for their own purposes. They were undoubtedly trying to forestall the emergence of a religious leadership that might become a national leadership, as the Palestinian religious leaders, both Moslem and Christian, had opposed the Zionists in the days of the British Mandate. Zionists saw the religious leaders as capable of sowing dissension, which they would find it difficult to oppose, considering Israel's proclaimed policy of noninterference in religious matters.

Official intervention took different forms for the various sects. For example, the authorities found it very difficult to influence the management of Christian Arab affairs since the responsibility for appointments and transfers is in the spiritual centers of the main Christian sects outside Israel. Further, Israel wants to remain on good terms with the

Christian nations and therefore takes great care not to treat its Christian community in any way that might forfeit the good opinion of the Christian world. Indeed, responsible government groups have made great efforts to establish contact with both Arab and other Christian priests, their eagerness bordering on flattery, and the Christians have in many cases responded with enthusiasm, or at least with an acceptance of peaceful coexistence with the Israeli regime. Some Orthodox Jewish groups have opposed Christian missions in Israel and have on occasion succeeded in pressing the government to restrict their work.

The situation is very different with regard to the Moslems. Under the British Mandate the Moslem community had complete freedom in the management of its religious affairs. The Israelis, on the other hand, at first seemed at a loss as to how to deal with the Moslems. The head of the Islamic department of the ministry of religions advocated the resumption of the former system, with supervision of Moslem affairs restricted to members of that faith.[117] But the government, after some hesitation, seized Islamic *waqf* property and took charge of setting up courts of Islamic law (one each in Nazareth and Acre in 1947, and one each in Jaffa and Taybeh at the beginning of 1950); the *qadis* or judges of the religious courts, were appointed by order of the minister of religions.[118] When the legality of these moves was questioned, the Knesset, at the suggestion of the government, hastily passed a law confirming them, over the objections of some members who felt that the Moslem community was not being treated on a par with other religious minorities, since it had not been consulted in the matter.[119] In 1961, when one of the *qadis* appointed by the minister of religions died and the other was on the point of retirement, the government passed the Law of Shari'a *Qadis*.[120] This law placed the appointment of Shari'a *qadis* in the hands of a committee of nine, at least four of whom could be non-Moslems.[121] This committee became the one and only body regulating the Moslem community's religious affairs, the government having rejected a proposal to reinstate a higher Moslem council similar to the one during the Mandate on the grounds that the request represented "a political rather than a religious aspiration."[122] The Israeli authorities do not always adhere to their traditional stance of nonintervention in religious matters. For example, although "a Moslem may take a Jewish or Christian wife ... and the wife may practice her own religion [under Islamic law], the laws of the state forbid us [Shari'a *qadis*] from marrying couples of different faiths. The wife has to embrace Islam."[123] This is a difficult step to take in Israel, especially for Jewish women. The real reason the Shari'a *qadis* cannot perform such mixed marriages is not "the laws of the state" but internal instructions issued by the Islamic department of the ministry of religions in 1952 to the effect that "mixed marriages between Jews and non-Jews are a disturbing problem from the Jewish perspective," being incompatible with the Zionist character of Israel.[124]

As far as possible, Israeli authorities have tried to keep religious matters in the Moslem community under their control. For example, they pay part of the salaries of Moslem religious leaders, as well as the expenses of administering the mosques. These are made as donations, although the money is actually income from the expropriated *waqf* properties. The decision to make the "donations" lies with a committee made up of representatives of the ministry of religions, the custodian of absentee property, and the advisor on Arab affairs, without consultation of any Islamic body.[125]

One reason for the authorities' behavior toward the Moslem minority is the identification, in the eyes of most Israelis, of Moslem with Arab. This has led on many occasions to senseless and inflammatory propaganda against Islam and the Moslems, both in and outside Israel.[126]

In contrast to the other Arab religious minorities, the government has treated the Druze with what is officially described as "friendliness." At first there was no differentiation between the Druze and the Arabs. The change came gradually, aided by the fact that some Druze leaders collaborated with Israel and a number of Druze fought alongside Israelis in 1948. Moslem and Christian Arabs had also fought, but the Druze leadership went much further and after 1948 organized petitions requesting that all young Druze enlist in the Israeli army to fight for their "fatherland," as a gesture of "loyalty and friendship" on the part of the Druze community. Not that the authorities needed such fawning gestures in order to recruit Druze—or any other Arabs—into the army since the minister of defense has the power to call up all Israeli citizens, with or without petitions. Of course, there was no objection to exploiting such an offer, and the government expressed its appreciation while the minister of defense announced that he would "grant" the Druze request and order compulsory military service for all young Druze males. However, the Druze are excluded from service in certain army units that are entrusted with "sensitive" missions, and the result has been a continuing rift in the community between those favoring and those opposing conscription.[127]

The Israeli government then developed a policy of distinguishing the Druze from the Arabs. In 1957, the Druze were recognized as "an independent religious sect" contradicting an announcement ten months earlier by the minister of religions.[128] Five years later the Knesset passed the Druze Religious Courts Law, 5723—1962, which was advertised as regulating the sect's religious matters in such a way as to make the Druze equal to other sects, their affairs having been governed by the Islamic Shari'a court till then.[129] This was part of a much larger plan: once the Druze were recognized as a separate sect, the description "Druze" began to appear under "nationality" on identification forms and other official Israeli documents where "Arab" had appeared before. When the minister of interior was asked the reason for this designation, he replied that "the leaders of the Druze sect [whose names he did not recall] had requested that their Druze origins be recorded as the nationality of the Druze community, and that the ministry of interior had found no reason to refuse."[130] The campaign emphasizing the differences between Druze and Arab was then officially intensified in the hope that such a distinction would affect their position, not only within Israel but in the neighboring Arab countries as well. This was an extension of the past policy of those Zionist groups that had advocated dealing with the peoples of the Middle East along religious lines, reducing them to a collection of minorities—among whom the Jews would hold a position of importance.

The Druze themselves, at any rate, derived no extraordinary benefits from this policy. Their standard of living, rural development, and general circumstances are not very different from the rest of the Arabs. And in many respects their lot is even worse.[131] For example, when Jabr Ma'di, as deputy minister, wanted to boast of the achievement of his people under Israeli rule, he announced that: "It was with great pleasure that I learned that there are ten doctors from our sect ... some lawyers and engineers and other professionals," who graduated during the twenty-four years of Israel's existence (until 1972).[132] The Druze then numbered thirty-five thousand. Land belonging to Druze villages has been just as vulnerable to seizure and expropriation as that of other Arab villages. The military government affected all the sects at first, though eventually Druze serving in the army did not come under its rule. Even today, many restrictions are imposed on young Druze who oppose the government's policy, for "security reasons," although most of them probably served in the Israeli army. Regardless of the relatively poor standard of living in the Druze villages, there continues to be mutual support between the Israeli authorities and a number of Druze leaders. In 1967, for example, the administration of Druze affairs was removed from the government department for Arab affairs because "the Druze are now 'equal' to the Jews, the obvious achievements of the sect in its organization and its social and cultural development indicating to the government that it is no longer in need of a special government department to handle its affairs."[133] As the years pass, it is obvious that this was mere public relations, since the advisor on Arab affairs is still in charge of the Druze.[134] In the same vein, an announcement was made that special schools would be opened for Druze pupils and that a history of their community was being prepared for use in these schools.[135] Such far-reaching interference has only been possible because of the very close cooperation of some of the traditional heads of Druze families at the expense of the Druze community. The prestige of the leaders has been boosted to the point where the authorities themselves cannot ignore them. For example, in 1966 when a judge of the Druze court had reached the age of seventy and was about to be pensioned off—according to Israeli practice in both civil and religious courts—he and his supporters objected and he was allowed to carry on until he reached seventy-five.[136] When the five years were up, the conflict between the members of the Druze community on the committee for appointing judges was so great (a situation for which the authorities were largely responsible) that it was impossible to replace the retired judge.[137] At this point, the Knesset modified the law, so as to permit the Druze court to settle cases coming before it with a panel of only one judge.[138] Such concessions would never be made, for such reasons, in any other court in Israel.

For all its relative tolerance, Israel's policy toward the Druze has been unpopular with many members of the community, who have objected to land expropriation and compulsory military service, especially when service in the army or with the police has resulted in casualties.[139] Opponents of the government have been few, however, and most have preferred to live with the policy. The attempt by the government to separate the Druze from the rest of the Arabs has succeeded, as have so many efforts to divide the Arab presence in Israel and absorb the community into the various Israeli parties.

8
Education, Economics, and Services

Whatever the differences of opinion regarding military government, land seizure, or the rights of the Arab minority, there seems to be an almost unanimous feeling at all levels of Israeli society that there has been "great achievement" and "extraordinary progress" in Arab education under Israeli rule. Though official boasts about such improvements have been less frequent recently, there continue to be announcements such as "government projects for developing [the Arabs in Israel] ... have been unmatched in any Arab country." [1]

Indeed, it would be inaccurate to deny that conditions have improved in many ways for the Arab minority, but to attribute these changes to the existence of Israel and to its efforts would be a gross exaggeration. Despite whatever progress has been made, the standard of life of the Arabs in Israel generally remains far below that of the Jews—even after a quarter century of living under one system of government. [2] Furthermore, if present-day life is compared with pre-1948 conditions (a favorite comparison in many Israeli groups), the improvement of Arab life in Israel falls short, in many ways, of that enjoyed by a considerable proportion of Palestinians living outside Israel. The exaggerated claims about progress seem to be the official reaction to charges that Israel has mistreated and oppressed its Arab subjects. The pages that follow deal with the main areas affecting the life and standards of the Arab minority; the Arab schools and the general level of education; the development of Arab agriculture and the condition of the Arab laborer—the two principal sources of livelihood for a majority of Arabs; and the development of the Arab village and the state of its services.

After the 1948 War and its chaos had dispersed a large number of teachers and administrators and paralyzed the school system, the first change in Arab education introduced by the Israeli government was the establishment of new elementary schools in addition to the existing local schools. Every Arab community was included, whether town, village, or Bedouin tribe, so that after one decade of Israeli rule there were 167 elementary schools (including the old and the new) and 141 kindergartens in 138 Arab settlements.[3] A major advance in Arab education was thus achieved. Every Arab student in Israel was able to receive elementary schooling, in Arabic, at a school near home. Unfortunately, this seems to have been the government's only noteworthy accomplishment in this field. In order to understand the shortcomings of its policies, a few general remarks about education in Israel may be useful.

In 1949 the Knesset passed a special law regulating elementary education for both Arabs and Jews.[4] According to this law the state, together with such local authorities as the municipalities and district councils, guarantees to provide eight years of free, compulsory education to children between the ages of five and thirteen. The state is responsible for supplying teachers, training and paying them, and for the curricula; the local authorities are in charge of school buildings, furniture, and other necessities. The students' guardians are obliged to send them to school as long as they are of school age and are liable to penalties for failing to do so. They are also responsible for the students' personal expenses, such as the purchase of books and paper.

Secondary education consists of four years after elementary school (ages 13 to 17) and is taken care of mainly by local authorities and private institutions, with some form of state subsidy in certain areas. Free compulsory education has recently been extended two years to include the ninth and tenth grades (ages 14 and 15). This came into effect after September 1, 1972, for the fourteen-year-olds, and will take effect after September 1, 1976, for fifteen-year-olds.[5] It is too early to assess its results.

Despite these arrangements, there has been no significant advance in Arab education in Israel. Statistics show that an average of 25 percent of school-age children either drop out of elementary school or fail to attend at all (see Appendix, Table 10). The authorities themselves are to blame, in that they do not enforce the compulsory education law. They are lax in taking action against parents who prefer to keep their children at home to help with their work, and they ignore "conservatives" who refuse to send their daughters to school. Only 44 percent of school-age Arab girls attend school.[6] In contrast, compulsory education is much more strictly enforced among the Jews. The administration of the Arab schools is also inadequate, with the result that the level of education remains unsatisfactory, even in the eyes of the Israeli authorities. Naturally, failures at this level have a detrimental effect on Arab life generally.

Of all the things that have hindered progress in Arab education, the most important has been a shortage of trained teachers. The absence of professional teachers was most sorely felt immediately after the establishment of Israel, when the authorities were forced to appoint dozens of untrained people—during the academic year 1949–50, 90 percent of the teachers working in Arab schools were untrained.[7] With the increase in the number of Arab schools, a number of secondary school graduates have been recruited as elementary school teachers. In the twenty-year period between 1949 and 1969, the proportion of professional teachers rose from 10 percent to 45 percent, but thus, at the beginning of the 1970–71 academic year, more than half the elementary teachers in Arab schools were still not trained.[8]

There has been no urgency on the part of the authorities to remedy the shortage. It was not until 1956 that a training college for Arab elementary and kindergarten teachers was opened in Jaffa. (It was moved to Haifa in 1965, after part of

the building it had been occupying collapsed.)[9] The number
of teachers who have graduated from the college so far
exceeds the number of untrained teachers currently working
in the elementary schools, but appointments have not always
been based on the fitness of the candidates, rather on such
considerations as the recommendation of the military government or other official bodies.[10] There is much pressure also
from the candidates themselves, since the position of elementary school teacher is one of the few white-collar jobs open
to an Arab high school graduate. For some of these reasons
trained graduates are not being appointed to jobs, and the
ministry of education has been pressured into keeping on
untrained teachers. This makes Arab teachers doubly vulnerable to the authorities, who can take advantage of the scarcity of jobs to intimidate them or, on occasion, dismiss them
for political reasons. The teachers seem to have resigned
themselves to the situation, even refraining from supporting
or participating in strikes organized by Jewish teachers for
better working conditions.

Other reasons for the low standards in Arab schools have
been ineffective teaching programs: school curricula have
been vague, incomplete, and subject to sudden change. By
1952 the ministry of education had decided on a new Arabic-
language curriculum for the first two grades. The other grades
continued to use the old curriculum until October 1957,
when a complete program, for grades one through four, was
adopted.[11] The program for grades five through eight was not
ready until November 1959. But changes continued from
time to time; the last modification was introduced in February 1971 on the recommendations of a committee appointed to reexamine the Arabic teaching programs.[12] The
Arab secondary schools, on the other hand, received programs related to specific subjects until the curriculum was
complete in 1967.

The serious shortage of Arabic textbooks, especially during
the first ten years, was also a big handicap. Teachers and
pupils had to use old books or copy down the subject of a
lesson from one of the few books available. By 1953 only

one new book had been published for use in Arab schools.[13] Conditions improved in the 1960s, when the authorities began to encourage the publication of textbooks and the translation of Hebrew books for use in Arab schools.[14] By the end of the year 1961-62, fifteen schoolbooks had been published, and twenty-five more came out in the following two years. All books required in elementary school were ready by 1966, and eighty elementary-level books were available during the 1970-71 school year.[15]

As for books required in secondary school, their preparation and publication has yet to be completed, but the situation for Arabic books in general has improved. During the early years of the state, it was almost impossible to find any books in Arabic. By the end of the 1950s, however, there was a resurgence of books written or translated into Arabic, and several publishing houses began to reprint Arabic books that had originally appeared outside Israel. By 1964 there were 179 books in Arabic in circulation, not counting schoolbooks, dictionaries, or official and government publications. Of these, 75 were written or translated in Israel; the rest were reprints which were printed without permission from either authors or publishers. By 1971 the number of books in Arabic had risen to 440, of which 128 were produced in Israel.[16]

Finally, inadequate buildings, services, and equipment, such as furniture, maps, and laboratories, contributed to the general slump in Arab education. This negligence can also be traced to overall Israeli policy toward the Arabs, which had a very damaging effect on the schools. The maintenance of school buildings and equipment are the responsibility of local authorities. These are respected personalities who represent the residents of their areas and who have the power to levy taxes and obtain loans from public and private foundations to meet the needs of the area, including the upkeep of schools. Where there is no local authority, as in a village or Bedouin encampment, the minister of interior and the minister of education can appoint a local education committee of one or more members to assume responsibility for the schools. This arrangement is prevalent in 66 of 104 Arab communities.[17] For reasons to be considered later, the minister of education was very reluctant to set up local councils in these communities. But experience has shown that the committees cannot carry out their responsibilities in a satisfactory way. Most are unable to exact taxes from local residents and lack the power to make funds available for building schools "because communities without municipalities or local councils cannot obtain loans," according to the minister of education, Abba Eban.[18] He admitted that "there are nearly eighty such communities and the school facilities in most of them are below acceptable standards."[19]

In 1964, the Communist Party and Mapam proposed a modification in the compulsory education law, transferring responsibility for school buildings in communities without local authorities to the state, together with the power to levy education taxes through the government tax-gathering apparatus, which is notoriously enthusiastic in its work. But the Knesset, adopting the government's position, did not approve the modification.[20] The Knesset also rejected a proposal to authorize the government to construct school buildings on behalf of local education authorities whenever they so request.[21] The situation has eased somewhat since then with an increase in the number of local councils, but on the whole it remains unsatisfactory. Insufficient funds for school construction have not helped. For example, in the decade 1960 to 1970, the government appears to have allocated nearly 10 million pounds for the extension and restoration of Arab school facilities. (There is conflicting information on this subject since it is difficult to ascertain which of the sums approved in the budget were actually spent for the purpose intended.)[22] One-quarter of the amount spent in this way was in the form of grants; the rest was government loans to be repaid over twenty-five years at an interest rate of 5.5 percent.[23] In 1971 a three-year plan for improving Arab school facilities was approved, with a budget of ten million pounds for the years 1971–74.[24]

The low standard of education in Arab elementary schools

has directly affected the secondary schools, with the result that a considerable proportion of Arab students fail the examinations at the end of their secondary education. To this day more than two-thirds of the candidates do not pass the examinations and cannot receive the diploma that would enable them to find work or go on to college (see Appendix, Table 11).

Considering the relatively small number of Arab students who make it as far as the secondary school examinations and the large proportion of these who fail, it is not surprising that the general level of teaching among the Arabs has been adversely affected. According to the statistics, the proportion of Arabs holding secondary school diplomas is nearly one-tenth that of the Jews (see Table 12), which means that even the minimum needs of the Arab community for educated people are not met.

The high percentage of failure in secondary school has a harmful effect at the university level, too. In the 1959-60 academic year, for example, 77 Arab students attended Israeli universities; this figure rose to 272 in 1964-65, 440 in 1968-69, and 607 in 1970-71. The proportion of Jewish students attending universities has been ten times as large during the same period. It is uncertain how many Arab students actually complete their studies, since official sources are uncharacteristically silent on the subject—there is no celebration of Arab "achievements" in this field. Clearly there is little to boast of.

> According to a study of higher education among the Arabs in Israel prepared by the prime minister's advisor for Arab affairs, it appears that during the last ten years, 1961-71, only 300 Arab students received degrees from institutions of higher learning in Israel, while in the previous ten years, 1950-60, the number of Arab university graduates did not reach 100. In 1949 there were only 50 Arabs in Israel with university educations. Altogether, the number of Arabs holding university degrees in Israel does not exceed 500. (It is assumed that of the hundreds who have gone abroad to study, only a few dozen have returned—there is no accurate estimate of their number.)[25]

It is obvious that the total of 500 university graduates in a population of 400,000 leaves the Arab community in dire need of university-trained specialists of every kind.[26]

The community has a plentiful supply of laborers, but even at the best of times only a small proportion of these are skilled. In vocational and technical training, the standard of teaching among the Arabs does not even measure up to the requirements of the Arab population and does not compare with similar training among the Jews. For example, in 1970–71 there were 7 schools for apprentices attended by 226 pupils in the Arab sector and 116 schools and 4,836 pupils in the Jewish sector; 19 vocational training schools with an attendance of 1,048 pupils in the Arab sector and 250 schools and 53,847 pupils in the Jewish sector; 1 agricultural school with 393 students for the Arabs and 30 schools with 7,462 students for the Jews; 1 teacher-training college with 358 students for the Arabs and 38 colleges with 5,191 students for the Jews.[27]

The responsible authorities do not deny that Arab secondary education is in a bad state, but their explanations differ. The ministry of education blames the schools for accepting any student who has completed elementary education, regardless of scholastic achievement or intelligence. It criticizes the leniency with which students are promoted from one class to the next, without tests of their ability, so that a large number inevitably take the final examination without adequate preparation. It does acknowledge, however, a lack of university-educated teachers in the secondary schools and a shortage of suitable books in Arabic on a wide range of subjects.[28] The Knesset education committee said in a report on secondary education among the Arabs "that the state of [Arab] secondary education is disturbing," and that "the ministry of education must make special efforts to help it reach the required standard within the next few years."[29] It offered a list of recommendations whose implementation it considered indispensable. Among other things, it suggested prompt action in setting up local councils, supervising the construction of schools, enlarging the Arab teacher-training college, raising the standards of future teachers, publishing suitable textbooks in all subjects for the secondary schools, and, finally, "ensuring that the appointment of teachers to Arab schools is based solely on the intellectual attainments of the candidates and their ability, without the intrusion of any other considerations." Ten years after these recommendations were drafted, Arab education, especially secondary education, is still in need of the same remedies. As long as the situation remains unchanged, it will be difficult to make any significant improvement in Arab university and elementary education.[30]

As a conclusion to this description of Arab education, it may be interesting to look at the curricula approved by the ministry of education for Arab schools. Extensive political themes are interwoven, especially in the Arabic and Hebrew history and language programs. Even a cursory study of the history program will show that it is geared to celebrating the history of the Jews and presenting it in the best possible light, whereas the view of Arab history is warped to a point bordering on falsehood. Arab history is represented as a series of revolutions, killings, and continuous feuds, in such a way as to obscure Arab achievements. Similarly, the time devoted to the study of Arab history is meager. In the fifth grade, for example, ten-year-olds spend ten hours (or periods) learning about the "Hebrews" and only five on the "Arabian Peninsula."[31] And even while studying the Arabian peninsula, attention is drawn to Jewish communities there, as stipulated in the program.[32] In the sixth grade, thirty out of sixty-four history periods are spent on "Islamic History," from its beginnings to the end of the thirteenth century, including a study of Moses Maimonides and the Spanish Jewish poet Ibn Gabirol.[33] There is no mention of Arab history in seventh grade, but a sixth of the history periods are devoted to studying relations between the Jews of the Diaspora and Israel. In the eighth grade, there are thirty hours for studying the "state of Israel" and only ten for the history of the Arabs from the nineteenth century to the present. This leaves a gap of five centuries in the history of the Arabs. Among the subjects covered in the eighth grade are the religious crises in Syria and Lebanon and the feud between the Druze and the Maronites in 1860.[34]

The status of Arab history is no better in the secondary schools. Only 32 hours, out of a total of 416 hours set aside for history during the four-year program in the arts division or 384 in the sciences division, are spent on the study of the history of the Arabs (without touching on Moorish Spain).[35] Jewish history, on the other hand, is taught broadly at every stage, alongside the history of ancient Egypt, Greece, and Rome, through the Middle Ages to the present, taking up a third of the history periods. Even more remarkable are the questions in the history examinations. Questions connected with Jewish history are complex, serious, and to the point, conforming to the official political line of the Israeli government, while questions on Arab history are mere riddles, emphasizing disputes and divisions in the Arab world. Excessive prominence is given to periods of decline in Arab history, while important Arab leaders are neglected—one finds no questions, for example, about the prophet Muhammad, or the Omayyad Caliph Muawiya, or about Harun al Rashid or Saladin.

But it is the Hebrew and Arabic language programs that show most clearly how the Israeli authorities make every effort to favor Hebrew at the expense of Arabic. Instructions for the teaching of Arabic are compressed into one paragraph, entitled "Objectives for teaching the language." For Hebrew the instructions are more detailed, taking up three paragraphs: "Objectives for teaching the language," "Realizing the objectives," and "Program and subject matter." In the last paragraph are the following words: "The Hebrew language is to be studied in accordance with a regular and permanent curriculum in the Arab elementary schools, starting in the fourth grade. It is also recommended that, in certain cases, the study of Hebrew start in the first grade, or even in kindergarten, by means of songs, games, and so forth."[36]

A comparison of the current curricula for Jewish and Arab

secondary schools is also revealing. For example, there is much emphasis in the Arab curriculum on Jewish history; Arabs and their history are largely ignored in Jewish schools. Similarly, Arabs must concentrate on Hebrew literature but Arabic literature courses do not include any works by Palestinian writers and poets. There is almost an excessive glorification of Israeli society and culture in the Jewish program, with no acknowledgment of the contributions of other cultures.[37]

It was a desire to create a generation of Arabs who would benefit the nation, or at least accept its existence, that motivated policy on Arab education in Israel. It is the same wish, largely unfulfilled so far, that periodically inspires the authorities to search for a new "foundation" for Arab education. One recent proposal, drawn up in February 1971, calls for the education of the Arabs "in the principles of peace . . . and loyalty to the state, by stressing the common benefit to all citizens and by underlining the isolation of the Arabs of Israel . . . and by instilling in them Arab, Israeli, and world values."[38] When applied, these suggestions become broader in scope and much clearer:

> In the Arab schools Arab history must be taught as part of Middle East history and its contributions to world culture and from the perspective of a diversity of peoples, kingdoms, civilizations, and religions in the area. . . . selections from the Torah must be studied and literature relating to the Jewish settlement of the country . . . the history of the land of Israel in particular . . . the permanence of Jewish settlement, and the importance of Arab–Jewish coexistence, both in Israel and outside it. As well as the history of Israel, a short but instructive history of the Jews in the Diaspora should also be taught.[39]

This kind of outlook, which basically reflects traditional Zionist convictions, does not even serve Israel's own purposes in the long run, since "the disregard of Arab nationalist desires in the schools of Israel will not kill such desires. The Arab student who finds no solution for his difficulties in school looks for, and finds, political leadership elsewhere"— outside Israel, in fact.[40]

All the planning behind Arab education has not had much success. Israel has neither fulfilled its own objectives through the school system nor supplied the Arab population with the kind of education it needs. Not only is the education of the Arabs unsatisfactory, but it is no exaggeration to say that in this field Israel's record, as far as official relations and attitudes to the Arabs are concerned, has been worse than in any other.

The economic situation of the Arabs differs from that of the rest of the population because it is directly dependent on two sectors of the Israeli economy: agriculture and wage labor. Like the rest of the Palestinians, the Arabs who stayed on in Israel were an agricultural people, and as late as the end of 1955 more than half of them were still living off agriculture (see Appendix, Table 13). A large proportion, however, had turned to wage labor for reasons to be discussed.

The expropriation of vast areas of Arab land was the major obstacle to the development of Arab agriculture. With suitable farmland severely diminished, the average family property-holding in the Arab villages, which had been 67.3 dunums in 1944, was reduced to 38.5 in 1949–50 and 26.9 in 1963, a decrease of about 60 percent.[41] There are thus fewer Arab landowners and, more important, far fewer Arabs owning enough land to make a living from farming. According to a census by the ministry of agriculture in 1963, in 104 Arab villages lying north of Lydda—which includes almost all the villages in Israel—95,406 of the 171,720 Arabs (55.5 percent) owned land, a total of 385,993 dunums.[42] This land was divided among 14,340 family units into such small plots that 72 percent of the families owned less than 30 dunums each (an average of 12); the remaining 28 percent owned 31 dunums or more (an average of 65)—"the smallest agricultural land area that can provide an independent livelihood."[43] This subdivision of farmland is probably more marked today, due to the distribution of land among heirs.

Almost as damaging as land expropriation was the indifference of the government to Arab agriculture, which seemed to "freeze" in its development. In the early years of the state, when agricultural food crops were in great demand, marketing was put under strict government control. A few companies, specially formed for the purpose, were allowed to monopolize the market and any farmer failing to comply with this arrangement was threatened with the confiscation of his crops.[44] The dominant company was Bustan al Jalil (Garden of Galilee) and its administration and shares were controlled by organizations marketing Jewish agricultural products.[45] Jewish agriculture had not yet taken over, and benefited from, the land left behind by the Palestinian refugees, and the monopolizing companies did not hesitate to take the necessary steps to hinder and block Arab agriculture until Jewish agriculture attained its full strength. Arabs were paid less than Jews for their produce, with the full acquiescence of the controller of supplies. The reason given was that "the outlay for growing foodstuffs in an Arab village was less than its Jewish equivalent, and it was therefore considered only proper to reserve a proportion of the price for developing" Arab villages.[46] The difference in price necessary to "equalize" Arab and Jewish agricultural profits meant 16-17 percent less for Arab goods.[47] This discrepancy was officially abolished in 1952, but the practice continues to this day.[48] Indeed, the difference seems to increase from year to year.

A look at the price of tobacco, a principal crop for the Arab farmer, may shed further light on this situation (see Appendix, Table 14). Although Arabs in Israel grow eight times as much tobacco as Jews, over a twenty-year period the average price paid to the Jewish farmer was 64.4 percent more than that paid to the Arab for the same quality of tobacco. The government, responsible for supervising the marketing and pricing of tobacco, in consultation with certain bodies, can easily set such a price difference, yet it comes about less directly. Arab tobacco is bought by certain Jewish companies, which pay the price set by the government; the Jewish crop, however, is sold to a specially formed company, Alei Tabac, owned by the Jewish Agency, which pays a supplement over and above the government price as a

bonus to encourage Jewish agriculture.[49] The Jewish Agency
does not deny the practice, claiming that it was created to
help Jews and no one else; the government's excuse is that it
cannot interfere or correct the situation since the Jewish
Agency is to a certain extent a "state" in its own right and
can take any measures it considers appropriate.

The Arab tobacco growers did not accept this state of
affairs passively but made several attempts to resolve, or at
least draw attention to, the injustice. Several Arab members
of the Knesset had a financial involvement in this branch of
agriculture and gave the problem their special attention. They
questioned the Knesset repeatedly, and more than one parlia-
mentary investigation was conducted at their request, bringing to light a number of issues affecting Arab agriculture in
general, as well as the facts on tobacco. Early in 1956 the
Knesset economic committee made a number of recommendations as a result of its study of tobacco farming. Among
other things, it suggested improving cultivation, tying the
price to the quality of the tobacco, implementing the old
marketing agreements, and setting up a council for growing
and marketing tobacco. At the end of the year, the economic
committee had to remind the government of the need to put
these suggestions into effect, especially the creation of a
tobacco council.[50] But it was not until six years later, in
1962, that the council was finally appointed.[51] The same
committee conducted another investigation in 1969. This
time it reported that "it was disturbed at finding no permanent organization responsible for tobacco and at the lack of
harmony between the two government departments in charge
of the crop, the ministry of agriculture and the department
of customs and excise."[52] It recommended more cooperation
between government sectors concerned with tobacco and
intensified guidance for the farmer. It suggested the appointment of a research committee to check the quality of the soil
devoted to tobacco cultivation and to improve the quality of
tobacco plants, a committee of experts to assist the tobacco
council, an appeals committee to settle farmers' grievances,
limitation of the buying season for companies interested in
the tobacco harvest, and the reassessment of taxes on the

farmer's profit.[53] Unfortunately, little has changed. If the economic committee were to make a third inquiry into tobacco it would surely find almost all the shortcomings it reported before.

What is true for tobacco applies to the two other major Arab products: olives and olive oil. So far the Arabs have been producing twice as much of these as the Jews, but the average price difference has been 41.1 percent in favor of the Jews (see Appendix, Table 13). The economic committee again drew the government's attention to the situation, demanding improvement, but with no result.[54] The same discrepancy in price is found in other crops. For example, the price of wheat per ton rose from 48.1 pounds for the Arab harvest and 55.1 pounds for the Jewish in 1948-49, to 308.6 and 339 pounds per ton respectively in 1970-71. Barley prices rose from 32 and 38 pounds per ton to 281.7 and 285.7 pounds per ton over the same period.[55] Such price differentials are typical of the whole range of agricultural products.

Beyond the obstacles already mentioned, the government's policy, although not deliberately planned to undermine Arab farming, goes a long way toward blocking its development. The basis for the creation of Israel is settlement and agricultural settlement in particular, an aim that is energetically supported by the government and World Zionist organizations. This ideal has led to a concentration of power in the hands of the representatives of the agricultural settlements. For example, there are many more Knesset members representing agricultural settlements than the proportion of settlers among the general population would warrant. The same disproportionate representation holds within the government, where those in high posts devote their efforts and influence to the interests of the agricultural sector, sometimes at the expense of the rest of the Israeli economy. So far their efforts have been irresistible. Even the Israeli army has to make a contribution to agricultural settlement in the form of the Nahal groups. From time to time the government has tried to encourage Arab agriculture, by providing instruction or loans, or by improving the soil or helping occasionally with marketing and the acquisition of agricultural machin-ery.[56] But compared to the assistance provided to the Jewish farmers, this becomes insignificant. With the support of the pro-agriculture members of the government, Jewish farmers have received subsidies, huge loans, and modern equipment. Highly effective marketing and producing institutions have been created with all necessary powers, including the power to determine the price of agricultural products. The result has been an enormous gap between Jewish and Arab agriculture. For example, Table 16 (see Appendix) shows the proportion of land cultivated with the help of irrigation—irrigation is used by the Jews ten times as often as by the Arabs.

The handicaps described above have had a devastating effect on Arab farming, which has gradually become unprof-itable and is practiced only by those who have no other choice. At the same time and due to the same factors, income per dunum in Jewish agriculture rose in the period 1950–51—1970–71 an average of 289 percent over the equivalent Arab income (see Appendix, Table 17).[57] Arab farmers and agricul-tural workers are not unaware of this difference and have tried to work in Jewish agriculture, but the Israeli govern-ment hastened to formulate a special law preventing them from doing so (Chapter 5). It is not surprising, then, that the proportion of Arabs engaged in agriculture has fallen from 48.8 percent in 1955 to 22.4 percent in 1971. In other words, more than half have moved into other occupations, leaving their land untilled. This has probably been the govern-ment's long-term hope—that the Arabs would be reduced to selling what land remained to them after its upkeep exceeded its income. More Jewish settlements could then be estab-lished and the Jewish way of life more firmly imprinted on the land.

When Israel was established, the situation of Jewish and Arab workers differed radically. Apart from a few labor unions limited to particular sectors or places of work, Arab workers had not been organized to any effective degree under the British Mandate. The few trade unions that came into existence were usually dissolved after a short period of activity. In sharp contrast, Jewish labor unions began to organize at the beginning of the century and by 1920 were in a position to found the Histadrut, the General Federation of Jewish Labor, which encompassed all trade unions. Over the years the Histadrut has gained power and prestige until it has become an important element in the Israeli system. It has done much to ensure the rights and look after the interests of Jewish workers, even venturing into areas not usually considered the business of a labor union. Thus in 1958, most Jewish workers belonged to the Histadrut, or to other labor organizations. Most of the Arab workers were not organized at all, although a very few belonged to the Congress of Arab Workers and the Union of Palestine Workers, which continued to function.[58]

The position of the Arab worker was further weakened by the unfriendly, even hostile, attitude of various Israeli authorities. Such negative feeling goes back to the early days of Jewish settlement when the Zionist desire for complete control of the land inspired the twin slogans "conquest of the land" and "conquest of work" (see Chapter 5), which in turn gave birth to a policy contained in the motto "Hebrew labor." Several Zionist factions tried to disguise the shamefully racist overtones of this notion, but it soon became the guiding light for a large majority of Zionists. Zionist workers' groups in particular used it as a justification for favoring Jewish over Arab workers, especially in Jewish places of work, and eventually for dismissing Arab workers and replacing them with Jews. A few small groups within the Zionist labor movement that belonged to the Zionist left or were supporters of rapprochement with the Arabs were not entirely in favor of "Hebrew labor." These groups believed in the need to organize Arab workers and helped to form the Union of Palestine Workers in 1927 in order to "organize" Arab workers under the supervision of the Histadrut.[59]

There were other considerations, such as security, that shaped Israeli attitudes toward the Arab worker in the early years of the state. The military government and the system of travel permits made life particularly difficult. Permits were consistently withheld from Arabs seeking to travel to Jewish areas in search of work; the police even opened fire on them when they demonstrated against this measure.[60] This practice continued as long as Jewish immigrants were in need of work, which remained the case for a considerable length of time.[61] Representatives of Jewish labor also objected to accepting Arab workers within the framework of organized labor, since the Arabs were content to receive less pay than the Jews for comparable work. Pressure was put on the military government to continue withholding travel permits as a way of checking such competition.[62]

Despite its proclaimed "sympathy" with the Arab workers, the Histadrut did little worth mentioning on their behalf. Its Arab department made a few further "organizational" efforts, with the help of the Union of Palestine Workers, but with no significant results. The Arabs' difficulties were not even mentioned during the Histadrut's seventh congress (the first after the establishment of Israel), at the end of May 1949.[63] It was not until 1953 that Arabs were allowed to join some of the trade unions attached to the Histadrut and to benefit from some of its services, such as health insurance. No Arabs were accepted as members of the Histadrut itself. Meanwhile, the small associations of Arab workers, especially the Congress of Arab Workers which was under Communist influence, were being harassed by the Israeli authorities. Congress members were hounded, meetings were prevented by the military government, and finally the Congress "agreed" to dissolve itself.[64] The Union of Palestine Workers soon did the same.[65]

The Arab workers were not in an enviable position. They were forbidden to work outside their villages or in the Jewish areas at a time when job opportunities in the villages were diminishing rapidly because sources of agricultural income were falling and the population was increasing. In time, the government became aware of the crisis and tried to solve it by setting up employment offices in the Arab communities. (This is in fact required by the law where hired laborers, especially those hired by the day, are employed.) But these employment offices did not cover all the Arab regions and could only handle a fraction of the problem. By the end of the 1950s there were nine offices altogether, four in Arab towns and large villages—Nazareth, Tayba, Baqa al Gharbiya, and Umm al Fahm—and five to serve Arabs in cities with mixed populations: Haifa, Acre, Jaffa, Lydda, and Ramle.[66] The military government also introduced a slight modification in its policy and began to give travel permits to Arabs who could prove that they had jobs to go to.

Needless to say, these changes did not approach a total solution of the problem. Many Arabs were forced to break the regulations of the military government and the employment offices and seek work surreptitiously, which made them vulnerable to shameless wage exploitation by employers. If discovered, such workers were brought before the military court and dismissed from their work for breaking employment regulations, being "unorganized" workers. In such conditions, Arab workers were forced into strenuous and low-paid jobs. Aharon Cohen has described the situation as follows:

In the period 1948-58, the Arab worker was driven into the unskilled, manual jobs that were the most exhausting and least well paid, jobs shunned by the Jewish worker such as mixing plaster, cleaning jobs, unskilled jobs in quarries and construction and the like. In practice, the difference between Arab and Jewish workers is still current as far as wages and social services are concerned, even when doing similar work. If, in a few special jobs, there is equality [highly skilled jobs, jobs in large offices or factories that have been organized since the days of the Mandate, jobs in the large municipalities or state offices], the rights of the Arab worker are usually suppressed as he progresses professionally. . . .

Most office and other work in the state was closed to the Arabs; their only opportunities lay within the narrow scope of Arab agriculture. . . . When an Arab managed to "snatch" a few days on a construction job or in other city work, in some primitive workshop, or on the margins of Jewish agriculture in some settlement, he was inevitably fired for not being "organized." "Attacks" on the Arab workers intensified during unemployment crises affecting the Jewish population, when even the meanest jobs were in demand. Sometimes the police were involved, sometimes unemployed Jewish workers were the instigators. As soon as the general employment situation improved, pressure against the Arabs was relaxed. The fact that the Arabs were forced to work surreptitiously and take the worst jobs meant that they were doomed to the worst possible working conditions.[67]

This situation continued until the late 1950s when there were several changes for the better. Travel restrictions became less stringent: Arab workers could travel to work without special permits during daylight hours. The economic situation in Israel had improved and there was a demand for more laborpower. Further modifications in the military government came soon after, and these were directly related to the need for more workers.

Not unconnected with these factors was the Histadrut's decision at the end of 1959 to admit Arabs as members with equal rights and obligations.[68] Mapai, controlling more than half the seats at the Histadrut congress, had made a similar decision a short time before. This step has been described as "neutralizing the propaganda of the Communist Party and of some of the Zionist parties ... and depriving the Arab countries of a major part of their ammunition in their propaganda against Israel."[69] The Employment Service Law, passed by the Knesset at the beginning of 1959, recognized that every worker in Israel had a right to employment, and this too influenced these developments.[70]

All these changes had a directly beneficial effect on the Arab workers, although improvements did not occur uniformly. Fluctuations in the economic situation continued to be felt more acutely by the Arabs than by any other sector of the population: in a crisis they were the first to find themselves without jobs. But the Histadrut decision removed once and for all the nightmare of not being "organized," pursued and dismissed by the employment offices. Henceforth, any Arab could be "organized" simply by applying for Histadrut membership. But although the Histadrut began to accept Arab members early in 1960, "the Arabs were very slow indeed to join, and we must admit that great efforts were required to induce them to do so," according to the head of the Arab department.[71] By the end of 1971 there were nearly forty-two thousand Arab members—some 40 percent of all Arab workers but only half the proportion of Jewish workers belonging to the Histadrut.[72] The main reason for Arab indifference seems to have been the feeling that since jobs were now open to them, they had no great need for the Histadrut's services.[73]

The Employment Service Law also improved matters for the Arabs by creating state employment offices required to handle the problems of Arabs and Jews jointly (replacing the separate offices for Arab employment). Some of the provisions of this law, however, affected the Arabs adversely, especially in times of general unemployment. For example, Israel was divided into labor areas, giving the residents of each area precedence over outsiders in finding employment. Only when there was a superabundance of jobs could outsiders come into an area to work. Since the regions inhabited by the Arabs usually did not have enough offices and factories to employ all the available laborpower, Arabs often were out of work. Further, the law required that workers find employment through the employment offices, but such offices were not created in all Arab areas, especially the more remote places and the small villages.[74]

Despite these shortcomings, various jobs were opened to Arab workers, who abandoned their agriculture to take them. The number of such jobs increased from year to year, especially in construction (Table 13). Not long after conditions improved, some Israeli groups were warning that the "Arabs are taking over the country's manual labor" and that many branches of work were becoming "monopolies of Arab labor."[75] Others pointed out that

if the Arabs ever decided not to go to work, or for any reason were unable to go to work, there would be vast problems in some areas . . . not to mention costly losses. The three main sources of employment for Arabs are agriculture, where they make up the majority of seasonal workers, construction, and services (restaurants, hotels, garages and gas stations). They also make up a large proportion of the watchmen.[76]

Obviously, the Arabs gravitated toward these particular jobs because they were the only ones they could get. And employers encouraged this trend:

> Arabs fill this kind of job because they are considered better laborers [than the Jews]. Even when he is an organized worker registered with the Histadrut, the Arab does not entertain great illusions, he comes primarily to work ... Another reason for the Jewish employer's preference for the Arab worker is that his wages are generally lower.[77]

But with the passage of time a considerable proportion of Arab workers no longer earn such low wages. Having acquired technical skills, they are in great demand. They insist on—and receive—wages that exceed the official tariff.[78]

With the changing conditions, new problems have emerged. Basically, there is not enough work near home, compelling a large proportion to travel great distances to work. They live under "strange conditions" in order to be near their work, sleeping in barracks, abandoned buildings, or even out of doors during the week and returning home only for the weekend.[79] According to an investigation by the Central Bureau of Statistics, by 1963 the number of these commuting workers had reached

> about 27,000, or half the number of Arab workers. 23,500 of them are male. The homes of 69 percent of commuting workers are in the rural areas and 13 percent in Nazareth and Shafa Amr; about 10 percent are from the Bedouin tribes; the remaining 8 percent live in the cities. Thirty-four percent of these commuters work in agriculture, forestry, and fishing, 24 percent in construction, 22 percent in factories, offices, mines, and quarries, and 20 percent in service capacities.[80]

Toward the end of 1963, the government appointed a committee at the ministerial level to study the possibility of founding a government company to build low-cost housing for Arabs near their work. The ministry of housing was entrusted with the "study of the possibility of helping needy Arab workers, living far from their work, who are ready to make a permanent move into the cities."[81] But all these projects had to be abandoned when a separate study by the ministry of labor demonstrated that the "number of Arab workers willing to move into low-rent housing near their work is very low indeed."[82] An alternative proposal was made to ensure cheap transportation between home and work. The Arabs must have disappointed a number of Israelis who had hoped that they would leave their villages for the cities. But the majority preferred to maintain ties with their villages and spend their incomes there. There is no doubt that this has affected the level of progress in the villages, especially in the improvement of housing.

Arab workers complain of a number of other problems but these are not so widespread. There is, for example, the exploitation of juveniles whose family circumstances force them to drop out of school and find work. They are considered "strong and silent" workers because, being employed illegally, they rarely find anyone who will protect their rights.[83] Women workers suffer similar exploitation, especially in the Triangle, but in their case it is Arabs who contribute to the process. Arab "work contractors" (bosses) supply Jewish employers with women workers in return for a commission deducted from the women's pay. Since the employers are paying wages lower than the official rate, both sides profit at the women's expense.[84] The "bosses" emerged during military government, when they used their relations with the authorities to procure travel permits for the women workers. The ministry of labor has tried to stop this practice —by bringing the bosses to trial, among other things—but the exploitation continues.[85] In 1972 there were fifty bosses still in business, compared to two hundred in the past.[86] Finally, the Arabs are still the first to be affected by a slump in the economy, though they return to work when conditions improve.[87]

In general, the number of Arab workers is continually increasing and the majority are still manual workers (skilled and unskilled; see Table 13) in the Jewish sector, since there are almost no factories in the Arab sector. The government "has not undertaken any industrialization projects, and has no plans for such projects" in the Arab sector, while offices not essentially dependent on manual labor are generally closed to Arabs.[88] Even government ministries discriminate against Arabs, employing only a small number. In 1951, for example, there were 353 Arab government employees (not counting laborers); in 1964 there were 320 Arabs out of a total of 11,878 employees in six ministries, or under 3 percent.[89] Most of the Arabs employed by the state are teachers in government Arab schools, and a remarkably large number work in the police department and prison administration. By 1964 there were 583 Arab policemen and jailers, and by 1969 there were 1,251, of whom 796 were Druze (including 19 officers), 281 Moslems (10 officers), and 184 Christians (4 officers).[90] This constitutes about 11 percent of the total number of policemen and jailers, the percentage of Arabs in the whole population—probably the only field with such a proportion.[91] One reason for this is that a number of Arabs who were soldiers or volunteers in the Israeli army were recompensed at the end of their service by appointments to the police department or prison administration.

The distribution of Arab laborers indicates that most of them hold jobs with low incomes. Finally, one cannot help pointing out that in spite of Zionist claims to a Jewish return to manual labor, and all that is implied in the slogan "Hebrew labor," after twenty-five years of Israeli rule it is the Arabs who continue to do a large part of the manual work. And it looks as if they will be continuing to do so for a considerable time in the future. Despite this, the circumstances of the workers are acceptable and even advanced when compared to other aspects of Arab life in Israel.

Local authorities, in the form of municipalities and local and district councils, play an important role in many areas of community life in Israel. They are empowered to supervise construction, road building, water and electric supplies, education and health care, the licensing of various trades, and the upkeep of a number of public services. They also have the right to levy taxes, obtain loans and grants, and sign contracts for services. With the establishment of Israel these authorities grew in importance, their powers expanded, and their number increased. Within a relatively short time every Jewish community was served by a local authority. Arab communities, on the other hand, fell far behind the Jews in this respect, with only two municipalities (Nazareth and Shafa Amr) and one local council (Kfar Yasif) among one hundred towns and villages in 1948.[92]

The matter of creating local authorities in the Arab sector was viewed with obvious indifference, if not with intentional neglect. At the beginning, there was even less opposition to elections in the existing municipalities. It was not until March 1954 that municipal elections were held in Nazareth, the largest center of Arab population, after the military government had withdrawn its objection.[93] Similarly, there was great reluctance on the part of the ministry of interior to create new local councils, and by 1950 only sixteen had been added to the existing three.[94] The process dragged on from year to year and in 1963 there were still seventy Arab villages without local councils.[95] Once the Arabs realized that the standard of services in the villages to a large extent depended on the existence of local councils, they made insistent and repeated demands for local government. The ministry of interior could hardly continue claiming that the Arabs "opposed" local councils, and they were created in the Arab sector in increasing numbers. By 1971 fifty-one Arab villages had local councils and twenty-three others were attached to a neighboring district council, and about 80 percent of the Arab population was living within the sphere of some form of local government (see Appendix, Tables 18 and 19).[96]

There seems to be some exaggeration, however, as to the rate of progress, and one should treat the available information with some reservation, no matter how official and high-placed the source. A signature on an order to set up a local council is often taken as proof that such a council exists, although a considerable length of time usually elapses before it actually begins to function. Furthermore, the sources include planned councils. If one considers as fully functioning local authorities those municipalities and local councils that have held at least one election, the total number established between 1948 and 1972 comes to forty-three, leaving about 60 percent of the Arab villages without effective local government.[97] In 1967 the Knesset rejected a bill proposed by Tawfiq Tubi authorizing the minister of interior to hold elections within three months for councils in every Arab settlement with a population over 250.[98] And yet the Knesset interior committee had already urged the ministry "to study the feasibility of creating additional legal and administrative powers to speed up the process" of establishing local councils since the current conditions "were hindering the orderly development of the Arab villages."[99]

Another factor undermining local government in the Arab sector was the government's abolition of the system of "mukhtars," on the grounds—to some extent justified—that the system prevented progress in the villages. When confronted with the administrative problems arising out of the lack of local government, however, the government instituted a system that differed from the mukhtars in name only. "Chiefs" were appointed, without consulting the local residents, to administer a number of villages. The Knesset interior committee expressed its reservations about this innovation and requested reports on the subject.[100] Nevertheless, the number of such "chiefs" rose from three in 1963 to sixteen in 1971.[101]

The unsettled state of local government naturally affected the standard of services available to the Arab inhabitants. For example, the first Arab village to receive electricity was Tayba in 1955. By 1961 lines had been laid to five more villages. By 1963, eighteen villages had electricity, twenty-eight had it in 1967, and a few more have acquired it since then. But over half the Arab villages in Israel are still without it.[102]

The demand for electricity was insistent:

As soon as the first few villages had been linked to the supply of electricity, pressure from the other villages increased. The required amount of money for this service has been collected by a large number of villages, but the power company finds it difficult to handle the large number of requests and work in all the villages that have fulfilled the required conditions for introducing electricity.[103]

However, the introduction of electricty into the rural areas is more advanced at this writing than transportation and road building. These are generally the province of the public works department, which collects a down-payment of 25 to 40 percent of the estimated cost of building a road, adding its share toward the funding just before the project is started.[104] The same is true for the water supply, which is controlled by cooperatives. After successful experiments with cooperatives in two villages, others responded, and by the end of 1959 there were twenty-seven. Members of a cooperative provide about 25 percent of the capital; the government and the Histadrut provide the rest in the form of long-term loans.[105] Health care and postal services, in the charge of the ministry of health, the health insurance service, and the ministry of postal services, are the best of the services in the rural Arab areas.

The Israeli government has also made efforts to improve the general condition of the Arab villages. In 1962 it announced a five-year plan for such development, with a budget of almost £71 million.[106] At the end of the five years, a second five-year plan, 1967/72, was announced with a budget of almost £115 million.[107] Nearly £10 million had already been spent during the years 1957/62.[108] In total, then, during a fifteen-year period the government spent £196 million, out of a total of billions of pounds, on the development of Arab villages. One-third of this sum was spent finding sources of income and employment in the rural areas; the rest was devoted to the development of water, electricity, roads, and schools. Part of the funds were in the form of grants, but the greater proportion were loans to be repaid with interest, by the villages.

Despite the amount spent—and it represents only a very small fraction of the Israeli development budget—the needs of the Arab villages were not met. A much more ambitious and comprehensive development program was needed. Yet at the close of the second five-year plan the project was not renewed. The explanation was that "the problems of national and social identity, and their integration into the society and culture of Israel, are the fundamental difficulties facing the Arab minority. Financial and economic problems are secondary. The focus has therefore . . . shifted from the economic . . . to the social and cultural level."[109]

One further obstacle to the efficient functioning of the Arab local councils should be noted: divisiveness and lack of cooperation among council members. In this case not only the government but the Arabs themselves are responsible. Whenever the government sets up a local council it appoints the council members. This is usually done on a family basis— that is, "representatives" of the leading families of a village are chosen. Every government body, from the ministry of interior to the Arab departments of the Labor Party, the intelligence service, and the Histadrut, intervenes, on behalf of their supporters, sharpening family rivalries and conflicts between candidates and adding to the number aspiring to membership. The seeds of discord seem to flourish spontaneously. The results of the elections for local councils in thirty Arab villages in 1965 and 1969 show that in 1965 there were 252 slates, of which 154 were successful.[110] This comes to about five slates per council, too many for a stable coalition. "Changes of government" are frequent, heads of councils and their deputies are replaced from time to time, and the councils are thus undermined and prevented from effectively carrying out their duties to the people.[111] The Israeli government does not seem to be very concerned about these political upheavals as long as they involve government supporters. However, as soon as Communists, or their supporters among critics of the government, appear to form part of a coalition on a council, the government promptly interferes, making clear that "such a move would lead to the limitation of

government assistance and loans to that council."[112] The
government made sustained efforts to weaken the councils of
Kfar Yasif and Yafa al Nasra and succeeded in dissolving the
coalitions there, which were led by Communists and nationalists.[113] For all their shortcomings, a number of the Arab
local councils seem to be well enough organized to act in
matters that are of no direct concern to them. For example,
several councils have called impromptu meetings to condemn
certain aspects of the "sabotage" carried out by Palestinian
guerrillas inside Israel.[114]

The reluctance of the Israeli authorities to set up local
councils in the Arab sector and their neglect of such councils
once they have been formed cannot be attributed to over-
sight alone. A principle dating to the beginnings of Zionist
settlement in Palestine led to the opposition to local councils,
since the creation of an Arab council in a village was in effect
official recognition of the existence of that village, and therefore a dangerous precedent. For example, the area controlled
by the council had to be defined, and this presented problems in the event of a decision to expropriate the land. There
was also the question of government subsidy of council
expenses and the guaranteeing of its basic needs. Interesting
in this respect is the absence of local outline schemes for
most Arab villages. These are used as a basis for granting
construction licenses, and so on, but by early 1971 the local
schemes for only three villages had been completed. Forty-
nine others were being studied; preparations for mapping the
remaining villages had not even begun.[115] It is also interesting
that only very small areas in the Arab villages have been
allotted to construction. These are far below the needs of the
villagers, and in spite of insistent demands for an extension of
these areas, the government rarely grants the necessary
permits.[116] As a result, hundreds of homes have been built
without licenses outside the permitted areas. In some cases
these have been destroyed by the government. The price of
new housing has risen noticeably in the rural areas because of
the scarcity of building sites. It has become easier and
cheaper to find a permanent home in the cities, even after

payment of key money, than to build one in a village. The migration of Arabs from the rural areas to the cities has been marked, and the proportion of Arabs is increasing in those cities with mixed populations (see Appendix, Table 3).

Thus the suppression of Arab agriculture by the Israeli government and its neglect of the development of the rural areas inhabited by Arabs, added to an increase in opportunities for work outside these areas, have combined to uproot the Arabs from their own areas and to transfer them to the cities. The current solution of the Arab problem in Israel depends on the completion of this process, with the Arabs finally giving up what land remains to them and Zionist settlements extending into every part of Israel. Although a deliberate policy to bring about these results has been followed since the late 1950s, events so far indicate that it will take a long while before these hopes are realized.

V
Conclusion

"No Israeli Arab looks upon himself, even for the length of one day, as a true Israeli citizen or a true member of the nation, or feels 'at home' . . . their hopes have been disappointed, first by the government and then by the Jewish population in general . . . there is no solution but the difficult one of a complete solution of the Palestine question as a whole."

—Uri Avneri,
Haolam Hazeh, November 26, 1969

The Arabs in Israel have now had twenty-five years' experience of Zionist rule, and the events of the period have made manifestly clear the nature of Israeli policy concerning them.

A basic fact that emerges from a study of the history of the last quarter of a century is that the Arab in Israel has been, and continues to be, a "different" citizen, "non-Jewish," belonging to the goyim and excluded from the rights enjoyed by Jewish citizens. This distinction, which affects every aspect of Arab life, has been officially implemented from the establishment of Israel to the present. With some intermittent adjustments to suit the changes in the times, the early measures adopted with regard to the Arabs have remained in effect. Where necessary, additional provisions have been drafted to protect the Zionist character of the country. For example, the law of return and the nationality law, which give the Jewish immigrant, merely on the basis of Jewish faith, rights exceeding those of the Arab who was born in the country and whose forefathers had lived there, have recently been extended to include Jews who do not even intend to immigrate. Jews living outside Israel can now obtain Israeli citizenship simply by making known their wish to hold such citizenship. In contrast, Arab refugees living inside Israel—not to mention those outside—are not permitted to return to their home villages, even where their present residence is only a few miles from their old homes. Despite modifications and improvements the military government still applies to the Arabs alone. The series of laws that legalized the expropriation of vast stretches of Arab property and turned them over to Jewish hands were considered insufficient because the Arabs were returning as hired laborers on their former properties. Suitable measures were soon passed to prevent even this contact between the Arabs and their land. When the government became aware of the "threat" from the natural increase of the Arab population in Israel, it took prompt measures. A special law was passed extending financial benefits to Jews who had large families. Arab families were excluded from this subsidy.

In addition to these measures, which affect such important areas of Arab life as the right to citizenship, personal freedom, ownership of property, work, and ability to raise children, there was an almost permanent policy of benign neglect as far as the educational, social, and economic problems of the Arabs were concerned. Not surprisingly, the standard of Arab life does not in any single aspect equal that of the Jews. A survey of the circumstances of the Arabs in Israel vindicates the statement that Israel is a Zionist-Jewish state whose officials are dedicated to the interests of the Jewish citizens above all others and that at best the Arab is only a second-class citizen.

Another important lesson from the Arab experience under Israeli rule is contained in the official reaction to any Arab opposition to government policy. Major changes came about only when the government felt the Arabs had reached a boiling point. Although there were occasional changes in accordance with the requirements of phases in Israel's history, they were always made with the welfare of Israel as a priority. To attribute any improvements to a sense of justice or goodwill on the part of the authorities would be misleading. It was rather the resistance of the Arabs themselves that induced the government to modify its measures. The struggle of the Arabs, day by day, against the restrictions they suffered, whether by ignoring them or petitioning and demonstrating against them, went on without interruption. Though the number of protesters varied at different times, the weight of the continuous protest had its effect. Even then changes were accompanied by shifts in Israel's "philosophy" of self-interest: the solution of Arab difficulties was presented as essential to the welfare of the country. It was always some time before the Arabs sensed that there had been a change in the official position.

Although the general policy of neglect continues, there are increasing efforts to find solutions to the problems facing the Arabs. There is no doubt that the occupation of further Arab territory in 1967 and the increase in the number of Arabs, Palestinians and others, living under Israeli rule has spurred these changes and the search for solutions. It seems as if the Israeli government has decided to deal first with the difficulties of its "own" Arabs, neutralizing them before facing such questions as the future of the occupied territories and the position it will take regarding the Arab world. As far as the Arab world is concerned, the experience of the Arabs in Israel has clearly demonstrated that struggle is not unproductive, and this should not be overlooked in future dealings with the Zionists.

There is a third lesson to be drawn from the "encounter" between the Arabs and Zionism. Despite all the obstacles officialdom has placed in their way, and despite the direct and indirect measures taken to hold them back, the Arabs have been able to make extensive progress in several fields of work, at times surpassing the rest of the population, in the face of Zionist claims to self-sufficiency. Because of their perseverance and energy, Arabs now command an important position in the field of manual labor, and although government policy played a role in driving them to this kind of work, several branches of the Israeli economy would now suffer considerable loss should the Arabs ever decide to stop working. This undermines the Zionist claim that a "normal Jewish society" is being created in Palestine, down to the use of Jewish manual labor. In the same way, there is no evidence of a Zionist attachment to what they call the "land of their ancestors." Despite all the financial incentives offered to Jewish settlers to attract them to farm work, the government has had to resort to special measures and restrictions to prevent a considerable proportion from leaving their land to be worked by the Arabs. The Arabs, on the other hand, have always appeared closely bound to their land.

Finally, the Zionist position on the political and national rights of the Arabs has become all too clear during the last twenty-five years. In the past there had been boasts of intentions to respect the rights of Arabs and live with them in peace and a spirit of cooperation. Israel's subsequent actions, and the means by which the Arabs have been contained both nationally and politically, leave no room for doubt that recognition of the national rights of the Arabs living in Israel would refute the basic principles of Zionism. In this, Israel's narrow-minded attitude exceeds the arrogance of most racist regimes and brings to mind the classic colonial way of thinking. The Jews—or, to be precise, the Zionists—believe in enjoying complete political rights while denying the same rights to the Arabs, especially the Palestinian Arabs, for no better reason than that the Zionist creed bases the solution of the Jewish problem on the existence of a Zionist state. Indeed, this creed has helped complicate rather than solve the problem, since it is based on both indirect and open violation of Arab rights. This feature of Israeli rule will gain special significance as far as the territories occupied in 1967 are concerned.

Israel's suppression of Arab national rights cannot hope to succeed in the long run. Opposition or denial of such rights has only led to a sharp increase in nationalist feelings; the racism implied in the Zionist emphasis on such ideas as the "chosen people" and the "land of Israel" has only inflamed popular feeling. At first, Israeli policy relied heavily on time, in the belief that the Palestinian Arabs, both inside and outside Israel, would eventually lose their national identity and be assimilated into the societies they happened to be living in. But events have proved the contrary. It took some time for the Palestinian nationalist movement to crystallize outside Israel and reach its present state of armed resistance and other forms of protest. This process was much swifter inside Israel; national awareness appeared among Arab political groups at an early stage, within sight and earshot of the Israeli authorities, and appears to run deeper.

There is no doubt that the basic aim of Israeli policy—whether through raw force, forceful persuasion, or "bribery" in the form of improvements in the Arabs' economic situation—was to eradicate Arab nationalism in Israel. But the emergence of armed Palestinian resistance and its spread among the Arabs inside Israel has killed such hopes. The experience of the last twenty-five years may well be an important factor behind the call by several Israeli factions for annexing the smallest possible amount of territory occupied in 1967 and for a solution that will not leave Israel face to face with large sectors of the Palestinian population. Israel does not seem to have benefited from its experiences with the Palestinians. Its policies have helped to keep the Palestine problem alive both inside and outside Israel. The Palestine question seems to have returned to its point of origin, proving to the Arabs in Israel that their problems cannot be solved until the case of Palestine as a whole is resolved.

Notes

Chapter 1: "For Security Reasons"

1. *The Palestine Gazette* 1442, no. 2 (27 Sept. 1945): 1058.
2. *Laws of the State of Israel* (LSI) [official English translation] 3 (1949): 56.
3. It should be pointed out, however, that although the Defense (Emergency) Regulations, 1945 are of British origin, as is the principle governing their interpretation—granting the military governors extensive powers—in Britain these regulations were put into effect during World War II for the duration of the actual fighting, and they were promptly repealed at the end of the war. They have been mockingly described as "the contribution of the House of Lords to the war effort" and Lord Atkin, a well-known judge, described supporters of such measures as "more royalist than the King" (*All England Law Reports* 3: 338, 361, Liveridge v. Anderson).
4. *The Palestine Gazette* 584, no. 2 (19 April 1936): 259.
5. Ibid. 675, no. 2 (24 March 1937): 267.
6. Ibid. 737, no. 2 (11 Nov. 1937): 1138; 914, no. 2 (26 August 1939): 659.
7. During the years 1944-47, the Mandate government banished some members of I.Z.L. and Lehi who had been arrested but could not be convicted, for lack of evidence, to some of its African colonies where they were held in detention. By early 1948 the number of such exiles had reached 250, some of whom had been held for years. The Latrun prison camp was used toward the end of June 1946 after the Haganah had joined I.Z.L. and Lehi in anti-British operations.
8. *Hapraklit (The Lawyer)*, February 1946, pp. 58-64.
9. Ibid. When Dov Joseph was reminded of his reference to "such an

official" during a Knesset debate, he said that he had only meant a "British" official (*Knesset Debates*, 15 May 1950, p. 1365).

10. Bernard Joseph, *British Rule in Palestine* (Washington: Public Affairs Press, 1948), p. 222. For his full comments on the defense regulations, see pp. 218-32.

11. *Hapraklit*, February 1946, pp. 58-64.

12. Ibid.

13. The illegal immigration section was, in effect, repealed the moment the establishment of Israel was announced on the evening of May 14, 1948: "[Ben-Gurion] passed on [after reading the Proclamation of Independence] to the reading of the 'Proclamation' of the Provisional State Council. As he came to the second passage revoking the legal enactments arising out of the 'White Paper' it seemed as every one were holding their breath, but then the storm of applause broke out again ... we are legally repealing sections. ... (Zeev Sharef, *Three Days*, London: W.A. Allen, 1962, p. 286). The sections mentioned were 102-7 of the emergency regulations and 13-15 of the 1941 Immigration Ordinance. The 1940 Land Registration Regulations, which restricted land ownership by Jewish settlers in many areas of Palestine, were also repealed. The repeal of these articles and laws was made retroactive to the date of their enactment. The prompt action on this particular legislation was no doubt related to its contradiction of the ideal of a Zionist presence in Palestine (see *Kouetz Ha-Takanot [Official Gazette]*, 5 May 1948, p. 3).

14. *Hamishpat (Justice)* 3 (1948/49): 307, Herzel Cook and Ziborah Wienerski v. the Minister of Defense et al., Files 1, 2/48, the Tel Aviv District Court sitting as a Supreme Court of Justice.

15. *Knesset Debates*, 8 July 1953, p. 1870.

16. This prompted the appeal reviewed by Shalom Kassan (fn. 14). See also *Debates of the People's Council and Provisional State Council*, 15 July 1948, p. 5 and 12 Aug. 1948, pp. 6-7, in Hebrew.

17. Ibid., *Debates*.

18. *Knesset Debates*, 12 July 1949, p. 975, Pinhas Rosenblatt (Rosen), minister of justice.

19. Ibid., 21-23, 28-30 May 1951, pp. 1802-92; 4, 6, 18 June 1951, pp. 1922-2001; 17 July 1951, pp. 2196-2201; 14 Nov. 1951, pp. 389-91; and 10 Dec. 1951, pp. 540-82.

20. Ibid., 28 March 1949, p. 239; 6 June 1949, p. 641; 1 Aug. 1949, p. 1190, David Ben-Gurion, prime minister.

21. Ibid., 3 July 1950, p. 2204, Rosen.
22. But Israeli occupation forces have applied many of them in the territories occupied since 1967.
23. The Emergency (Security Zones) Regulations 5709—1949 place the same restrictions over the security zones as the defense regulations do over the closed areas; neither may be entered without a written permit from the military authorities. They were promulgated by special legislation in the Knesset. The powers the minister of defense can assume under these laws are extremely dangerous, especially his power to expel the permanent residents of any of the security zones from their homes (see Chapter 4).
24. The military government used its control over the licensing of arms to favor the Israeli Intelligence Service, granting licenses to Arab collaborators in "appreciation" of their services.
25. Since the 1967 War they have been convened almost regularly to try Palestinian *fedayeen.*
26. *Judgments of the Supreme Court* (in Hebrew) 7:913, Ismail Ali v. the Inspector of Police et al.
27. *Judgments* 10: 105, Subhi Ayyubi et al. v. the Minister of Defense et al.
28. *Judgments* 31: 272, Hasanein et al. v. the Minister of Defense et al.
29. *Judgments* 7: 534, Kaufmann v. the Minister of Interior et al.
30. *Judgments* 13: 473, Appeal 53/188, Abu Ali et al. v. Verben et al.
31. Ibid.
32. *Judgments* 30: 103, Iraqi et al. v. the Military Governor in the Central Region et al.; 30: 321, Abdul Fattah et al. v. the Minister of Defense et al.
33. *Judgments* 31: 272, Hasanein.
34. Sabri Jiryis, *Democratic Freedoms in Israel* (Beirut: Institute for Palestine Studies, 1971), pp. 45-47.
35. According to Article 3 (par. 2) of the regulations: "It shall not be necessary to publish any emergency legislation in *Reshumot* [*Kouetz*]."
36. *State Controller's Report on Security for Financial Year 1957/58* 9 (15 Feb. 1959): 52, in Hebrew.
37. It became apparent in 1965, however, when the regulations were enforced against the Arabs in Haifa, that on October 29, 1956, on the eve of the Sinai War, "the General Chief of Staff, with the confirmation of the minister of defense, appointed the Commander of the Northern Region military governor over area (A),"

which though its exact boundaries were not known "does include the city of Haifa." This means that there had been military government over Haifa since 1956.

38. This does not mean that the Jewish inhabitants of the area are subject to military government; what it does mean is that the Arab inhabitants are forbidden to enter it.

39. The closed areas were later numbered in Hebrew letters.

40. *State Controller's Report*, p. 52.

41. Zeev Schiff, "The Pros and Cons of the Military Government," *New Outlook*, March-April 1962, pp. 65-66.

42. *State Controller's Report*, p. 56.

43. When a permit was granted, its instructions might forbid the bearer to enter any Jewish colonies on the way to his destination, to do any work other than that mentioned in the permit, and to change his permanent address.

44. For a satirical description of these procedures see Tawfiq Muammar's novel *Bithun* (Nazareth, 1959) and *Al Rabitah* magazine. See also the review of this novel in *Haaretz*, 5 Nov. 1959 and Abraham Yanon, "Some Basic Themes in Arab Literature in Israel," *Hamizrah Hehadash* (*The New Orient*) 15, no. 1-2 (1965): 57-84.

45. According to available information, the number of Arabs convicted in military courts for breaking the emergency regulations, most of whom had infringed the travel restrictions, in the period March-December 1951, was 2,028; their total fines amounted to 13,606 Israeli pounds (*Knesset Debates*, 19 Aug. 1953, p. 2397, Pinhas Lavon, deputy minister of defense). In 1958 there were 2,125 convictions; in 1959, 1,602; in 1960, 3,270; in 1961, 2,516; in 1962, 1,947; in 1963, 2,767; in 1965, 1,574; in 1966, 1,341; and in 1967, 1,476. Then in 1968 after the changes in the military government, there were only 827. See Central Bureau of Statistics, *Criminal Statistics* (1958), special series 121: 39; (1959): 52; (1960, 1961) 167: 26-27; (1962, 1963) 233: 26-27; (1964, 1965) 247: 24; (1966) 266: 18; (1967) 315: 20; and (1968) 344: 18.

46. During the British Mandate, a person in exile received an allowance for self and family for the duration of the banishment even though it was not required by law. The Israeli government, however, did not follow this tradition.

47. *Knesset Debates*, 19 Aug. 1953, p. 2398, Rustum Bastuni.

48. Ibid., 9 Jan. 1957, p. 715, Tawfiq Tubi.

49. Ibid., 23 Dec. 1953, p. 399, Emil Habibi.

50. Ibid., 12 May 1954, p. 1646, Tubi.

51. Ibid., 30 May 1956, p. 1902, Moshe Sneh.

52. *State Controller's Report*, p. 55.

53. *Knesset Debates*, 28 Aug. 1952, p. 3194, Ben-Gurion, minister of defense.

54. Article 20 of the emergency regulations.

55. *Knesset Debates*, 12 July 1949, pp. 975-78.

56. Ibid., 21 Nov. 1950, p. 283.

57. Ibid., 15 May 1950, pp. 1364-6, see Zisling's statement and the response of the minister of justice.

58. Ibid., 16 May 1951, p. 1787.

59. Ibid., 22 May 1951, pp. 1828, 1833.

60. Ibid., 3 Dec. 1951, p. 1322.

61. Ibid., 12 Feb. 1952, p. 1275.

62. For more information on that period see Don Peretz, *Israel and the Palestine Arabs* (Washington: The Middle East Institute, 1958), pp. 90-120. See also *Abolishing Military Government* (Haifa, 1956), a pamphlet presented to the Committee on Military Government by the Central Committee of the Israeli Communist Party.

63. *Knesset Debates*, 1 Dec. 1954, p. 241.

64. *Haaretz*, 11 October 1955.

65. Yorma Ben-Porath, *The Arab Labor Force in Israel* (Jerusalem: The Falk Institute for Economic Research in Israel, 1966), pp. 51-52, 55. Until 1953 the military government determined the wages of Arab laborers in the area under its control because, according to Levi Eshkol, minister of finance, "there are no labor offices in the area" (*Knesset Debates*, 7 Nov. 1953, p. 465).

66. *Knesset Debates*, 18 May 1955, p. 1664.

67. *Al Hamishmar*, 14 March 1956.

68. Peretz, *Israel*, p. 101.

Chapter 2: Toward a New Policy, 1959-66

1. See the debate in *Knesset Debates*, 29 July 1959, pp. 2771-79.

2. The following ministers were members of the committee: Dr. Joseph Burg (National Religious Party), Mordechai Bentuv (Mapam), Israel Bar-Yehuda (Achdut Haavoda), Kadish Loz (Mapai), Pinhas Rosen (Progressives), and Bikhur Shitrit (Mapai),

with Rosen, minister of justice, as chairman. Dr. Burg resigned
from the committee when his party withdrew from the government coalition.

3. *Davar*, 26 March 1959.

4. *Knesset Debates*, 5 Aug. 1959, p. 2923.

5. Ibid., 20 Feb. 1962, p. 1319, as quoted by Pinhas Rosen during the
debate on military government.

6. *Ner*, July-August 1958.

7. *Lamerhav*, 25 Aug. 1958.

8. *State Controller's Report on Security for Financial Year 1957/58* 9
(15 Feb 1959): 57-58.

9. In the summer of 1955, for example, on the eve of the third Knesset elections, the military governor of Galilee ordered the arrest
of the chairman of the Tamra local council—who had been appointed by the minister of interior, Itzhak Rokah of the General
Zionist Party—because he supported the General Zionists against
Mapai. In the summer of 1956, the military governor in the Triangle ordered the banishment of two members of the Tira local
council to prevent them from voting in the election of the chairman, thus guaranteeing a majority for his own candidate. In 1957
there was a sharp conflict between the military governor in the
Triangle and Israel Bar-Yehuda (then minister of the interior and
a member of Achdut Haavoda) over influence in some of the local
councils. The dispute eventually had to be settled at the national
level. In another instance, after the 1959 elections, the legal advisor to the government demanded that the military prosecutor
take measures against Emanuel Shababo, the military governor's
representative in Umm al Fahm, whom he accused of "using
threats and acting in excess of his powers" to induce Arab voters
in his district to vote in favor of the list attached to Mapai. See
Emil Habibi in *Knesset Debates*, 29 Nov. 1955, p. 411, and *Judgments of the Supreme Court* 30: 103, Appeal 56/136, Iraqi et al.
v. the Military Governor in the Central Region et al. See also the
newspaper *Yediot Aharonot*'s defense of the military governor in
its 22 Aug. 1959 issue and *Haaretz*, 12 Nov. 1959.

10. *Knesset Debates*, 18 June 1958, p. 2122, Bikhur Shitrit, minister of
police.

11. Ibid., 26 May 1958, p. 1900 and 18 June 1958, p. 2120, Ben-
Gurion and Esther Wilenska.

12. More than forty demonstrators in the two cities received sentences
of two years' imprisonment (*Knesset Debates*, 26 May 1958, p.

1900; 18 June 1958, p. 2120). The noted Israeli poet Nathan Alterman, a close associate of Ben-Gurion's who has been dubbed "court poet" by some, wrote a poem on the subject that appeared originally in *Davar:*

> No! That same unknown Arab who cursed in blind rage
> And beat and lashed out and was dragged to the battered
>   police van
> Is really, in truth, the only one blameless in this whirlpool of
>   passions—
> Though he sits in jail . . .
>
> What now must be changed is the approach (a vague concept
> But a very real thing), the whole line which now for ten years
> Has humbled and hurt the Arabs in Israel
> Oppressed and humbled! This is the bitterness which broke
>   out in rioting. . . .

(*New Outlook*, July-August 1958, pp. 48-49).

13. The difficulties they encountered were typical of those confronting Arabs as they searched for a means of livelihood. Vast stretches of Arab agricultural land had been expropriated, limiting the possibility of farm work, while travel restrictions prevented workers from reaching the cities and working there.

14. See also Walter Schwarz, *The Arabs in Israel* (London: Faber, 1959), p. 65.

15. *Knesset Debates*, 5 Aug. 1959, p. 2923.

16. Ibid., 24 Feb. 1960, pp. 663-67.

17. Herut's desire to abolish the Defense (Emergency) Regulations has a distinctly emotional tone, since these laws were used under the British Mandate against members of I.Z.L., some of whom were condemned to death. Immediately after the creation of Israel, the government used the laws again against I.Z.L. members and sent some of them to prison. Thus Herut has always called and still calls for the replacement of the laws with "suitable Israeli laws."

18. *Knesset Debates*, 14 Nov. 1962, p. 145.

19. The most important of these rallies was a mass meeting in the Moghrabi Cinema in Tel Aviv on 9 Feb. 1963, which was attended by several thousand Jews and Arabs (*Al Ittihad*, 8, 12 Feb. 1963).

20. *Maariv*, 19 Feb. 1963.

21. *Knesset Debates*, 20 Feb. 1962, pp. 1315-39, 1359-65 and 20 Feb. 1963, pp. 1207-24. In 1962 bills were introduced by the Israeli

Communist Party, Mapam, the Liberal Party, Herut, and Achdut Haavoda. Agudat Israel also proposed its own bill which was turned over to the Security and Foreign Affairs Committee. In 1963 bills were proposed by the Israeli Communist Party, Herut, Mapam, and Achdut Haavoda.

22. During the debate that day four orthodox members of Agudat Israel abstained, thus swinging the vote in favor of military government. The Council of Torah Scholars, the highest authority in the movement, had stated that the military government was equivalent to "self-preservation." But on several previous occasions Agudat Israel had openly expressed disapproval of the military government. It was later revealed that the reason for the change in position was a promise by the government that it would grant the movement a license to open a bank, the Agudat Israel Bank, later dubbed the Military Government Bank (*Maariv*, 24 Nov. 1964). But even the "blessing" of the Council of Torah Scholars was unable to save the bank which failed in 1972 and was taken over by the main Israeli bank, The Bank of Israel (*Maariv*, 16 Jan. 1972 and *Haaretz*, 18 Jan. 1972). See also Zeev Schiff, "How the Military Administration Was Saved," *New Outlook*, March-April 1963, pp. 6-8.

23. *Knesset Debates*, 20 Feb. 1963, pp. 1215-16.
24. Ibid., p. 1218.
25. Ibid., p. 1222.
26. Yigal Allon, *Curtain of Sand* (Tel Aviv, 1960), pp. 327-28.
27. *Knesset Debates*, 20 Feb. 1962, pp. 1322-23.
28. Ibid., 20 Feb. 1963, p. 1211.
29. Ibid., 20 Feb. 1962, p. 1317.
30. Aharon Cohen, *Israel and the Arab World* (Tel Aviv: Sifriat Poalim, 1964), p. 509, in Hebrew. Assaf is one of Mapai's most prominent Arabists, who looks for the negative aspects of international Arab policy and Arab nationalism. He has pursued this subject since the early 1930s and has written several books. He wrote on Arab affairs for the newspaper *Davar* and was one of the founders and the first editor of the newspaper *Al Yaum* in 1948. Though one of the opponents of military government, he did not express his opinions on this in *Al Yaum*, which was intended for Arab readers.
31. *Knesset Debates*, 20 Feb. 1963, p. 1209, as summarized by Menachem Begin.
32. Ibid., 20 Feb. 1962, p. 1320.

33. The government had begun to exempt Druze soldiers from having to obtain travel permits in 1959 and 1960. Villagers from the Circassian village of Kfar Kama in Galilee were similarly exempt because many were serving in the army. Eventually the exemption was extended to include all members of the two sects except those out of favor with the authorities.

34. *Knesset Debates*, 20 Feb. 1962, p. 1326, Ben-Gurion. One year after the creation of these committees—although there were hundreds who had been harmed by the activities of the military government—only twenty people had gone to the committees, mainly because of a lack of confidence in their effectiveness.

35. Achdut Haavoda, a different party from that later known by the same name, was the largest Zionist party in Palestine during the British Mandate.

36. The system of mukhtars, instituted by the Turks and adopted by the British in Palestine, comprises the most reactionary elements among the Arabs. Furthermore, "most of those who call themselves 'mukhtars' assume the title illegally" (*Knesset Debates*, 22 July 1959, p. 2655, minister of interior). Apart from eighteen mukhtars in the Bedouin tribes of the Negev, there were only three officially recognized mukhtars in small Arab villages. In practice, however, the military government recognized some one hundred mukhtars from eighty Arab villages in Galilee and the Triangle.

37. Cohen, *Israel and the Arab World* (New York: Funk & Wagnalls, 1970), p. 494.

38. *Haaretz*, 21 Feb. 1963.

39. *Knesset Debates*, 20 Feb. 1963, p. 1219.

40. In the memoirs of former Knesset member Moshe Unna (National Religious Party), it is clear that he considers these two parties to have had an influential role in the government's periodical decisions to introduce improvements in the military government. When the agreement for a government coalition was signed in 1961, Mapam and Achdut Haavoda insisted on reserving the right to vote against the government, if necessary, over the military government. Unna was an opponent of military rule "on principle" objecting to the system "whose unlovely stamp the ministers could recognize among the Arab population, in carrying out their work" (*Hatzofeh*, 22 July 1971, as quoted from the periodical *Amudem*).

41. *Maariv*, 29 Dec. 1961.

42. *Davar*, 26 Jan. 1962.
43. *Knesset Debates*, 20 Feb. 1963, p. 1217.
44. Ibid., 27 Nov. 1963, p. 354, Emil Habibi.
45. Ibid.
46. *Maariv*, 19 Jan. 1966.
47. Ibid., 20 Jan. 1966 and *Haaretz*, 19, 20 Jan. 1966.
48. *Knesset Debates*, 20 July 1966, pp. 2231-34.

Chapter 3: The Velvet Glove

1. See, for example, *Maariv*, 13 Jan. and 15 Aug. 1966.
2. *Maariv*, 15 Aug. 1966.
3. *Haaretz*, 3 Dec. 1965 and *Maariv*, 3 Dec. 1965.
4. *Davar*, 7 Nov. 1965.
5. *Haaretz*, 10 Feb. 1966.
6. *Maariv*, 10 July 1966.
7. Ibid. See also the *Jerusalem Post* of the same date.
8. For some aspects of daily life under the military government, see Baruch Geltz, *The Ugly Governor* (Tel Aviv, 1966), in Hebrew. The author worked with the military government of the Negev during his military service.
9. The mingling of police and Arab affairs may seem strange but it appears to have come about by chance. The first candidate for the post of minister of interior, Yitzhak Greenbaum, refused to be responsible for police and intelligence, having, in his opinion, suffered greatly at the hands of these departments in his land of origin, Poland. So the police was separated from the ministry of interior and a special ministry of police was created. Since the minister of police, Bikhur Shitrit, was regarded by the government as altogether its best administrator for Arab affairs, the minorities division was attached to his ministry.
10. *State Controller's Annual Report for Financial Year 1963/64* 15 (1965): 106, in Hebrew.
11. The office did not then have a single Arab on its staff. *Knesset Debates 1966/67* (Beirut: Institute for Palestine Studies, 1971), 20 July 1966, p. 2228, in Arabic, Levi Eshkol.
12. *Haaretz*, 4 April 1961.

13. *Haolam Hazeh*, 14 April 1965.

14. Haganah was an organization in the tradition of Lehi and I.Z.L.

15. For example, on 12 Jan. 1953, Palmon said at a news conference that "democratic elections do not suit the situation in the Arab sector" and that "it would be best not to allow the Arab minority too much democracy" (*Knesset Debates*, 9 March 1952, p. 884, as quoted by Hanan Rubin). He also said that he "opposed the government's policy of equal prices for Arab and Jewish agricultural products" (ibid., 15 July 1953, p. 1947, Emil Habibi). A government spokesman denied that Palmon had made these statements, but Palmon himself wrote an article in the periodical *Ner* (Feb. 1953, pp. 3-5) expressing such opinions. And twenty years later, as advisor to the mayor of Jerusalem, he declared his opposition to political activity and electioneering among the Arabs in the Old City of Jerusalem (*Haaretz*, 15 May 1972).

16. For example, in a lecture on the state of the Arabs in Israel, Lubrani said: "It very probably would be better if there were no Arab university students. It probably would be easier to govern them if they continued to work as wood cutters and waiters. But these things are not influenced by our wishes. There is nothing we can do except find a way of dealing with the problems" (Zeev Schiff, "If I Were an Arab," *Haaretz*, 4 April 1961). In a previous press conference he had complained that some of the Arabs in Israel had "Nazi ideas" (*Haaretz*, 31 Aug. 1960). See also the discussion in *Knesset Debates*, 16 Nov. 1960, p. 236.

17. *Haaretz*, 6 April 1965.

18. *Maariv*, 14 May 1965.

19. Ibid., 1 Nov. 1965.

20. The call for Arab-Israeli awareness had begun in 1962 on the initiative of the Arab department in Mapai and prominent Arabs cooperating with it. This "awareness," according to a pamphlet with an introduction by Seifeddin Zu'bi, mayor of Nazareth, consisted of being "Israeli Arabs proud of their Arab heritage, and at the same time loyal to their Israeli nationality, [believing] that the absence of peace between Israel and her Arab neighbors gave Israel the right to defend herself against her enemies, like any other nation in the world, whether the enemies were inside the country or outside." The group also "believed in the historic right of the Jewish people . . . to its homeland" and "as Social Democrats, we consider Israel in the vanguard of social democratic government" (Jacob M.

Landau, *The Arabs in Israel*, New York: Oxford University Press, 1969, pp. 231-36).

21. *Maariv*, 15 Aug. 1966.

22. *Haaretz*, 6 Feb. 1966.

23. For Amnon Lin's opinion on the Labor Party's activity among the Arabs, see Jacob Landau, *The Arabs in Israel* (Tel Aviv: Maarahoth, 1971), pp. 307-24. Lin had left the Labor Party and had resigned from the Knesset when his position became shaky after the death of his brother-in-law Abba Hoshi. In the end he joined the Greater Eretz Israel movement.

24. Eshkol was further spurred to adopt the new policy by the fact that most of the important officials in charge of Arab affairs had been supporters of Ben-Gurion and this was an opportunity to rid himself of them, or at least to limit their influence.

25. *Knesset Debates 1966/67*, p. 136.

26. Ibid., pp. 137, 167.

27. For example, after 1967 the Israeli authorities forbad many of the Arab students at the Hebrew University in Jerusalem from going into the Old City, to prevent them from having contact with its Arab inhabitants. Those who were students at colleges that were moved into the Old City after the war were forced to follow prescribed routes to reach their schools.

28. See also Michael Bar-Zohar, *Spies in the Promised Land: Isar Harel and the Israeli Secret Service* (Boston, 1972), pp. 101-2.

29. *Knesset Debates 1966/67*, p. 158, Uri Avneri; see also pp. 153-57, Tawfiq Tubi's speech.

30. Ibid., 1 Aug. 1967, p. 2813, Moshe Dayan.

31. Ibid., 29 Oct. 1968, p. 117.

32. For more details on the nature of these restrictions and who suffered them, see *Al Ittihad*, 14, 18, 21, 25, 28 July 1967.

33. *Knesset Debates*, 10 Jan. 1968, p. 683. When he was deputy minister of defense, Shimon Peres refused to answer a comparable question for the same reasons (ibid., 7 Jan. 1964, p. 692).

34. *Knesset Debates*, 29 Oct. 1968, p. 117. The number of people living under restrictions in the district of Acre at the end of 1972 had reached 200 (*Haaretz*, 3 Jan. 1973). On 30 Jan. 1973, *Al Ittihad* published a memorandum, signed by seventy-six Arabs and addressed to the United Nations, objecting to the residence restrictions. Zeev Schiff's estimate of the number of Arabs living under such restrictions at the end of 1970 was about 830 (*Haaretz*, 22 Jan. 1971).

35. Even before 1967, the number of Arabs directly under military government restrictions was never more than this. In 1963, Ben-Gurion stated that "only some two thousand persons are known to be restricted by the military government, able to obtain only temporary permits or permits for one journey only" (*Knesset Debates*, 20 Feb. 1963, p. 1217).

36. *Al Ittihad*, 7, 14, 30 April 1970.

37. "Orders, announcements and publications put out by the command of Israel's defense forces in the West Bank," order concerning security instructions, 7 June 1967, p. 5 (pars. 65-70); Golan Heights, 18 June 1967, p. 9; Gaza strip and northern Sinai, 10 June 1967, p. 7; and the Shlomo region (southern Sinai), 11 June 1967, p. 8.

38. *Haaretz*, 3 April 1970 and *Maariv*, 6 April 1970.

39. *Al Ittihad*, 7, 14 April 1970.

40. *Davar*, 27 July 1970.

41. *Knesset Debates*, 29 Oct. 1968, p. 117, Moshe Dayan; *Davar*, 26 Nov. 1969; *Haaretz*, 15 Feb. 1970, Shmuel Toledano's statement; *Davar*, 21 Nov. 1971; *Skira Hodishit* (periodical), January 1973, p. 10, Toledano.

42. *Davar*, 28 March 1969, interview with Eliahu Sasson, minister of police.

43. *Haaretz*, 24 Feb. 1970, Shlomo Hillel, minister of police.

44. *Davar*, 2, 3 Feb. 1970, the results of a poll.

45. *Maariv*, 28 Nov. 1969.

46. Ibid.

47. *Knesset Debates 1966/67* p. 159.

48. Jacob Landau, *The Arabs in Israel*, pp. 308-9, Hebrew edition, quoting the diary of Amnon Lin (1 May 1968) on the activity of the Labor Party among the Arabs.

Chapter 4: "Redeeming" the Land

1. For the proposals and debates on this subject, see *Minutes of the First Zionist Congress* (Jerusalem, 1946), pp. 142-44, in Hebrew.

2. Keren Keymeth Leisrael, *Report on the Legal Structure, Activities, Assets, Income and Liabilities of Keren Keymeth Leisrael* (Jerusalem, 1963), p. 17. In 1954 a special law on Keren Keymeth was passed (Keren Keymeth Leisrael Law, 5714—1953, *Laws of the*

State of Israel [LSI] 8 [1953/54]: 35, in Hebrew), and the wording of the clause quoted was changed, so that the region in which the company operated was defined as "the state of Israel, in any area within the jurisdiction of the government of Israel or in any part thereof." See Article 3(a) of Memorandum of Association of Keren Keymeth Leisrael, *Report...*, p. 56.

3. For details on the way bribery was used, see the memoirs of an employee of the company, Musa Goldenberg's *Ve-ha-keren Odena Keyemet* (*And the Fund Still Stands*) (Tel Aviv, 1965), pp. 101, 107, 109, 110, 115, and 162.

4. A. Granott, *Agrarian Reform and the Record of Israel* (London: Eyre & Spottiswoode, 1956), p. 28.

5. 26,305,000 dunums.

6. Zeev Sharef, *Three Days* (London: W.A. Allen, 1962), p. 165.

7. *Israel Government Yearbook* 5719 (1958): 234.

8. Ibid.

9. See also Don Peretz, *Israel and the Palestine Arabs* (Washington, D.C.: The Middle East Institute, 1958), pp. 168-87; Rony E. Gabbay, *A Political Study of the Arab-Jewish Conflict* (Paris, 1959), pp. 348-62.

10. LSI 4 (1949/50).

11. *The State Controller's Report for Financial Year 1966/67* 18 (1968): 114, 301-2.

12. *Israel Government Yearbook* 5715 (1954): 113.

13. Aharon Liskovsky (Layesh), "The Absentees Present in Israel," *Hamizrah Hehadash* 10:3 (1960), 189.

14. Granott, *Agrarian Reform*, pp. 107-11.

15. See Joseph Weitz, *Diaries and Letters to the Children* (Tel Aviv, 1965), 3: 343-45.

16. *Israel Government Yearbook* 5723 (1963/64): 107.

17. United Nations General Assembly, *Progress Report of the United Nations Conciliation Commission for Palestine*, 23 January-19 November 1951, A/1958, p. 11 and Annex, part I, Ch. II, pp. 10-13; United Nations General Assembly, Doc. A/AC. 25/W. 84, 28 April 1964. See also Sami Hadawi, *Palestine: Loss of a Heritage* (San Antonio, Texas, 1963), pp. 18-23, 50-61.

18. Joseph Weitz, *Struggle for the Land* (Tel Aviv, 1950), pp. 226-27, in Hebrew. See also Granott, *Agrarian Reform*, p. 89.

19. For information on these properties see *Israel Government Yearbook* 5711 (1950): 134-35; 5713 (1952): 118-19; 5715 (1954): 113-15; 5716 (1955): 170-72; 5717 (1956): 224-25; 5718

(1957): 235-37; 5720 (1959/60): 259-60; 5721 (1960/61): 189-99.

20. This estimate is approximate because centers of population owning no land and Bedouin tribes are not counted, and adjoining villages are counted as one settlement. For a list of towns, villages, and tribes in Palestine see the 1945 Administrative Divisions Proclamation published by the British Mandate in *The Palestine Gazette* 1415, no. 2 (7 June 1945): 621, in English.

21. For a list of Palestinian villages and towns in the West Bank and the Gaza strip see Israel Defense Forces, *Census of Population 1967*, *conducted by the Central Bureau of Statistics: West Bank of the Jordan, Gaza strip and northern Sinai, Golan Heights*, Publication No. 1 (Jerusalem, 1967), pp. 45-49, 163-65.

22. In the *Israel Government Yearbook* 5719 (1958): 235, the number of these towns and villages is mentioned as having reached a rough total of 350.

23. *Maariv*, 5 Aug. 1965 and *Haaretz*, 6 Sept. 1966. See also Levi Eshkol, prime minister, answering questions, *Knesset Debates 1966/67*, p. 386, in Arabic.

24. Representatives of Keren Keymeth usually participated in drafting all laws related to land in Israel, especially those concerning the expropriation of Arab land or the means of carrying out such laws. See Weitz, *Diaries* 4: 162, 193, 208, 225, 237, 258-59, and 5: 184.

25. LSI 14 (1960): 48.

26. Ibid., p. 49, Israel Lands Law, 5720—1960.

27. Ibid., p. 50, Israel Lands Administration Law, 5720—1960.

28. Keren Keymeth Leisrael, *Report . . .* , pp. 78-83.

29. *Debates of the People's Council and Provisional State Council*, 24 June 1948, p. 25, in Hebrew. The custodian for absentee property had called a press conference in Tel Aviv early in January 1949 at which he spoke of "dangerous charges of looting of abandoned [Arab] property being leveled against large sectors of the population. . . . and excessive . . . talk . . . about theft and plunder . . . since the prevailing mood of the public makes it difficult to bring those guilty of such acts before the courts" (*Haaretz*, 6 Jan. 1949). Joseph Weitz notes that "the looting of Arab property was the subject of conversation in various circles and while everyone expressed indignation, in practice everyone was stealing and plundering" (*Diaries* 3: 291). See also Joseph Nahmani, *A Man of Galilee* (Ramat Gan, 1969), p. 250.

30. For further details on the expulsion of the Arab population and land seizures in this period, see the statements and questions of Knesset members Tawfiq Tubi, Meir Vilner, Eleizer Beari, and Moshe Aram and the responses of Israeli ministers in *Knesset Debates*, 9 March 1949, pp. 84-85; 28 March 1949, p. 225; 1 Aug. 1948, pp. 1189-90; 8 Sept. 1949, p. 1634; 26 Nov. 1949, pp. 71-75; 7 March 1951, p. 1293; 29 Aug. 1953, p. 2398. See also the newspaper *Al Ittihad*, which published many articles and news items on the subject during 1949-51. See also the editorial in *Haaretz*, 7 Aug. 1949.

31. In many cases, however, when the families of the banished men appealed to the Supreme Court, it ordered the return of some of them. The court decisions on the appeals were not published, but a study of several files of cases (nos. 79, 93, 152, and 163 in 1950; 41, 78, 80, 92, 192, 236, 237, 247 in 1951; and 13 and 141-45 in 1952) showed that 865 of the banished men were allowed to return by order of the court. It is, of course, not known how many did not make attempts to return and how many were refused permission to do so.

32. The missions of Unit 101 of the Israeli Army against the Negev Bedouins between 1953 and 1954, which succeeded in expelling some of the Bedouins (the Azazmeh tribe) to Sinai, were described as such: "The army's desert patrols would turn up in the midst of a Bedouin encampment day after day dispersing it with a sudden burst of machine-gun fire until the sons of the desert were broken and, gathering what little was left of their belongings, led their camels in long silent strings into the heart of the Sinai desert. . . ." (*Haaretz*, 3, 19 Nov. 1959).

    "And Moshe Dayan [who was commander of the southern region] came from Tel Aviv to congratulate them . . . on their victory" (Michael Bar-Zohar, *The Paratrooper's Book*, Tel Aviv, 1969, p. 71).

33. Among these were the villages of Batat, Amqa, Saffuriya, Majdil, Mansura, Ma'ar, Kuweikat, Barwa, Damun, and Ruweis. For their fate and that of other Arab villages and the Jewish settlements built on their lands, see *Haaretz*, 28 July 1972.

34. LSI 4 (1949/50): 68.

35. *Kouetz Ha-Takanot* (*Official Gazette*) 37 (12 Dec. 1948): 91, in Hebrew.

36. Peretz, *Israel . . .*, p. 152.

37. "Village property," belonging to all Arab absentees whether they

are outside the country or living in Israel, "acquired by the custodian of absentee property, includes some three hundred million dunums. . . . The agricultural property includes eighty thousand dunums of citrus groves and more than two hundred thousand dunums of orchards. . . . Urban property includes 25,416 buildings consisting of 57,497 residential apartments and 10,729 stores and light industry workshops" (*Israel Government Yearbook* 5719, 1958, p. 235).

The custodian of absentee property had stated in 1949 that he had in his keeping 223,000 dunums of Arab orchards including "85,000 dunums of citrus plantations and . . . 80,000 dunums of olive groves, 15,000 dunums of vineyards, 14,000 dunums planted with fig trees and smaller areas of almond and apricot orchards and banana plantations" (*Haaretz*, 6 Jan. 1949).

38. In *Israel and the Arab World* (Tel Aviv: Merhavya, 1964), pp. 514-15, Aharon Cohen says: "Inasmuch as the law for absentees' property has also been enforced in the case of Arab property in the mixed towns, where the majority of the population were forced to change their places of residence, this means, in practice, that all Arab property in the towns is regarded as 'absentees' property' unless the contrary can be proved. It is by no means unusual for an Arab who has moved from one quarter in the same town to another to be forced to pay the custodian of absentee property rent for the house he has moved to, as the house has been acquired from the custodian from other persons, while at the same time he receives no rent for his former house, in which others are now living and paying their rent to the custodian."

39. Absentees' Property (Amendment) Law, 5716—1956, LSI 10 (1955/56): 31.

40. Absentees' Property (Amendment 5) (Increase of Payments to Absentees' Dependents and to Absentees) Law, 5727—1967, LSI 21 (1966/67): 138.

41. *Arab-Israeli Armistice Agreements* (Beirut: Institute for Palestine Studies, 1967), p. 56.

42. *Judgments of the Supreme Court* 26: 209, the Custodian of Absentee Property v. Sammara, Jayyusi, and Al Rabi, Civil Appeals 25/55, 145/55, and 158/55.

43. See the discussions in *Knesset Debates*, 27 Feb. 1950, pp. 867-72 and 7 March 1950, pp. 950-65.

44. For more details on Israel's original policy regarding absentee property, see Peretz, *Israel*, pp. 141-67.

45. *Knesset Debates*, 16 Jan. 1951, pp. 789-90.

46. Ibid., 3 Dec. 1952, p. 245.

47. See the debate and findings of the Finance Committee in *Knesset Debates*, 3 Feb. 1954, pp. 834-36 and 28 July 1954, pp. 2245-46.

48. Ibid., 22 Feb. 1956, p. 1159.

49. Ibid., 10 July 1957, pp. 2373-76.

50. Ibid., 30 July 1958, p. 2467.

51. *Judgments* 6: 284, Jamal Aslan et al. v. the Military Governor of Galilee, Appeal 220/51.

52. *Kouetz* 225 (6 Dec. 1951): 242.

53. *Judgments* 9: 689, Aslan, Mahmud et al. v. the Military Governor of Galilee, Appeals 288/51, 33/52.

54. LSI 3 (1949): 56.

55. Ibid., 664 (6 Jan. 1972): 25.

56. The term "protected area" began to be used after the United Nations decision on the partition of Palestine, since the UN partition placed part of this area inside Arab borders. No doubt this explains Herut's repeated requests to change this term whenever the Knesset renewed the law.

57. *Kouetz* 18 (8 June 1949): 230; 215 (2 Nov. 1951): 144.

58. See Articles 8 and 10 in the Emergency (Security Zones) Regulations.

59. Weitz, *Diaries* 3: 373-74.

60. According to a statement by one of the villagers as reported in *Al Ittihad*, 4 July 1972.

61. *Judgments* 4: 461, Mbada Daoud et al. v. the Minister of Defense et al., Appeal 64/51.

62. Ibid., 11: 102, Mbada Daoud et al. v. the Security Zones Appeals Committee, 239/51.

63. Ben-Gurion, minister of defense, stated during a Knesset debate after the destruction of the village: "As for the destruction of the houses . . . the order for this did not come from me even though the army carried it out" (*Knesset Debates*, 16 Jan. 1952, p. 1012). See also Rustum Bastuni on the subject during the same debate. Mukhtar Mbada Daoud was forced to watch the annihilation of his village from a hill nearby.

64. *Kouetz* 309 (3 Sept. 1953): 1446.

65. See the report of the Israeli officer in charge of the evacuation of the village in *Haaretz*, 11 Aug. 1972.

66. *Kouetz* 307 (27 Aug. 1953): 1419.

67. The residents of Kfar Berem were also Christian, belonging to the Maronite sect.
68. *Israel Government Yearbook* 5725 (1964): 32.
69. See *Davar,* 16 Aug. 1972 for a photograph of part of the compensation agreement and Metropolitan Hakim's comments in an interview with *Al Jarida* (Beirut) 18 Aug. 1972.
70. *Haaretz,* 24 July 1972; *Yediot Aharonot,* 30 June 1972.
71. *Haaretz,* 2 Aug. 1972.
72. Ibid., 3 Aug. 1972.
73. Ibid., 24 Aug. 1972.
74. See the report of the deputy head of the Israel Lands Administration in *Davar,* 16 Aug. 1972.
75. *Judgments* 13: 203, Attiya Juweid et al. v. the Minister of Defense et al., Appeal 132/52. See also the statement of Zvi Dinstein, deputy minister of defense, asking for an extension of the validity of the regulations, *Knesset Debates,* 24 Jan. 1966, p. 467.
76. *Kouetz* 27 (15 Oct. 1948), supplement 2: 3.
77. LSI 2 (1948/49): 77.
78. *Debates of the People's Council,* 6 Jan. 1949, pp. 8-9.
79. *State Controller's Report 1963/64* 15: 287.
80. *Kouetz* 41 (7 Jan. 1949).
81. LSI 27 (23 Nov. 1949): 1.
82. Ibid., 106 (22 Aug. 1952): 391.
83. Ibid., 188 (8 July 1955): 191.
84. Ibid., 7 (1952/53): 43.
85. *Knesset Debates,* 3 June 1952, p. 2202.
86. *Haaretz,* 5 Feb. 1953. See also Gabbay, *A Political Study,* pp. 362-64.
87. *Knesset Debates,* 15 June 1955, pp. 1899-1900, 1911.
88. See the discussion in *Knesset Debates,* 4 March 1953, pp. 856-62 and 9 March 1952, pp. 888-95, especially the reservations of Tubi, Hanan Rubin, and Masad Qassis.
89. *Maariv,* 25 Dec. 1953 (reprinted in the issues of 15 Feb. 1966 and 3 July 1972).
90. *Knesset Debates,* 7 Nov. 1960, p. 132, Moshe Dayan, minister of agriculture, proposing the bill. See also Mahmud Bayadsi, "Israel Land Reform and the Arabs," *New Outlook,* February 1961, pp. 18-22.

Chapter 5: "Liberating" the Land

1. *Knesset Debates*, 5 Aug. 1959, p. 2923.
2. *Maariv*, 8 Feb. 1963, Shmuel Segev.
3. *Yediot Aharonot*, 28 Aug. 1965, Y. Ben-Borat. See also the discussion of the Judaization of Galilee project in *New Outlook*, November-December 1963, pp. 56-73.
4. *Davar*, 26 Jan. 1962.
5. Joseph Nahmani, *A Man of Galilee* (Ramat Gan, 1969), pp. 117-20.
6. Ibid., pp. 134-40.
7. Joseph Weitz, *Diaries and Letters to the Children* (Tel Aviv, 1965), 5: 89-96. No doubt he also took part in the discussions about the reorganization of Zionist settlement foundations and Israeli policy on land ownership in general. Eventually, with the help of his supporters, he was able to induce the government to follow the original principle that "state land" was not to be sold.
8. Ibid., pp. 240, 248, 303-8.
9. Ibid., pp. 258, 264, 312-15.
10. *Maariv*, 29 Aug. 1965, Emmanuel Mareuveni.
11. The 1943 law was again invoked in 1961 for the expropriation of some two thousand dunums in the Battuf Plain belonging to the villages of Arava and Sakhnin for use in the Diversion of the Jordan Waters Project.
12. See Emil Habibi's protest against the land expropriation, *Knesset Debates*, 31 July 1957, p. 2625.
13. Allon was later appointed head of the Arab department in the Labor Party.
14. *Knesset Debates*, 31 Jan. 1962, pp. 1126-30.
15. Ibid., 31 Oct. 1962, p. 24.
16. Ibid., 4 April 1962, p. 1797 and 25 June 1962, p. 2421: see Emil Habibi's statement and Shimon Peres's response.
17. *Maariv*, 17 Jan. 1963.
18. *Al Ittihad*, 15 Feb. 1963 and 12 March 1963.
19. *Knesset Debates*, 2 Dec. 1964, p. 486.
20. *Maariv*, 14 Feb. 1965.
21. Ibid., 30 Jan. 1972 and *Davar*, 10, 16 Feb. 1972.
22. *Statistical Abstract of Israel* (1970), p. 36.
23. *State Controller's Report for Financial Year 1963/64* 15 (1965): 336.
24. LSI 12 (1957/58): 129.
25. *Al Ra'ed* (periodical, Haifa), September 1957, p. 118.

26. *Israel Government Yearbook* 5724 (1963/64): 208; 5725 (1964/65): 214. See also Dov Joseph's statement in *Knesset Debates*, 13 June 1962, p. 2306 and the *Report of the Israel Lands Administration for Financial Year 1964/65* 4 (Jerusalem, 1966): 66-68.
27. *Judgments of the Supreme Court* 15: 906, Ahmad Bednan v. the State of Israel, Appeal 482/59.
28. For a comprehensive study of the land survey and the Israeli government's aims in undertaking it, see Yitzhak Oded, "Land Losses among Israel's Arab Villagers," *New Outlook*, September 1964, pp. 10-25. See also Oded's "Bedouin Lands Threatened by Takeover," *New Outlook*, November-December 1964, pp. 45-52.
29. *Israel Government Yearbook* 5732 (1971/72): 237.
30. *Israel Government Yearbook* 5727 (1966/67): 201. The *Report of the Lands Administration* 4: 66, in its description of the progress of the land survey to date notes that "the government's claims in forty-two Arab villages (in the north of Israel) totaled some 276,000 dunums and the claims of the custodian of absentee property and the development authority some 124,000 dunums, or about 400,000 dunums altogether out of the original 702,000 dunums.

"By 31 March 1964 (following court action) 178,000 dunums of the 400,000 claimed were surveyed with 134,000 going to the state and 44,000 to the development authority. The conflict over an area of 114,000 dunums continues, while 108,000 dunums are still in the process of being surveyed."

On page 68 the report adds with a note of pride that "it can be said that the state has won more than 85 percent of the cases resulting from claims made during the land survey."
31. See Articles 2, 5, and 9 in the Leasing of Land (Temporary Provisions) Law, 5719—1959, LSI 13 (1958/59): 210.
32. *Kouetz Ha-Takanot (Official Gazette)* 2486 (27 Nov. 1969): 509-12, in Hebrew. The villages were Ein Mahil, 960 dunums; Daburiya, 2007 dunums; Yafa al Nasra, 2730 dunums; and Al Maghar, 5837 dunums.
33. *Knesset Debates*, 16 May 1949, p. 502.
34. See the article by Habib Kanan in *Haaretz*, 21 April 1952 and Rashid Hussein's poem in *Al Mirsad*, 7 Jan. 1960. However, after the annexation of the Old City of Jerusalem by Israel in 1967, a special law was promptly passed to stay the expropriation of the

holy places in that city. See Article 2 of the Legal and Administrative Matters (Regulations) Law (Consolidated Version), 5730—1970, LSI 24 (1969/70): 144.

35. *Judgments* 6: 1198, Yacoub Hassuneh v. Custodian for Absentee Property et al., Appeal 332/52. See also *Judgments* 23: 151, Boulos Boulos v. the Minister of Development et al.

36. *State Controller's Report 1966/67* 18 (1968): 302.

37. Ibid.

38. An Israeli study has estimated the different kinds of *waqf* land in Palestine to be somewhere between 750,000 and 1.1 million dunums, half of it inside Israel. Yaacov Shimoni, *Palestine Arabs* (Tel Aviv, 1947), p. 90, in Hebrew and Atallah Mansour in *Haaretz*, 13 Dec. 1965, apparently based on a conversation with Aharon Layesh, head of the Islamic department of the prime minister's advisor on Arab affairs.

39. *Knesset Debates*, 3 June 1952, p. 2193, Ben-Gurion.

40. See also the statement of Haim Cohen, minister of justice, in reply to the proposal made by Rustum Bastuni (Mapam) that *waqf* property be freed, *Knesset Debates*, 3 Dec. 1952, p. 249.

41. *Knesset Debates*, 27 May 1957, p. 1981, Zirach Werhaftig, minister of religion.

42. For details on government aid, especially for the restoration of mosques, see the *Islamic News Bulletin* published by the ministry of religions (Jerusalem), December 1971, p. 20.

43. 7 Sept. 1971.

44. *Knesset Debates*, 7 July 1959, p. 2455.

45. *Knesset Debates*, 12 Dec. 1962, pp. 449-51.

46. Ibid., 4 March 1964, pp. 1295-99.

47. Absentee's Property (Amendment No. 3) (Release and Use of Endowment Property) Law, 5725—1965, LSI 19 (1964/65): 55.

48. By 1970 committees had yet to be appointed for Nazareth and Shafa Amr (*Israeli Government Yearbook* 5731, 1970/71: 317).

49. See the questions asked of the minister of religions and his response in *Knesset Debates*, 7 Jan. 1963, p. 709 and 18 Feb. 1963, p. 1149.

50. *Maariv*, 3, 12 Sept. 1971. For more information on how the Israeli government dealt with the *waqf* see Aharon Layesh, "The Islamic *Waqf* in Israel," *Hamizrah Hehadash* 15, no. 1/2 (1965): 38-56.

51. *Haaretz*, 22 Sept. 1972.

52. Bedouin elders in the Negev, during a press conference, as reported in *Haaretz*, 13 June 1965. See also Weitz, *Diaries* 3: 355, 357,

and 359; 4: 8, 9, 15, and 22, and Emanuel Marx, "Bedouin of the Negev," *Hamizrah Hehadash* 7, no. 2 (1966): 89-98. See also Ben-Gurion's statements in *Knesset Debates*, 6 Feb. 1952, pp. 1222-23.

53. Emanuel Marx, *Bedouin of the Negev* (Manchester University Press, 1967), p. 35.

54. *Knesset Debates*, 9 June 1952, p. 2235, Moshe Shapira, minister of interior, responding to questions.

55. Ibid., 6 Nov. 1951, p. 338; *Al Hamishmar*, 18 May 1972.

56. Marx, *Bedouin*, pp. 38-46.

57. For further information on the relocation of the Bedouins see the statements of Moshe Aram and Rustum Bastuni in *Knesset Debates*, 13 May 1953, p. 1320 and 4 Dec. 1954, p. 282.

58. Weitz, *Diaries* 4:23.

59. Weitz, *Diaries* 5: 183, 194, 206, 211, and 292. See also the statement of Shimon Peres, deputy minister of defense, in response to questioning in *Knesset Debates*, 3 April 1962, p. 1757.

60. *Knesset Debates*, 17 July 1963, p. 2424. See also 20 May 1964, p. 1840.

61. See Bikhur Shitrit, minister of police, responding to questioning in *Knesset Debates*, 4 May 1952, pp. 2025-26.

62. *Maariv* reported the situation as follows 4 June 1956: "The department of defense is taking administrative measures against the Suaed Arab Bedouins, in the hills of central Galilee, who have resisted a military order and refuse to leave their tents which are in a closed area.

"The restrictions imposed on the tribe include a ban on leaving their place of residence, the cancellation of all government permits in their possession, such as hunting, grazing, and travel, the closing of their elementary school, a ban on independent food supplies to the tribe as well as a ban on the sale of the tribe's products outside their area.

"The tribe claims that 'as long as the blood runs in our veins, we shall not leave the land we have owned for generations. . . .'

"In the last few days dozens of peasants from the villages of Majd al Kurum, Araya, Deir al Asad, Sachnin and others have been arrested for 'invading' closed areas. The military court before which they were brought has sentenced them to six months in prison and fines of five hundred to one thousand pounds."

63. *Knesset Debates*, 5 Dec. 1962, p. 383, Ami Asaf, deputy minister of education. See also 24 Nov. 1962, p. 244 and 3 July 1963, p.

1085, a report on the incident by the Knesset Education Committee.

64. *Knesset Debates*, 2 Dec. 1964, p. 504, Tawfiq Tubi.

65. See *Davar*, 26 March 1964.

66. *Maariv*, 26 Sept. 1965.

67. *Israel Government Yearbook* 5727 (1966/67): 33. See also *State Controller's Report 1965/66* 17 (1967): 294-96.

68. *Israel Government Yearbook* 5727 (1966/67): 33, 181; 5732 (1971/72): 39; *Davar*, 26 May 1972.

69. *Al Hamishmar*, 18 May 1972.

70. *Haaretz*, 19 and 20 March 1973.

71. Weitz, *Diaries* 5: 258.

72. *State Controller's Report 1965/66* 17 (1967): 292 and *Report of the Lands Administration 1964/65* 5 (1966): 165-68 and ibid., 1965/66 5 (1967): 185-88. See also *Israel Government Yearbook* 5732 (1971/72): 67.

73. 22,056,000 Israeli pounds were paid as compensation for 123,193 dunums.

74. *Report of Lands Administration 1964/65* 4 (1966): 166-67.

75. See the findings of the Knesset Finance Committee and Levi Eshkol, minister of finance, responding to questioning, *Knesset Debates* 28 July 1954, pp. 2245-46; 30 July 1958, p. 2467; 20 July 1959, p. 2581; and 10 Aug. 1960, p. 2167.

76. *Knesset Debates*, 15 March 1965, p. 1539, report of the Finance Committee.

77. As quoted by *Ner*, Feb.-April 1960, quoting Israel Hertz in an article in *Al Hamishmar*.

78. *State Controller's Report 1966/67* 18 (1968): 304-5.

79. See *Village Statistics 1945, A Classification of Land and Area Ownership in Palestine*, with Explanatory Notes by Sami Hadawi (Beirut: Palestine Liberation Organization Research Center, 1970), pp. 7-36, for Hadawi's reservations.

80. Central Bureau of Statistics, *Census of Agriculture, 1949/50. Part A — Farm Economy of the Arabs, Druzes and other Minority Groups*, special series no. 8 (Jerusalem, 1952).

81. *Yalkut Ha-Pirsumim (Official Gazette)* 288 (23 April 1953)—355 (13 June 1954); *Report of Lands Administration 1964/65* 4 (1966): 165 and *Report of Lands Administration 1965/66* 5 (1967): 185. According to the British classification, twenty-five of the villages lie in the Acre district; ten in Nazareth; seventeen

in Tiberias; thirty-one in Safad, eight in Beisan, thirty-one in Haifa; thirty in Tulkarm; six in Jenin; twenty-one in Jaffa; forty-five in Ramle; seventeen in Jerusalem; and four in Hebron. The minister of finance, Levi Eshkol, had previously stated that the expropriated land totaled 1,234,785 dunums (*Knesset Debates*, 2 Feb. 1955, p. 715).

82. See Collective Planning Center for Agriculture and Settlement and the Ministry of Agriculture, Nazareth Branch, *Results of the Census and Project A for Agricultural Development* (Nazareth, July 1963), pp. 12-24, in Hebrew.

83. *Yalkut* 355 (13 June 1954): 1220-23.

84. Marx, *Bedouin*, p. 56.

85. *Haaretz*, 28 Aug. 1972.

86. *Report of Lands Administration 1964/65* 6 (1966): 166 and *State Controller's Report 1965/66* 17 (1967): 292.

87. *Al Ittihad*, 10 July 1964, Tawfiq Tubi, but Tubi does not mention his sources for this estimate.

88. *Knesset Debates*, 22 Feb. 1965, p. 1298.

89. Ibid., 16 June 1965, pp. 2193-94.

90. *Haaretz*, 7 Dec. 1964.

91. Agricultural Settlement (Restrictions on Use of Agricultural Land and of Water) Law, 5727—1967, LSI 21 (1966/67): 105.

92. For part of the debate on this law, see *Knesset Debates 1966/67*, pp. 119-31. See also Sabri Jiryis, "Recent Knesset Legislation and the Arabs in Israel," *Journal of Palestine Studies*, Autumn 1971, pp. 53-67.

93. *Davar*, 3 Feb. 1972.

94. *Haaretz*, 5 Nov. 1971.

95. *Maariv*, 26 Oct. 1971.

96. *Hatzofeh*, 20 Dec. 1971.

97. *Kouetz* 1043 (30 Jan. 1973): 160, introduction to the bill (1043) amending the Agricultural Settlement Law, 5733—1973.

Chapter 6: *From Deir Yasin to Kfar Kassim*

1. For further information see *Sefer Toldot Ha-Haganah* (A History of the Haganah), edited by Ben-Zion Dinor (Tel Aviv, 1964), Bk. 2, 2: 795-97, 833-50, and 1053-72.

2. For details see David Niv, *Haarakhot Ha-Irgun Ha-Zvai Ha-Leumi* (History of the National Military Organization) (Tel Aviv, 1965), 2: 238-57.

3. Several Zionist historians have cited the massacre at Deir Yasin as one of the causes for the departure of large numbers of Palestinians in 1948. See, for instance, the "official" history of the 1948 War by the history section of the General Staff: *Toldot Melhemit Ma-Kumamyout* (History of the War of Independence) (Tel Aviv, 1959), 17th printing 1970, pp. 116-18.

4. Unit 101 later merged with a company of paratroopers and changed its name to Unit 202.

5. For a description of these operations and their purpose by some leaders of the units who took part in them, see Meir Har-Zion, *Chapters from a Diary* (Tel Aviv, 1969), pp. 143-221, in Hebrew; and Moshe Yanoka, *From Kibya to Mitleh* (Tel Aviv, 1967), pp. 9-177.

6. *Judgments of the District Courts of Israel* 17, pp. 99-101, Military Attorney General v. Major Melinki et al., File 3/57, District Court of Israel Defense Army, Center Command. For a description of the trial sessions, see also *Eleven Green Berets on Trial* (Tel Aviv, 1959), in Hebrew.

7. Ibid., p. 101.

8. Ibid.

9. Ibid., p. 102.

10. Ibid., p. 104.

11. That same night two more Arabs were killed in the village of Kfar Barra.

12. Ibid., p. 106.

13. Ibid., pp. 108-10.

14. Ibid., p. 111.

15. Ibid., pp. 114-15.

16. Ibid., pp. 117-18.

17. *Davar*, 7 Dec. 1956.

18. *Knesset Debates*, 12 Dec. 1956, p. 462.

19. *Ner*, August-October 1959, Boaz Evron; and *Haaretz*, 18 Nov. 1959.

20. *Knesset Debates*, 10 Feb. 1960, p. 603, Shimon Peres, deputy minister of defense, answering questions.

21. *Yediot Aharanot*, 27 April 1967.

22. This was not the first time that Justice Halevy had embarrassed the Israeli authorities. During a case stemming from the Kastner

affair—Rudolf Kastner was a well-known senior official in the Mapai Party—Halevy did not hesitate to charge him with collaboration with the Nazis during the war, causing a sensational scandal for the party. In another case, he was not deterred from disclosing corruption in the Israeli ministry of police while Ben-Gurion's son, Amos Ben-Gurion, was inspector of police.

23. *Judgments* 17: 208. See also the testimonies of Melinki and Dahan and Shadmi's own testimony in *Haaretz*, 22, 23, 26-28 Jan. 1959 and 6 Feb. 1959.
24. *Lamerhav*, 24 Oct. 1958.
25. *Knesset Debates*, 6 Dec. 1960, p. 429 and 4 Jan. 1961, p. 644, Shimon Peres.
26. *Debates of the People's Council and Provisional State Council*, 14 Oct. 1948, p. 4, the interrogation of Shmuel Mikunis. Defense Minister Ben-Gurion's explanation was that "ten [of those arrested] tried to escape and were shot" (p. 5).
27. *Knesset Debates*, 14 Nov. 1951, p. 393.
28. Ibid., 5 March 1952, p. 1525, Bikhur Shitrit, minister of police.
29. Ibid., 26 March 1952, p. 1692, Rustum Bastuni.
30. Ibid., 28 Aug. 1952, p. 3203, Ben-Gurion.
31. *Haaretz*, 19, 21, 24 Sept. 1961.
32. Ibid., 9, 10, 11 Nov. 1959.
33. These incidents are taken from *Al Ittihad*, which showed concern over the wave of bomb findings, reporting them at once.
34. *Knesset Debates*, 23 Dec. 1957, p. 467.
35. See Tawfiq Tubi's questions and Shimon Peres's replies in *Knesset Debates*, 9 July 1963, p. 2322 and 21 July 1964, pp. 2418-19.
36. *Haaretz*, 30 Jan. 1970. See also Moshe Dayan's answers to questions, *Knesset Debates*, 31 March 1970, p. 1470.
37. *Knesset Debates*, 2 Nov. 1971, p. 113, Dayan.
38. Ibid., 7 March 1961, p. 1220 and 5 Nov. 1968, p. 168, Peres and Eliahu Sasson, minister of police, answering questions.
39. Ibid., 2 Nov. 1971, p. 113, Dayan.

Chapter 7: Political and Societal Circumstances

1. Asher Zidon, *The Knesset: Israel's Parliament* (Tel Aviv, 1971), 6th edition, p. 40, in Hebrew.
2. Ibid., pp. 41-44, 477, 513.

3. *Haaretz*, 7, 26, 27 Jan. 1949.

4. Michael Assaf, "Arab Integration into the State of Israel," *Hamizrah Hehadash* 1, no. 1 (1949): 4.

5. *Haaretz*, 14 Jan. 1966, Yehoshua Palmon.

6. The Israeli Labor Party has recently begun to issue membership cards to many of its Arab supporters, especially those who "served in the security agencies" (*Maariv*, 14 Sept. 1972). Some Israeli leaders had made the suggestion, before that, that an independent Arab labor party be founded in Israel (*Davar*, 24 Feb. 1972).

7. For the results of these elections and the composition of the Arab lists taking part, see Zidon, *The Knesset*, pp. 382-99 and 514-15.

8. *Davar*, 6 Oct. 1968, an interview with Zu'bi.

9. *Haaretz*, 14 Jan. 1966.

10. Ibid., 2 Jan. 1971.

11. *Yediot Aharonot*, 5 March 1970.

12. Ibid. By early 1972, eighty-two Arabs had been awarded such decorations by the Israeli authorities (*Davar*, 13 Aug. 1971, 2 March 1972).

13. Shabtai Teveth, *Moshe Dayan* (Jerusalem, 1972), pp. 133-34.

14. *Al Hamishmar*, 26 Feb. 1971, supplement.

15. *Haaretz*, 15 July 1944.

16. *Knesset Debates*, 7 Jan. 1952, p. 893, minister of agriculture and *Maariv*, 7 Oct. 1955.

17. *Knesset Debates*, 21 Jan. 1952, p. 1029; 13 May 1959, p. 2480, minister of agriculture and minister of finance. See also interview with Zu'bi in *Davar*, 6 Oct. 1968.

18. *Knesset Debates*, 5 July 1960, p. 1767, minister of industry and commerce.

19. *Haaretz*, 30 April 1958.

20. This is the opinion of former Knesset member Moshe Unna, from his memoirs as quoted by *Hatzofeh*, 22 July 1971 from the periodical *Amudem*.

21. *Haaretz*, 28 Oct. 1965, quoting an interview in *Al Yaum*, 20 Oct. 1965.

22. Ibid., Atallah Mansour.

23. *Al Hamishmar*, 26 Feb. 1971, supplement.

24. Theodore Herzl, *Altneuland, Kitvei Herzel* (Jerusalem, 1960), 1: 165-72, Hebrew translation.

25. In *Haaretz*, 4 Nov. 1965, Joseph Ariel describes the sorting of

votes in the district of Acre, which has a large Arab population. Those present were looking out for ballot sheets that "were folded and marked in a certain way by whole families from the minority villages, to indicate the number of family members voting for a certain list." Heads of families and leaders of the various parties come to some kind of agreement before the elections. It is a highly effective way of influencing voters since they know that the number of votes in a family can determine the kind of treatment the family can expect.

26. *Al Ittihad*, 10, 24, 31 Oct. 1969 gives details of a charge that Arab activists supporting the Communist list were detained on the eve of the 1969 elections.

27. *Knesset Debates*, 23 March 1961, p. 1468, Hanan Rubin (Mapam).

28. Ibid., 30 Oct. 1968, pp. 124-29.

29. *Davar*, 21 Jan. 1973.

30. *Al Yaum* was originally published by a group of Oriental Jews under the editorship of Michael Assaf, reporter on Arab affairs for Histadrut's newspaper *Davar*, with help from the ministry of minorities. For Assaf on this paper, see *Hamizrah Hehadash* 1 (1949/50): 6. In April 1953 a special Al Yaum Society was created to run the paper (*Knesset Debates*, 2 July 1962, p. 2526, Hayim Moshe Shapira).

31. *State Controller's Report for Financial Year 1963/64* 15 (1965): 107-8.

32. Assaf, *Hamizrah Hehadash* 1 (1949/50): 6 and "Collected Information on Histadrut's Activities Among the Arabs," *Hamizrah Hehadash* Nov.-Dec. 1962, p. 1; *Knesset Debates*, 18 July 1962, p. 2761, Ben-Gurion.

33. In its "obituary notice" on the demise of *Al Yaum*, *Al Ittihad* said on 11 June 1968: "The notorious *Al Yaum* has been forced off stage. Its owners announced its collapse last week. Does anyone mourn it apart from those who nursed it and fostered it financially and politically, hoping to use it to deceive Arab people and undermine their spirits. . . . *Al Yaum's* failure is not financial but a political bankruptcy; it was unable to win the sympathy of its readers, being no more than a mouthpiece for official propaganda. . . ."

34. *Knesset Debates*, 30 Dec. 1968, p. 980, Israel Shlomo Ben-Meir, deputy minister of the interior.

35. For an account of the Arab press in Israel and the occupied

territories and the political leanings of each paper, see *Yediot Aharonot*, 30 July 1972. See also Tawfiq Khouri's article on *Al Anba'* in *Davar*, 5 Dec. 1971.

36. *Al Ittihad*, 28 Aug. 1964.
37. Ibid., quoting *Maariv*, 23 Aug. 1964.
38. Ibid., 1 July 1966, quoting Bastuni's statement in *Al Yaum*, 24 June 1966.
39. Peretz Mirhav, *History of the Workers' Movement in Eretz Israel* (Tel Aviv, 1967), p. 143, in Hebrew.
40. *Haaretz*, 7, 26, 27 Jan. 1949.
41. For further details see Mirhav, *Workers' Movement*, pp. 165-73. See also Moshe Braslavski, *The Workers' Movement in Eretz-Israel* (Tel Aviv, 1962), part 4, pp. 201, 208, in Hebrew.
42. Having once been a member of the Knesset, Bastuni's opinion of the Arab members is interesting: "The truth is that as party candidates they do not represent the Arabs in Israel, but within the party their views on minority problems are listened to. . . ." ("Arab Society in Israel," *Hamizrah Hehadash* 15, no. 1/2 (1965): 2.
43. See Mahmoud Yonis, "Arab Pioneer Youth Movement," *New Outlook*, February 1958, pp. 54-56. See also Abdul Aziz Zu'bi, "Discontent of Arab Youth," *New Outlook*, January 1958, pp. 12-17.
44. *New Outlook*, Sept. 1958, pp. 55-56.
45. The incident that made the party particularly vulnerable on this point was the establishment of its Kibbutz Berem on the land of the village of Kfar Berem (see Chapter 2).
46. *Davar*, 6 Oct. 1968.
47. *Al Hamishmar*, 21 May 1971. See also Shlomo Avineri in *Maariv*, 6 Aug. 1971.
48. See Jacob M. Landau, *The Arabs in Israel* (New York: Oxford University Press, 1969), pp. 190-201.
49. Knesset member Uri Avneri's comment on the appointment of Jabr Ma'di as deputy to the minister of transportation was: "He appears in the Knesset once every quarter and speaks once a year. I doubt whether I listened to the six speeches he delivered in the six years I have spent in the [Knesset]. . . . The Sheikh speaks in Arabic, reading with difficulty from a typed manuscript. From a practical point of view, it is hard to imagine what the Sheikh will do . . . in a ministry which, more than any other, relies on modern technology, a ministry of computers, satellites, complex

telephone equipment and up-to-date broadcasting stations. . . . To put the Sheikh in this position is a mistake bordering on a crime, it would be less wasteful to let a bull into a china shop" (*Haolam Hazeh*, 13 Oct. 1971).

50. *Al Hamishmar*, 21 May 1971.

51. See *Haaretz*, 10 Aug. 1955, for Jacob Aviel's analysis of the Arab vote in that election.

52. See also Landau, *The Arabs*, pp. 119, 125, 132, 144.

53. Ibid., p. 139.

54. *Maariv*, 10 Oct. 1965.

55. See, for example, *Haaretz*, 1 Dec. 1965 and 20 Nov. 1966 on the party's methods during the general election and the Nazareth municipal election. See also the party organ *Hatzofeh*, 8, 10, 11 Dec. 1970, for comments on party activities during the Nazareth municipal election in 1970.

56. See Atallah Mansour's article "The Two Faces of *Haolam Hazeh*" in *Haaretz*, 23 March 1966.

57. See their statement "Tug of War with Avneri" in *Al Ittihad*, 2 Sept. 1966.

58. See Yehoshua Porat, "League for National Liberation," *Hamizrah Hehadash* 4 (1964): 354-66. See also Yaacov Shimoni, *Palestine Arabs* (Tel Aviv, 1947), pp. 343-45.

59. *Debates of the People's Council and Provisional State Council* 1 (2 Sept. 1948): 6.

60. Ibid., 2 (6 Jan. 1949): 4 and 2 (13 Jan. 1949): 4.

61. See Yochanan Peres and Nirah Davis, "On the National Identity of the Israeli Arab," *Hamizrah Hehadash* 18, no. 1-2 (1968): 106-11. See also Peres, "Modernization and Nationalism in the Identity of the Israeli Arab," *The Middle East Journal*, Autumn 1970, pp. 472-92.

62. For details on the two viewpoints and the differences between the two groups, see their statements in Mirhav, *Workers' Movement*, pp. 89-100.

63. Aware of this fact, the Israeli authorities have tried to hinder the work of the Communist papers by periodically banning them. When the matter was brought before the Supreme Court (*Judgments of the Supreme Court*, 7: 871, *Al Ittihad* and *Kol Haam* v. the Minister of Interior, Appeal 73 & 87/53), it ruled in favor of a wide interpretation of the Press Ordinance, making it difficult for the minister of interior to ban newspapers. In accordance with the emergency regulations the Communist papers have to be

submitted to military censorship, and they occasionally appear with the marks of the censor's pencil.

64. In spite of this, Ben-Gurion ignored him until 1966 when, on the point of retirement, he invited Tubi to his home in Tel Aviv. He wanted to confer with Tubi and "to explain his own views, which had on occasion been misrepresented, as well as listen and understand the views of others" (*Al Ittihad*, 28 Oct. 1966).

65. See, for example, Zeev Schiff in *Haaretz*, 21 Oct. 1965 and Misha Maisels in *Maariv*, 6 Nov. 1969.

66. Knesset and Local Elections (5730) (Financing, Limitation of Expenses and Audit) Law, 5729—1969, LSI 23 (1968/69): 53, 218. See also Emil Habibi's statement in support of this law, *Knesset Debates*, 19 Feb. 1969, p. 1666.

67. See Landau, *The Arabs*, pp. 72-75 and Walter Schwarz, *The Arabs in Israel* (London: Faber, 1959), pp. 26, 59, and 68.

68. *Haaretz*, 6, 7 July 1958.

69. This meant inducing officials to use Arabic when dealing with Arabs, since the Arabs themselves normally use Arabic when contacting government offices. A few departments, like the Internal Revenue Service, did use Arabic, which is an official language in Israel. A Herut Knesset member, Esther Raziel-Naur, introduced a bill abolishing official use of Arabic, but it was rejected (*Knesset Debates*, 2 July 1952, p. 2520). Arabic's popularity with the Israeli authorities varies: at one moment it is enthusiastically regarded as a language that must be taught in all Jewish schools and then entirely forgotten the next. The latest official position is that it should be compulsory in all Jewish schools (*Maariv*, 24 May 1972). See Shmuel Mikunis' statement and Kalman Kahana's response in *Knesset Debates*, 6 May 1964, pp. 1718-20. On the general subject, see also Habib Qahwaji, *The Arabs in the Shadow of Israeli Occupation since 1948* (Beirut: Palestine Liberation Organization Research Center, 1972), p. 439.

70. *Knesset Debates*, 7 Jan. 1959, p. 806, Ben-Gurion.

71. Ibid.

72. Ibid.

73. See Schwarz, *The Arabs*, pp. 122-23.

74. *Haaretz*, 28, 29 June 1959 and 3, 5 July 1959. See also Tawfiq Tubi's speech and Ben-Gurion's reply in *Knesset Debates*, 15 July 1959, pp. 2546-48.

75. *Jerusalem Post*, 1 Feb. 1960.

76. *Haaretz*, 2 Feb. 1960.

77. *Judgments* 15: 1151, Mansour Kardosh v. the Registrar of Companies, Appeal 241/60.

78. *Judgments* 16: 1209, Registrar of Companies v. Mansour Kardosh, Appeal 16/61.

79. Article 94 (2) Defense (Emergency) Regulations, 1945.

80. *Judgments* 18, part 2: 344, Al Ard Company Ltd. v. District Commissioner in the North, Appeal 39/64. See also *Jerusalem Post*, 11 March 1964.

81. *Haaretz*, 24 July 1964.

82. *New Outlook*, Nov.-Dec. 1962, p. 61.

83. Ibid., p. 62.

84. *Al Ittihad*, 14 Aug. 1964, quoting a talk given at the sports club in Tira.

85. Mansour Kardosh, "For a Palestinian Arab State," *New Outlook*, May 1966, p. 43.

86. *Al Ittihad*, 11 Aug. 1974, quoting an interview with Mansour Kardosh by *Haolam Hazeh*.

87. Saleh Baransi, "To Face Facts and Confess Faults," *New Outlook*, March-April 1963, p. 67.

88. *Judgments* 18, part 4: 670, Sabri Jiryis v. the Haifa District Commissioner, case 253/64. See also the *Jerusalem Post*, 17 Nov. 1964.

89. Ibid., p. 677.

90. Ibid., p. 680.

91. *Haaretz*, 15 Nov. 1964.

92. *Yalkut Ha-Pirsumim (Official Gazette)* 1134 (23 Nov. 1964): 638.

93. See Uri Avneri in *Haolam Hazeh*, 7 April 1964 and Yigal Ilam in *Haaretz*, 7 April 1964.

94. *Al Ittihad*, 13 Nov. 1964, editorial.

95. Ibid., 17 July 1964.

96. *Haaretz*, 5 Sept. 1965.

97. *Haolam Hazeh*, 22, 29 Sept. 1965.

98. *Judgments* 19, part 3: 365, Yacob Yaridor v. the Chairman of the Central Elections Committee of the Sixth Knesset, Elections Appeal 1/65. See also the *Jerusalem Post*, 14 Nov. 1965.

99. *Judgments* 19, part 3: 384-90.

100. For the views of one of Al Ard's leaders, see Qahwaji, *Arabs in the Shadow*, pp. 446-75. See also "The Complete History of the Al Ard Movement," *Palestine Affairs* (Beirut), March 1971, no. 1: 112-20 and Landau, *The Arabs*, pp. 92-107.

101. For details see *Knesset Debates*, 8 July 1964, pp. 2299-2300,

"Conclusions of the Cultural and Education Committee on Arab Youth."

102. See, for example, Dan Mirkon, *Haaretz*, 30 Oct. 1966.

103. *Al Ittihad*, 28 April 1964.

104. *Maariv*, 25 Sept. 1966.

105. Ibid., 10 Oct. 1966. See also a letter from Mordechai Stein, lawyer, to the club members, in *Maariv*, 18 Oct. 1966.

106. *Al Ittihad*, 9 Jan. 1969.

107. Commenting on the measures taken against Al Ard, one said: "By tracing the administrative development of the affair, we will find that it is all Mapai-made. The minister of justice (a Mapai member) provided the legal basis. The minister of defense (a Mapai member) supplied security information. It is probable that the latter 'ordered' the legal justification from the very beginning. The minister of defense received the information from his deputy (a Mapai member) or his ministry's director general (a Mapai member), who in turn obtained it from their subordinates. The investigation will lead us to the military government people and the security services, all of whom are Mapai activists in the Arab sector. It is needless to point out that Mapai's position among the Arab population has nothing to lean on ideologically speaking. . . . Mapai also has a theory which it has developed over the years . . . and it is this very theory that frightened them. An Arab party would have caused Mapai serious trouble. Hence the conclusion: to make Al Ard its whip against all those who might ever dare to rebel against it. . . ." (Muhammad Watad, "Why was Al Ard Banned?", *New Outlook*, Sept. 1964, pp. 47-48).

108. See also Sabri Jiryis, "Democratic Freedoms in Israel," *New Outlook*, Sept. 1964, pp. 88-90, 98-100.

109. In almost identical circumstances, the change of government policy at the end of the 1950s was a result of the formation of the (Arab) Popular Front.

110. *Maariv*, 6 Aug. 1971.

111. See *Al Ittihad*, 4 Jan. 1966, for various activities of the Arab Students' Committee at the Hebrew University in Jerusalem. See also Landau, *The Arabs*, pp. 54-55.

112. See interview with Arab Students' Committee leaders in *Maariv*, 27 July 1965 and *Haaretz*, 16 Jan. 1966.

113. *Al Ittihad*, 17 Dec. 1971.

114. *Davar*, 23 Aug. 1971, Michael Assaf.

115. *Al Anba'*, 15 Dec. 1971.

116. *Davar*, 12 Dec. 1971 and *Haaretz*, 15 Dec. 1971.

117. See Dr. Haim Zaif Hirschberg's article, "[Islamic] Legal Problems in the State of Israel," *Hamizrah Hehadash*, Jan. 1950, no. 2: 97-108; see also July 1950, no. 4: 264.

118. *Knesset Debates*, 3 Nov. 1953, p. 40, the minister of religions.

119. Shari'a Courts (Validation of Appointments) Law, 5714—1953, LSI 8 (1953/54): 42. See Knesset members Emil Habibi, Rustum Bastuni, and Yohanan Badr (Herut) in *Knesset Debates*, 3 Nov. 1953, pp. 40-47.

120. *Knesset Debates*, 11 May 1960, p. 1217, minister of religions' introduction of the law.

121. Article 4, *Qadis* Law, 5721—1961, LSI 15 (1960/61): 123.

122. *Knesset Debates*, 20 Jan. 1964, p. 810, minister of religions. See also Aharon Layesh, "Muslim Religious Jurisdiction in Israel," *Hamizrah Hehadash*, no. 1-2 (1963): 19-37 and Layesh, "Muslim Religious Jurisdiction in Israel," *Asian and African Studies* (Jerusalem, 1965), pp. 49-79.

123. Muhammad Hebeshi, Shari'a *Qadi* of Acre, in an interview with *Yediot Aharonot*, 24 July 1972.

124. *Knesset Debates*, 6 July 1971, p. 3101, minister of religions. See *Davar*, 28 Jan. 1972, supplement, on official efforts to prevent mixed marriages.

125. See *State Controller's Report for Financial Year 1965/66* 17 (1967): 197.

126. One example is the statement by Dr. Israel Karlbach, editor of *Maariv*, in his article "You can't get on with Allah," *Maariv*, 7 Oct. 1955: "Islam is the enemy of all fruitful ideas, all well-intentioned initiatives and all creative thought. . . . It has contributed nothing of value nor will it do so in future . . . it represents darkness, reaction and the imprisonment of five hundred million beings. . . ."

127. For details, see the periodical *Ramzur*, 19 April 1971.

128. *Kouetz Ha-Takanat (Official Gazette)* 695 (21 April 1957): 1280 and *Knesset Debates*, 19 June 1956, p. 2053.

129. LSI 17 (1962/63): 27. See also Salman H. Falah, "Druze Communal Organization in Israel," *New Outlook*, March-April 1967, pp. 40-44.

130. *Knesset Debates*, 19 Dec. 1962, p. 527.

131. See, for example, Emmanuel Mareuveni in *Maariv*, 8, 9 June 1966 and *Haaretz*, 11, 13, 14 Nov. 1966.

132. *Yediot Aharonot*, 8 Dec. 1972.

133. *Knesset Debates*, 17 June 1968, p. 2260, Levi Eshkol, prime minister, responding to questions.
134. Ibid., 19 Jan. 1972, p. 1052, Golda Meir, prime minister, responding to questions.
135. Ibid., 9 Dec. 1970, p. 447 and 12 May 1971, p. 2479, Yigal Allon, minister of education.
136. Druze Religious Courts (Special Provisions) Law, 5727—1967, LSI 21 (1966/67): 134.
137. *Knesset Debates*, 4 July 1972, pp. 3190-92, minister of religions introducing the bill and Tawfiq Tubi's response.
138. Druze Religious Courts (Amendment 3) Law, 5732—1972, LSI 26 (1971/72): 165.
139. See *Al Ittihad*, 9 Feb. 1971, for example of objection to land expropriation. For examples of objections to military service see *Davar*, 20, 27 Jan. 1972 and *Haaretz*, 28 Jan. 1972, 8 Feb. 1972. By 1970, 108 young Druze had been killed while serving in the Israeli Army and Frontier Guard. For details, see Misbah Halabi, *Brit Damim* (Bloody Oath) (Tel Aviv, 1970).

Chapter 8: Education, Economics, and Services

1. *Israel Government Yearbook* 5722 (1961/62): 25.
2. See, for example, Simha Flapan, "National Inequality in Israel," *New Outlook*, Nov.-Dec. 1964, pp. 24-36.
3. See the statements of the Knesset Education Committee, *Knesset Debates*, 24 Jan. 1962, p. 1057.
4. Compulsory Education Law, 5709—1949, LSI 3 (1949): 125 (Articles 2, 4, 6, 7, and 8).
5. Compulsory Education (Temporary Provision) Law, 5731—1971, LSI 25 (1970/71): 139.
6. *Israel Government Yearbook* 5731 (1970/71): 143. See also *Knesset Debates*, 21 Dec. 1971, p. 705, Avner Shaki, deputy minister of education.
7. *Israel Government Yearbook* 5731 (1970/71): 143; 5727 (1966/67): 100.
8. See also *Statistical Abstract of Israel* (1971): 552.
9. See also *Knesset Debates*, 31 Dec. 1963, p. 625, Kalman Kahana, deputy minister of education, responding to questions.
10. Compare with *Statistical Abstract* (1972): 581, 590; (1971): 552,

555. See also Knesset Debates, 4 Feb. 1970, p. 686, Yigal Allon, minister of education.

11. *Knesset Debates*, 26 Aug. 1952, p. 3131, Ben-Zion Dinor, minister of education.

12. Ibid., 12 May 1971, p. 2383, Allon. See also *Haaretz*, 9 March 1971.

13. Ibid., 5 May 1953, p. 1230, Dinor.

14. Dr. Haveh Lystros-Yafeh, professor of Oriental Studies at the Hebrew University in Jerusalem, commented on the standard of these books and the way they were written in a letter published in *Haaretz* 11 March 1971. She warned of "academic, moral, and political gaps, resulting from the publication of studies about the Arabs and textbooks for Arabs compiled by writers who do not have a thorough knowledge of Arabic and have not studied the history of the Arabs or Islamic culture," adding that "it is impossible to achieve any results merely by having a discussion with an Arab through an interpreter, or by asking a few questions. . . . in the same way it is impossible to study curricula relating to national aspects of the Arab minority in Israel without taking into consideration the problems that confront the Arabs and the Arab countries in this respect. Superficial and marginal proposals are inadequate when confronting such basic problems."

15. *Knesset Debates*, 19 Oct. 1966, p. 52, Aharon Yedlen, deputy minister of education; *Israel Government Yearbook* 5731 (1970/71): 143.

16. Shmuel Moreh, "A catalogue of books, papers, and magazines published in Israel in the Arabic language, from 1948 until the end of April 1964," *Hamizrah Hehadash* 14, no. 2-3 (1964): 296-309 and "A catalogue of books, papers, and magazines published in Israel in the Arabic language from May 1964 until 1971," *Hamizrah Hehadash* 21, no. 2 (1971): 218-30.

17. *Knesset Debates*, 13 May 1964, p. 1787, Zalman Aranne, minister of education, answering questions.

18. Ibid., 5 Aug. 1953, p. 2157, Dinor, on taxing power.

19. Ibid., 21 July 1961, p. 1401.

20. See discussions in *Knesset Debates*, 13 May 1964, pp. 1785-90, 1794-95.

21. Ibid., 24 June 1964, pp. 2157-60, 2173.

22. See *Israel Government Yearbook* 5731 (1970/71): 144; 5728 (1967/68): 125; 5727 (1966/67): 100; 5726 (1965/66): 108; and 5725 (1964/65): 111.

23. *Knesset Debates*, 1 July 1970, p. 2304, Allon.

24. Ibid., 21 Dec. 1971, p. 707, Shaki.

25. *Haaretz*, 16 Aug. 1971. See also Butrus Abu Mana, "Spotlight on Arab Students," *New Outlook*, March 1965, pp. 45-48 and Anis Abu Hanna, "Arabs at the Hebrew University," *New Outlook*, July-August 1958, pp. 54-56.

26. By 1964 there were only ten Arab doctors who had completed their studies in Israeli universities and eighteen others who were finishing their studies at the Medical School of the Hebrew University in Jerusalem (*Knesset Debates*, 23 June 1964, p. 2141, Yitzhak Rafael, minister of health, answering questions).

27. *Statistical Abstract* (1972): 578, 580.

28. *Knesset Debates*, 24 Feb. 1960, p. 717, statement of Ami Asaf, deputy minister of education.

29. For the findings of the committee see *Knesset Debates*, 24 Jan. 1962, pp. 1057-59.

30. For a comprehensive picture of Arab education in İsrael through 1972, see the articles by Nahman Fabian in *Haaretz*, 5, 6, 7, 8 Dec. 1972.

31. Ministry of Education and Culture, "Curriculum for Elementary Government Arab Schools; Grades Five to Eight," November 1959, p. 50.

32. Ibid., p. 47.

33. Ibid., pp. 160-61.

34. Ibid., pp. 389, 401.

35. Ministry of Education and Culture, Department of Arab Education, "History Program," 1 Jan. 1961.

36. Ministry of Education and Culture, "Teaching Program for Grades One to Four," October 1957, pp. 2-3 and "Teaching Program for Grades Five to Eight," November 1959, p. 6.

37. For details, see Yochanan Peres, Avishai Ehrlich, and Nira Yuval-Davis, "National Education for Arab Youth in Israel: A Comparative Analysis of Curricula," *The Jewish Journal of Sociology* (London), December 1970, pp. 147-63.

38. *Knesset Debates*, 12 May 1971, p. 2383, Allon.

39. From the recommendations of a government committee for modifications in the Arab curricula, as quoted in *Haaretz*, 9 March 1971. For a sample of the Arab curricula in various subjects, with the books used in class, see Majed Ursan Kilani, *Zionist Inspiration in Curricula for the Arabs in Israel* (Amman, 1972).

40. Peres et al., "National Education for Arab Youth," p. 162.

41. These figures are from 1950 and 1963 statistics as cited by *Knesset Debates*, 30 June 1964, p. 2192, Tawfiq Tubi proposing a bill to guarantee land for Arab peasants. See also Haim Halperin, *Changes in Israeli Agriculture* (Tel Aviv, 1957), pp. 107-23, in Hebrew.

42. The Collective Planning Center for Agriculture and Settlement and the Ministry of Agriculture, Nazareth Branch, *Results of the Census and Project A for Agricultural Development* (Nazareth, July 1963), pp. 2, 3, in Hebrew. See, for comparison, Central Bureau of Statistics, *Census of Agriculture, 1949/50 Part A—Farm Economy of the Arabs, Druze, and other Minority Groups*, special series no. 8 (Jerusalem, 1952).

43. *Results of the Census*, p. 2.

44. See, for example, the debate following the confiscation of the olive harvest in the village of Rama, *Knesset Debates*, 6 Aug. 1952, pp. 2858-59.

45. *Knesset Debates*, 18 Dec. 1951, p. 686, Levi Eshkol, minister of agriculture and development.

46. Ibid.

47. Ibid., 7 May 1952, p. 1946.

48. Ibid., 13 Aug. 1952, p. 2923, Peretz Naphthali, minister of agriculture.

49. Ibid., 23 June 1959, p. 2331 and 29 March 1971, p. 2121, Kadish Loz, minister of agriculture, and Ben-Zion Halfon, deputy minister of agriculture.

50. For the committee's recommendations see *Knesset Debates*, 5 Dec. 1956, pp. 424-25.

51. *Knesset Debates*, 5 June 1962, p. 2179, Moshe Dayan, minister of agriculture, in a progress report.

52. *Knesset Debates*, 20 March 1969, p. 2138, the findings of the Economic Committee concerning the cultivation, marketing, and pricing of tobacco.

53. Ibid., pp. 2138-39.

54. See the committee's findings on the marketing of Arab crops in *Knesset Debates*, 27 June 1962, p. 2503.

55. *Statistical Abstract* (1972): 352; (1963): 234-37, 240-43.

56. For details see reports by various ministers of agriculture: *Knesset Debates*, 31 March 1959, p. 1781; 5 June 1962, p. 2179; 17 April 1967, p. 1696; 8 Feb. 1968, p. 1211; 4 March 1968, p. 1261.

57. Research into the condition of agriculture in Israel in 1960 revealed that the average income of an Arab working in agriculture at that

time ranged between 1500 and 1700 pounds per annum, while the average income of his Jewish equivalent was 3,123 pounds per annum (Shaul Zarhi and A. Achiezra, *The Economic Conditions of the Arab Minority in Israel*, Givat Haviva, Center for Arab and Afro-Asian Studies, 1966, p. 16).

58. See also Yaacov Shimoni, *Palestine Arabs* (Tel Aviv, 1947), pp. 359-71.

59. On Histadrut's actions during the British Mandate see Zvi Ben-Shoshan, *The History of the Labor Movement in the Land of Israel* (Tel Aviv, 1966) 3: 156-64, in Hebrew. See also Moshe Braslavsky, *The Labor Movement in the Land of Israel* (1959) 3: 440-42.

60. *Knesset Debates*, 23 Dec. 1953, p. 454, Moshe Sneh.

61. See Yoram Ben-Porath, *The Arab Labor Force in Israel* (Jerusalem: The Falk Institute for Economic Research in Israel, 1966), pp. 51-52.

62. Ibid., p. 55.

63. See Michael Assaf, "Development of Arab Integration into the State of Israel," *Hamizrah Hehadash* 1 (1949): 5. See also Yosef Fashitz, *Hamizrah Hehadash* 4 (1950): 260-61; Moshe Braslavsky, "The Labor Movement in the Land of Israel," *Hamizrah Hehadash* 4 (1959): 177, 219-21, 224.

64. *Knesset Debates*, 20 Nov. 1950, pp. 265-66, Meir Vilner and Jonah Kiseh.

65. Ben-Porath, *Arab Labor Force*, p. 56.

66. *Knesset Debates*, 15 May 1961, p. 1684 and 26 March 1957, p. 1513, Giora Josephthal and Mordechai Namir, ministers of labor.

67. Aharon Cohen, *Israel and the Arab World* (Tel Aviv: Merhavya, 1964), pp. 530-32.

68. At the tenth congress of the Histadrut held in early January 1966, a motion was carried (558-91) to remove the word "Jewish" from the Histadrut's name. The majority of those opposing the motion were Rafi members acting on Ben-Gurion's instructions. Another motion to substitute "Israel" for "Land of Israel" was rejected. Since then the Histadrut's name has been the General Federation of Workers in the Land of Israel (*Maariv*, 7 Jan. 1966 and *Al Ittihad*, 11 Jan. 1966).

69. *Haaretz*, 18 Jan. 1959, Habib Canaan.

70. Employment Service Law, 5719—1959, LSI 13 (1958/59): 29.

71. Moshe Bartal, "The Histadrut and the Arabs," *New Outlook*, March-April 1963, p. 48.

72. Arab department, Histadrut's Executive Committee, "Collected Facts on the Activities of the Histadrut among the Arabs," June-December 1971, 34: 7.
73. See also Y. Gilboa's article, *Haaretz*, 19 Jan. 1960.
74. Compare with Yigal Allon, minister of labor, in *Knesset Debates*, 10 July 1962, p. 2655.
75. *Yediot Aharonot*, 4 Jan. 1963.
76. Zeev Schiff, *Haaretz*, 19 Oct. 1962.
77. Ibid.
78. Bartal, "The Histadrut and the Arabs," p. 48.
79. *Knesset Debates*, 14 July 1964, Allon. For more details about these working conditions, see the complaints of Arab Knesset members and ensuing debates: *Knesset Debates*, 9 Feb. 1960, pp. 599-600; 14 Jan. 1964, 769-71; 14 July 1964, pp. 2355-61; 13 Feb. 1965, pp. 135-37; and 1 Feb. 1967, pp. 1123-27.
80. *Israel Government Yearbook* 5724 (1963/64): 32, 38.
81. *Knesset Debates*, 22 June 1964, p. 2124, Joseph Almoghi, minister of labor.
82. Ibid., 3 Jan. 1968, p. 622, the findings of the labor committee.
83. *Maariv*, 24 Nov. 1964.
84. See *Maariv*, 8 Feb. 1963, for a description of this system.
85. *Knesset Debates*, 4 Dec. 1963, p. 425, Allon.
86. Ibid., 18 July 1972, p. 3418, Almoghi.
87. See findings of the labor committee on Arab unemployment in the years 1967, 1968 in *Knesset Debates*, 18 Dec. 1968, p. 789.
88. *Knesset Debates*, 31 July 1968, p. 2981, Zeev Sharef, minister of trade and industry.
89. Ibid., 23 July 1956, p. 2356, Ben-Gurion, prime minister, and statements by the ministers of interior, trade and commerce, communications, labor, agriculture, and religions in *Knesset Debates*, 4, 10, 11, 17 March 1964, pp. 1294, 1347, 1378, 1419; 28 April 1964, p. 1621; and 13 May 1964, p. 1775.
90. *Knesset Debates*, 23 March 1964, p. 1503, Bikhur Shitrit, minister of police.
91. *Knesset Debates*, 8 June 1970, p. 2022, Shlomo Hillel, minister of police, in a progress report.
92. Moshe Maoz, "Local Government in the Arab Communities in Israel," *Hamizrah Hehadash* 12, no. 3 (1962): 235.
93. See statements of Emil Habibi and Rustum Bastuni and the response of the minister of interior in *Knesset Debates*, 29 July 1953, pp. 2067-68 and 10 Aug. 1953, p. 2170.

94. *Knesset Debates*, 30 June 1955, p. 2216, findings of the interior committee.
95. Ibid., 28 March 1963, p. 1736, findings of the interior committee.
96. Ibid., 20 Jan. 1971, p. 1064, Joseph Burg, minister of interior.
97. Central Bureau of Statistics, *Results of the Elections to the Sixth Knesset and Local Authorities . . . and Results of the Elections to the Seventh Knesset . . .* , special series nos. 216, 309: 283-381, 202-65. See also *Kouetz Ha-Takanot (Official Gazette)* 1510, 1511 (4 Feb. 1969): 997, 1013; 1832 (23 May 1972): 1879-89; 1835 (8 June 1972): 1772-73.
98. See debate over bill in *Knesset Debates*, 27 Dec. 1967, pp. 549-62.
99. *Knesset Debates*, 28 March 1963, p. 1736.
100. Ibid.
101. Ibid., 20 Jan. 1971, p. 1064, Burg.
102. *Israel Government Yearbook* 5727 (1966/67): 34. See also *Knesset Debates*, 24 July 1963, p. 2500 and 6 March 1967, p. 1553, Moshe Kohl and Joseph Almoghi, ministers of development.
103. Benjamin Shidlovsky, "Changes in the Development of the Arab Village in Israel," *Hamizrah Hehadash* 15 (1965): 26. At the beginning of 1973, the responsible Israeli authority was studying a project for tying forty Arab villages in northern Israel to the electric power network (*Davar*, 25 March 1973).
104. Shidlovsky, "Changes," p. 29.
105. Abraham Daniel, *Cooperatives—A Prophecy and its Realization* (Tel Aviv, 1972), p. 262, in Hebrew. See also pp. 251-63 for general information on Arab cooperatives. See also Gad Ben-Meir, "The Development of Arab Cooperatives in Israel," *New Outlook*, July 1961, pp. 31-36 and "Trial and Error in Arab Cooperatives," *New Outlook*, July 1959, pp. 54-57.
106. For details see *Israel Government Yearbook* 5726 (1965/66): 31. See also "The Economics of Integration," *New Outlook*, March-April 1962, pp. 7-33.
107. For details see Uri Standel, *Minorities* (Jerusalem: Ministry of Education and Culture, 1970), p. 57.
108. Based on Shidlovsky's estimates, "Changes," p. 28.
109. *Haaretz*, 23 Sept. 1971. See also summaries of the views of what is called the "intellectual circle" of the Labor Party in *Davar*, 21 Jan. 1973.
110. Central Bureau of Statistics, *Results of the Elections*, special series nos. 216, 309: 283-381, 202-65.
111. See articles by Elie Alad, "Family Rule in Minority Villages,"

Haaretz, 14 Nov. 1969 and Atallah Mansour and Nahman Fabian, *Haaretz*, 10 Nov. 1965 and 23 May 1972.

112. *Davar*, 15 Dec. 1969. See also statement by Tawfiq Tubi and response by Josef Goldschmidt, deputy minister of interior, in *Knesset Debates*, 7 Jan. 1970, pp. 436-39.

113. One of the measures taken by the ministry of interior in 1965 to depose Yammi Yammi, chairman of the local council in Kfar Yasif and a founder and leading member of the (Arab) Popular Front, was an order demoting the council (which is the oldest Arab council in Israel, dating back to 1925) from class A to class B. This was followed by a second order, "in the interest of the residents," appointing two new members to the council—both belonging to the minister's party—which resulted in the "election" of a new chairman. The Supreme Court, however, subsequently annulled these measures. See also *Knesset Debates*, 6 Jan. 1965, p. 846, for statements by Ben-Meir, deputy minister of interior, and pp. 857-60 for further discussions.

114. See, for example, *Al Ittihad*, 24 March 1969.

115. *Knesset Debates*, 20 Jan. 1971, p. 1064 and 12 Jan. 1972, p. 981.

116. See, for example, requests made to the government by representatives of the Arab local authorities in *Al Ittihad*, 25 Feb. 1966, 3 May 1967, and 30 July 1968.

Appendix

Tables

Table 1
Jewish and Arab Population of Israel[1]

Year	Total population	Jews	Arabs	% Arabs
11/8/1948	834,317	716,678	117,639	14.1
1949	1,173,871	1,013,871	160,000	13.6
1950	1,370,094	1,202,993	167,101	12.2
1951	1,577,825	1,404,392	173,433	11
1952	1,629,519	1,450,217	179,302	11
1953	1,669,417	1,483,641	185,776	11.1
1954	1,717,814	1,526,009	191,805	11.2
1955	1,789,075	1,590,519	198,556	11.1
1956	1,872,390	1,667,455	204,935	10.9
1957	1,975,954	1,762,741	213,213	10.8
1958	2,031,672	1,810,148	221,524	10.9
1959	2,088,685	1,858,841	229,844	11
1960	2,150,358	1,911,189	239,169	11.1
1961 (May 22)	2,179,491	1,932,357	247,134	11.3
1962	2,331,801	2,068,882	262,919	11.3
1963	2,430,125	2,155,551	274,574	11.3
1964	2,525,562	2,239,177	286,385	11.3
1965	2,598,424	2,299,078	299,346	11.5
1966	2,657,410	2,344,877	312,533	11.8
1967	2,708,082	2,383,554	324,528	12.8
1968	2,772,012	2,434,832	337,180	12.1
1969	2,847,745	2,496,438	351,307	12.3
1970	2,928,056	2,561,400	366,656	12.5
1971	3,018,900	2,636,600	382,300	12.7

Table 2

Distribution of the Arab Population According to Geographic/Administrative Regions[2]
(in numbers and percentage)

Date	Total	Northern District (Acre, Nazareth, Safad and Tiberias)	District of Haifa	Central District (Ramle and Petah Tikvah)	District of Tel Aviv (Jaffa)	District of Jerusalem	Southern District (Beer Sheba)
11/8/1948	117,634	86,378	9,876	2,616	3,772	1,575	13,417
12/31/1955	198,456	131,669	20,845	22,567	6,500	3,375	13,500
5/22/1961	247,134	142,743	48,016	26,932	6,662	4,172	18,609
12/31/1966	312,533	180,169	61,646	34,618	7,381	4,837	23,882
12/31/1971	382,300	219,500	74,600	43,300	8,800	5,400	30,700
11/8/1948	100	73.4	8.4	2.2	3.2	1.4	11.4
12/31/1955	100	66.3	10.5	11.4	3.3	1.7	6.8
5/22/1961	100	57.8	19.4	10.9	2.7	1.7	7.5
12/31/1966	100	57.6	19.7	11.1	2.4	1.6	7.6
12/31/1971	100	57.4	19.5	11.4	2.3	1.4	8.0

Table 3
Distribution of the Arab Population
According to Type of Settlement[3]
(in numbers and percentage)

Date	Total population	Total in cities	Arab cities	Cities of mixed population	Villages	Nomads
12/31/1955	198,556	52,050	20,406	31,644	125,214	21,292
5/22/1961	247,134	63,450	32,272	31,178	156,670	27,014
12/31/1966	312,533	98,947	39,200	59,747	181,108	32,478
12/31/1971	382,300	119,400	49,400	70,000	222,800	40,100
12/31/1955	100	26.2	10.3	15.9	63.1	10.7
5/22/1971	100	25.7	13.1	12.6	63.4	10.9
12/31/1966	100	31.7	12.6	19.1	57.9	10.4
12/31/1971	100	31.2	12.9	18.3	58.3	10.5

Table 4
Division of Arab Population
According to Religious Affiliation[4]
(in numbers and percentages)

	Total	Moslems	Christians	Druze
12/31/1955	198,556	136,256	43,300	19,000
5/22/1961	247,134	172,309	50,543	24,282
12/31/1966	312,533	223,000	58,507	31,026
12/31/1971	382,300	345,000		37,300
12/31/1955	100	68.6	21.8	9.6
5/22/1961	100	69.7	20.5	9.8
12/31/1966	100	71.4	18.7	9.9
12/31/1971	100	90.2		9.8

Table 5
Land Lost by Some Arab Villages in Israel Between 1945 and 1962[5]
(in dunums)

Village	Land area in 1945	Land area in 1962	Land expropriated 1953-54	Source: Israeli Facts		
				Number	Date	Page
1. Abu Sinan	12,871	5,434	1,811	298	6/25/1953	1157
2. Aksal	13,666	4,396				
3. Umm al Fahm						
4. Mu'awiya						
5. Masmas	68,311	12,006	34,600	324	12/17/1953	298
6. Al Mshirfa						
7. Ein Ibrahim						
8. Baqa al Gharbiya	21,116	8,228	10,400	319	11/12/1953	155
9. Beisan						
Ein al Asad	25,594	10,204				
10. Beit Naqubah	1,958	807				
11. B'einya	6,793	1,882				
12. Bi'na	14,839	3,679				
13. Buqai'eh	10,276	3,500	235	352	5/30/1954	1116
14. Al Jadidah	5,215	1,728	1,148	352	5/30/1954	1118
15. Juless	12,835	6,010		350	5/23/1954	1035-36
16. Jaljulya	11,873	2,237	11,411	352	5/30/1954	1129
				355	6/13/1954	1257

17. Jisr al Zarqa	2,531	309	268	355	6/13/1954	1230
18. Jish	12,430	2,026	4,062	352	5/30/1954	1099-1105
19. Jatt (Galilee)	5,907	1,727				155
20. Jatt (Triangle)	9,623	5,415	4,975	319	11/12/1953	
				350	5/23/1954	1037
21. Dalyet al Karmel	19,741	13,026				
22. Daburiya	13,373	2,974				
23. Dahi	3,011	2,029				
24. Deir al Asad	8,366	2,251				
25. Deir Hanna	15,350	5,090				
26. Zalfa	1,285	807				
27. Harfish	14,623	5,254	2,950	298	6/25/1953	1154
28. Tubah (Heib Bedouins)	13,684	1,772				
29. Tayba (Triangle)	32,750	13,343	4,540	322	12/3/1953	241
				325	12/24/1953	325-26
				337	3/11/1954	710
				347	5/12/1954	938, 949
				350	5/23/1954	1040
				352	5/30/1954	1127
				355	6/13/1954	1240, 1250, 1258, 1263
30. Tayba (Nazareth)	7,127	2,135				
31. Tira	26,803	8,599	5,232	231	1/28/1954	525-26
				347	5/12/1954	938-40
				350	5/23/1954	1033, 1037, 1055
				352	5/30/1954	1123-25
				355	6/13/1954	1263

Village	Land area in 1945	Land area in 1962	Land expropriated 1953–54	Source: Israeli Facts		
				Number	Date	Page
32. Tamra (Nazareth)	3,604	1,269				
33. Tamra (Acre)	30,549	14,489				
34. Tar'an	13,104	7,150				
35. Yanuh	12,466	1,343				
36. Yafa al Nasra	16,521	4,887	542	319	11/12/1953	156
37. Yarka	30,597	10,701				
38. Kabul	10,320	5,345	2,260	331	1/28/1954	527
39. Kawkab	2,134	1,235				
40. Kfar Barra	3,956	1,816	828	350	5/23/1954	1039
				355	6/13/1954	1245
41. Kfar Yasif	6,729	4,581	763	352	5/30/1954	1115
42. Kfar Kama	8,395	6,338				
43. Kfar Kana	18,869	7,868				
44. Kfar Manda	12,703	4,998				
45. Kfar Masr	4,629	1,889	423	335	2/25/1954	639
46. Kfar Samai	7,150	2,436				
47. Kfar Kassim	12,718	3,924	3,880	352	5/30/1954	1140
48. Kfar Kara	14,543	2,618	12,964	352	5/30/1954	1121-23
59. Majd al Kurum	17,828	4,237				
50. Mazra'a	3,116	298	1,548	319	11/12/1953	156
				355	6/13/1954	1225
51. Makr	8,661	3,884	2,554	352	5/30/1954	1117

52. Mi'lya	19,136	2,997	12,800	317	10/29/1953	107
53. Muqiblah	2,687	2,196				
54. Mashhad	9,852	4,236				
55. Maghar	45,590	12,227				
56. Na'urah	5,535	3,482				
57. Nazareth	12,599	8,325				
58. Nahf	15,654	4,454				
59. Nin	3,737	1,887				
60. Sajour	8,172	1,533	2,640	331	1/28/1954	528
61. Sulim	2,358	1,629				
62. Sachnin	70,181	25,775				
63. Ablin	16,019	10,206				
64. Azir	764	566				
65. Ailbun	11,190	3,772				
66. Elot	10,891	2,359	4,125	352	5/30/1954	1108
67. Ein Mahil	8,268	2,576	387	332	2/4/1954	552
68. Assifiya	16,811	9,681	550	317	10/29/1953	107
				355	6/13/1954	1217
69. Arava	30,852	18,421	8,236	307	8/27/1953	1422
70. Ar'arah (and Arah)	29,537	7,269				
71. Frideis	4,220	1,595				
72. Sandala	3,217	1,255				
73. Qalansuwa	17,249	6,620	5,505	332	2/4/1954	554
				347	5/12/1954	946, 949
				350	5/23/1954	1055
				352	5/30/1954	1127, 1139
				355	6/13/1954	1232, 1240

Village	Land area in 1945	Land area in 1962	Land expropriated 1953-54	Source: *Israeli Facts*		
				Number	Date	Page
74. Rama	23,701	7,322				
75. Rihaniya	6,112	1,607				
76. Rineh	15,899	5,880				
77. Ramana	1,485	271				
78. Shafa Amr	58,725	10,371	7,579	326	12/31/1953	349
Total	1,080,984	376,686	149,216			

Table 6
Arab Knesset Members and Their Affiliations[6]

Knesset	Date elected	Number of Arab members			Total (out of 120)
		Arab lists	Israel Communist Party	Mapam	
First	1/25/1949	2	1	—	3
Second	7/30/1951	5	2	1	8
Third	7/26/1955	5	2	1**	8
Fourth	11/3/1959	5	1	1	7
Fifth	8/15/1961	4	2*	1	7
Sixth	11/2/1965	4	2	1	7†
Seventh	10/28/1969	4	2	1	7

* One member, Emil Habibi, began on 10/4/1961 and resigned on 2/15/1972.
** After 9/21/1955.
† Starting on 5/5/1964 and until the end of the sixth Knesset in 1965, another Arab, Saleem Jabbara, was a member of the Knesset; he took the place of a Jewish member of Achdut Haavoda who resigned.

Table 7

Distribution of Arab Votes Among Election Lists[7]

(in Arab districts only)

List	Fourth Knesset (1959)		Fifth Knesset (1961)		Sixth Knesset (1965)		Seventh Knesset (1969)	
	Number of votes	Percentage	Number of votes	Percentage	Number of votes	Percentage	Number of votes	Percentage
Total votes	71,723	100	76,918	100	88,102	100	101,109	100
Arab lists	42,029	58.6	35,026	45.5	37,799	42.9	41,205	40.8
Israeli Communist Party (Maki)	8,097	11.3	17,287	22.5	511	0.6	744	0.7
New Communist List (Rakah)	—	—	—	—	20,691	23.5	29,871	29.5
Mapai	3,304	4.6	6,268	8.1 }		7,487	8.5 }	13,464	13.3 }
Achdut Haavoda	647	0.9	3,682	4.8				
Mapam	10,363	14.4	9,232	12.0	9,087	10.3 }		
Kafi	—	—	—	—	2,475	2.8	992	1.0
Religious parties	2,762	3.9	3,236	4.2	4,868	5.5	8,834	8.7
Rightist parties	3,474	4.8	2,078	2.7	3,017	3.5	3,429	3.5
Haolam Hazeh (Avineri)	—	—	—	—	1,797	2.0	1,233	1.2
Others	1,047	1.5	109	0.2	370	0.4	1,337	1.3

Table 8

Distribution of the Arab Vote in the Arab Districts According to Settlement and List[8]

	Arab cities		Large Arab villages		Small Arab villages		Bedouins	
	Number of votes	Percentage	Number of votes	Percentage	Number of votes	Percentage	Number of votes	Percentage
Fourth Knesset (1959)								
Total votes	11,153	100.0	31,819	100.0	21,643	100.0	7,108	100.0
Arab lists	5,725	51.3	19,867	62.4	13,141	60.7	3,269	46.0
Communists	2,959	26.5	3,978	12.5	1,100	5.1	60	0.8
Other lists	2,469	22.2	7,974	25.1	7,402	34.2	3,779	53.2
Fifth Knesset (1961)								
Total votes	12,005	100.0	34,286	100.0	22,465	100.0	8,162	100.0
Arab lists	4,426	36.9	15,912	46.4	10,267	45.7	4,421	54.2
Communists	5,399	45.0	8,753	25.5	2,918	13.0	217	2.7
Other lists	2,180	18.1	9,621	28.1	9,280	41.3	3,524	43.1
Sixth Knesset (1965)								
Total votes	20,468	100.0	39,737	100.0	19,821	100.0	8,076	100.0
Arab lists	7,672	37.5	17,559	44.2	8,540	43.1	4,028	49.9
Communists	8,552	41.8	9,181	23.1	2,593	13.1	365	4.5
Other lists	4,244	20.7	12,997	32.7	8,688	43.8	3,683	45.6
Seventh Knesset (1969)								
Total votes	23,349	100.0	50,865	100.0	16,784	100.0	10,111	100.0
Arab lists	8,647	37.0	19,292	37.9	8,055	48.0	5,211	51.5
Communists	11,056	47.4	16,103	31.7	2,197	13.1	515	5.1
Other lists	3,646	15.6	15,470	30.4	6,532	38.9	4,385	43.4

Table 9
Communist Votes in Knesset and
Local Government Elections
in Some Arab Settlements[9]

Town/ Village	1965		1969	
	Knesset	Local government	Knesset	Local government
Shafa Amr	1,090	265	1,671	575
Abu Sinan	—	—	551	385
Aksal	270	113	519	400
Umm al Fahm	—	—	1,491	753
Baqa al Gharbiya	474	92	583	109
Tayba	1,423	542	2,320	556
Tira	835	160	1,592	303
Tamrah	—	—	696	176
Yafa al Nasra	—	—	863	467
Qalansuwa	—	—	746	102
Rameh	243	107	630	203
Total	4,335	1,279	11,662	4,029

Table 10
Number of Youths of Compulsory School Age,
Those Attending School, and Percentages of Each Group in School[10]

Year	Population aged 5-14		Students in elementary school and kindergarten				Percentage			
				Arabs				Arabs		
	Jews	Arabs	Jews	Public schools	Private schools	Total	Jews	Public schools	Private schools	Total
1954/55	316,009	53,504	288,876	24,625	9,099	33,724	91.4	46	17	63
1957/58	412,092	59,000	394,830	30,393	8,655	39,048	95.8	51.5	14.7	66.2
1960/61	463,159	66,836	436,702	39,285	11,047	50,332	94.3	58.8	16.5	75.3
1963/64	501,855	81,315	473,811	49,773	11,804	61,577	94.4	61.2	14.5	75.7
1966/67	491,150	95,432	480,127	61,050	13,658	74,708	97.8	64	14.3	78.3
1968/69	493,464	126,875	482,131	71,335	27,908	99,243	97.7	56.2	22	78.2
1970/71	502,400	138,000	477,375	—	—	104,343	95	—	—	75.6
Average 1954/55 to 1970/71	455,591	84,373	441,082	46,338	12,976	61,923	96.8	54.9	15.4	70.3

Table 11
Percentage of Arab Students
Passing Baghrot *Examinations*[11]

School year	Percent passes	School year	Percent passes
1957/58	8.6	1963/64	21
1958/59	6.7	1964/65	27
1959/60	9.5	1965/66	no data
1960/61	13.1	1966/67	23.6
1961/62	10.3	1967/68	29.8
1962/63	16.7	1968/69	30.4

Table 12
Number of Secondary School Students and Holders of Baghrot Diploma
and Their Proportion Among Jews and Arabs[12]

Year	Population		Students in secondary school		Per 10,000 of each population		Students attaining Baghrot diploma		Per 10,000 of each population	
	Jews	Arabs	Jews	Arabs	Jews	Arabs	Jews	Arabs	Jews	Arabs
1954/55	1,590,519	198,556	14,469	710	91.0	35.8	2,520	38	15.8	1.9
1957/58	1,810,148	221,524	16,728	945	92.4	42.6	2,698	60	14.9	2.7
1960/61	1,932,357	247,134	30,015	1,086	155.3	43.9	3,464	94	17.9	3.8
1963/64	2,239,177	286,385	42,296	1,340	188.9	46.8	7,173	82	32.0	2.9
1966/67	2,383,554	324,582	53,577	1,846	224.8	56.9	10,588	144	44.4	4.4
1968/69	2,496,438	422,734	59,033	2,961	236.5	70.0	10,347	164	41.4	3.9
1970/71	2,636,600	458,500	58,199	6,933	220.7	151.2	10,693	250	40.6	5.5
Average 1954/55 to 1970/71	2,126,685	296,599	37,557	1,838	176.6	62	6,228	112	29.3	3.8
Total number of students holding Baghrot diploma from 1954/55 to 1970/71 and their proportion among the population up to 12/31/1971							105,868	1,903	401.5	41.5

Table 13
Workers According to Economic Sector[13]

	Agriculture, forestry, fishing	Manufacture, metals, stone quarries	Electricity, water	Construction, public works	Trade, hotels and restaurants	Transportation, communications, storage	Public service and office workers	Personal service, entertainment, etc.	Not known	Total number of workers
November 1955										
Jews	81,000	121,200	11,700	48,800	75,300	34,500	119,300	47,000	3,500	542,300
Percentage	14.9	22.3	2.2	9	13.9	6.4	22	8.7	0.6	100
Arabs	21,200	5,800	200	5,500	3,300	1,500	4,000	1,100	800	43,400
Percentage	48.8	13.4	0.4	12.7	7.6	3.6	9.2	2.5	1.8	100
1959										
Jews	89,000	149,400	15,200	57,300	77,500	45,100	143,000	48,800	2,500	627,800
Percentage	14.2	23.8	2.4	9.1	12.3	7.2	22.8	7.8	0.4	100
Arabs	21,400	7,700	700	6,300	3,300	1,900	4,400	1,700	200	47,600
Percentage	45	16.2	1.5	13.2	6.9	4	9.2	3.6	0.4	100
1962										
Jews	89,500	186,600	15,500	64,100	94,200	45,600	163,400	58,300	2,200	719,400
Percentage	12.4	26	2.2	8.9	13.1	6.3	22.7	8.1	0.3	100
Arabs	26,000	8,300	400	11,100	4,400	2,200	4,000	1,700	—	58,100
Percentage	44.7	14.3	0.7	19.1	7.6	3.8	6.9	2.9	—	100

1965

Jews	89,000	211,400	14,800	77,200	105,200	56,400	192,500	61,800	2,200	810,500
Percentage	11	26.1	1.8	9.5	13	7	23.7	7.6	0.3	100
Arabs	25,400	11,500	700	14,800	5,200	3,700	5,500	1,800	100	68,700
Percentage	37	16.7	1	21.5	7.6	5.4	8	2.6	0.2	100

1968

Jews	76,100	223,000	18,300	57,500	112,500	61,100	206,900	70,300	2,400	828,100
Percentage	9.2	26.9	2.2	6.9	13.6	7.4	25	8.5	0.3	100
Arabs	25,600	13,700	1,000	15,500	8,100	5,200	9,200	4,400	100	82,800
Percentage	30.9	16.6	1.2	18.7	9.8	6.3	11.1	5.3	0.1	100

1971

Jews	63,300	227,300	10,800	66,300	169,300	67,900	227,500	67,800	2,300	902,500
Percentage	7	25.2	1.2	7.4	18.8	7.5	25.2	7.5	0.2	100
Arabs	21,200	12,300	200	22,000	13,800	6,100	13,800	5,000	200	94,600
Percentage	22.4	13	0.2	23.2	14.6	6.5	14.6	5.3	0.2	100

Table 14
Tobacco Production and Prices[14]

| Year | Tons | | Tens of thousands of pounds | | Price per ton of Jewish tobacco | Price per ton of Arab tobacco | Price difference per ton between Jewish and Arab crop | |
	Jewish crop	Arab crop	Value of Jewish crop	Value of Arab crop	Pounds		In pounds	As percent of Arab price
1950/51	105	1800	158	1530	1505	850	655	77.0
1954/55	185	2150	403	2752	2178	1280	898	70.1
1958/59	300	2100	745	2856	2483	1360	1123	82.5
1962/63	50	60	198	133	3960	2217	1743	78.6
1966/67	280	1920	1248	6340	4457	3302	1155	35.0
1970/71	200	900	1000	3200	5000	3556	1444	40.6
Average 1950/51 to 1970/71	208	1642	683	328	3284	1998	1286	64.4

Table 15
Olive Production and Prices[15]

Year	Jewish crop	Arab crop	Value of Jewish crop	Value of Arab crop	Price per ton of Jewish olives	Price per ton of Arab olives	Price difference per ton between Jewish and Arab crop	
	Tons		Tens of thousands of pounds		Pounds		In pounds	As percent of Arab price
1950/51	950	1750	275	340	289.5	194.3	95.2	49.0
1954/55	1000	1800	518	725	518.0	402.7	115.3	28.3
1958/59	4000	4000	2125	1464	531.3	368	163.3	44.4
1962/63	4800	8200	4235	4906	882.3	598.3	284.0	47.4
1966/67	8000	16500	7580	10417	947.5	631.4	316.1	50.2
1970/71	6000	6500	8800	6900	1466.6	1061.5	405.0	38.1
Average 1950/51 to 1970/71	4190	8924	3130	4113	704.9	499.7	205.2	41.1

Table 16
Area of Cultivated Land in Israel[16]
(in thousands of dunums)

Year	Jewish agriculture			Arab agriculture		
	Total area cultivated	Area under irrigation	Percentage	Total area cultivated	Area under irrigation	Percentage
1950/51	2705	464	17.1	645	10	1.5
1954/55	2965	873	29.4	625	17	2.7
1958/59	3350	1209	36.1	755	26	3.4
1962/63	3185	1474	46.3	850	31	3.6
1966/67	3273	1548	47.3	865	40	4.6
1970/71	3387	1282	37.9	773	53	6.9
Average 1950/51 to 1970/71	3172	1214	38.3	759	28	3.7

Table 17
Cultivated Area and Value of Agricultural Crops[17]

Year	Area under cultivation (in thousands of dunums)		Value of agricultural crop (in thousands of pounds)		Value of crop per dunum (in pounds)		Difference in value of crop between Jewish and Arab agriculture	
	Jewish agriculture	Arab agriculture	Jewish agriculture	Arab agriculture	Jewish agriculture	Arab agriculture	Pounds	As percent of Arab value
1950/51	2,705	645	65,172	5,798	24.09	8.99	15.10	168
1954/55	2,965	625	353,237	24,168	119.13	38.67	80.46	208
1958/59	3,350	755	671,245	41,767	200.36	55.32	145.04	262
1962/63	3,185	820	1,102,997	58,330	346.31	71.13	275.18	387
1966/67	3,273	865	1,516,272	98,563	463.27	113.95	349.32	307
1970/71	3,387	773	2,393,200	116,700	706.58	150.97	555.61	368
Average 1950/51 to 1970/71	3,169	754	948,480	57,991	299.30	76.91	222.39	289

Table 18
Comparison of Centers of
Population and Local Government[18]

| | Number of towns, villages, and settlements | | Towns, villages, and settlements without benefit of local government | | | |
| | | | Number | | Percentage of each | |
Year	Jewish	Arab	Jewish	Arab	Jewish	Arab
1953	742	112	93	89	12.5	79.5
1957	802	111	40	81	5	73
1960	780	112	23	67	2.9	59.8
1966	774	103	13	46	1.7	44.7
1971	781	104	9	30	1.1	28.8

Table 19
Comparison of Population and Local Government[19]

| | Total population | | Population without benefit of local government | | | |
| | | | Number | | Percentage of each | |
Year	Jewish	Arab	Jewish	Arab	Jewish	Arab
1953	1,483,641	185,776	83,245	104,630	5.6	56.3
1957	1,762,741	213,213	19,944	114,953	1.1	53.9
1960	1,911,189	239,169	14,264	90,909	0.7	38
1966	2,344,877	312,533	5,775	85,828	0.2	27.5
1971	2,636,600	382,300	3,300	77,800	0.1	20.4

Notes for Tables

1. Israel, Central Bureau of Statistics, *Statistical Abstract of Israel,* 1972, p. 28; 1970, p. 38; 1969, p. 38; 1968, p. 28; 1967, p. 30; 1966, p. 30; 1965, p. 30; 1964, p. 22; 1962, p. 45; 1961, p. 39; 1959/60, p. 7. Total population figures are at year end unless otherwise stated. Figures for 1948 and 1961 are Census figures.

   The relatively large increase in the Arab population in 1949 as compared to 1948 was due to Israel's annexation of the Arab villages of the Triangle at the beginning of that year. After 1967 the total population of Israel in fact includes Arabs living in the Old City of Jerusalem, but they are not included in these calculations. Arab residents of the Old City are estimated at 65,756 at the end of 1967; 69,063 in 1968; 71,427 in 1969; 73,344 in 1970; and 76,200 in 1971. These figures were arrived at by subtracting the population living in Jerusalem before 1967 from the overall figure for the Arab population of Jerusalem and allowing for an increase in population based on the rate of population growth for the five years preceding 1967.

2. *Statistical Abstract of Israel,* 1972, p. 34; 1962, p. 36; and 1955/ 56, p. 9. The figures for 1948 and 1961 come from the Census.

   The increase of the Arab population in the Central District resulted from Israel's annexation of Arab villages of the Triangle in 1949. The 1971 figures for Jerusalem do not include the Arabs in the Old City of Jerusalem.

3. *Statistical Abstract of Israel,* 1972, pp. 36, 39-40; 1967, pp. 30-33; 1962, pp. 39, 42; 1955/56, p. 9. The 1961 and 1971 figures come from the Census. The Arab cities include Nazareth and Shafa Amr. Cities of mixed population include Acre, Haifa, Lydda, Ramle, Tel Aviv/Jaffa, New Jerusalem, and since 1961 Tarshiha-Maalot.

4. *Statistical Abstract of Israel,* 1972, p. 51; 1967, pp. 36-7; 1962, p. 45; 1959/60, p. 7. The 1961 figures come from the Census. There is no separate information regarding Moslem and Christian Arabs inside the 1967 border for the year 1971. The number of Arabs in Israel plus the Arabs in the Old City of Jerusalem (an estimated 72,000) totalled 458,500, of whom 343,900 were Moslem, 77,300 Christian, and 37,300 Druze; that is, 75 percent Moslem, 16.86 percent Christian, and 8.14 percent Druze.

5. For 1945, see *Village Statistics 1945, A Classification of Land and Area Ownership in Palestine,* with explanatory notes by Sami Hadawi (Beirut: Palestine Liberation Organization Research Center, 1970), pp. 40-77; for 1962, see *Israel Government Yearbook* 5724 (1963/64), pp. 32 and 38. The land was expropriated according to the Land Acquisition (Validation of Acts and Com-

pensation) Law, S713—1953. The total for 1945 includes
351,657 dunums classified as No. 16, which is quasi-agricultural
land that is not taxed. Such land is considered national property,
although compensation is paid to any Arab willing to relinquish
his rights to it.

6. In the first Knesset the Arabs entered one list; in the second, third,
and fourth, three lists; and in the fifth, sixth, and seventh, two
lists. The lists were attached to Mapai until the fifth Knesset; in
the sixth they were attached to Mapai-Achdut Haavoda, and in
the seventh to Mapam-Labor Party. From the sixth Knesset
onwards, Israel Communist Party became Raqah.

7. Israel, Central Bureau of Statistics, *Results of the Elections to the
Fifth Knesset . . .* , Special Series No. 166 (Jerusalem, 1964), pp.
20-25; *Results of the Elections of the Sixth Knesset . . .* , Special
Series No. 216 (Jerusalem, 1967), pp. 96-103; and *Results of the
Elections to the Seventh Knesset . . .* , Special Series No. 309
(Jerusalem, 1970), pp. 60-62. The Arab districts included cover
about 90 percent of Arab voters in Israel; it is impossible to
ascertain the distribution of Arab voters in cities of mixed population since Jewish and Arab votes are counted together. In the
fourth Knesset, there were three Arab lists; in the fifth, sixth, and
seventh, two lists.

The religious parties include the National Religious Party,
which wins most votes, Agudat Israel and Workers of Agudat
Israel. The rightist parties include: in the fourth Knesset, Herut
and General Zionist; in the fifth Knesset, Herut and the Inde-
pendents; in the sixth Knesset, Gahal, Herut, and separate inde-
pendents; in the seventh Knesset, the Independent Center was
added.

8. Same as Table 7. The Arab cities include Nazareth and Shafa Amr,
and since 1965 Umm al Fahm and Tayba in the Triangle. Results
of Arab votes in cities of mixed population resemble those in
Arab towns. Large villages include those with populations over
2,500, while small villages include those with populations under
2,500. In 1959 and 1961 the Communists included the Israel
Communist Party (Maki) and in 1965 and 1969 the new Communist list (Rakah).

9. Israel, Central Bureau of Statistics, *Results of the Elections of the
Sixth Knesset and Local Authorities . . .* , and *Results of the
Elections to the Seventh Knesset and Local Authorities . . .* ,
Special Series Nos. 216 and 309 (Jerusalem, 1967, 1970), pp.
47-48 and 21-32. Those towns and villages are included in which
the Communists gained at least 500 votes, except Nazareth where
the votes were almost even. In some villages there are no election
results for 1965, either because there were no local elections that

year, or because the Communists did not take part in the elections with lists of their own, or because they joined some other local faction.

10. For the population aged 5-14: *Statistical Abstract of Israel*, 1971, p. 43; 1970, pp. 44-45; 1968, pp. 38-39; 1964, pp. 30-31; 1962, pp. 45-49; 1959/60, pp. 21-24; 1957/58, pp. 19-20; and 1956/57, pp. 12-13. Since there is a difference of one year between fourteen year olds in the population and those completing elementary education at the age of thirteen, the figures refer to the population aged 5-14 as it stood at the end of the second year. For students in elementary school and kindergarten: *Statistical Abstract of Israel*, 1972, p. 580; 1970, p. 545; 1969, p. 550; 1966, p. 587; 1964, p. 503; and 1963, p. 634. Private schools are mostly Christian parochial schools.

The noticeable increase in the number of Arab students attending private schools after 1968/69 is due to the inclusion of the number of Arab students in the Old City of Jerusalem, for whom there are no separate figures. The information available for 1970/71 does not differentiate between students in private and public schools.

11. Based on information given out by Ministers of Education during questioning reported in *Knesset Debates*, 3/27/1963, p. 1668 and 2/4/1970, p. 685; and also in *Israel Government Yearbook*, 5728 (1967/68), p. 125. Since there are differences in the figures from official Israeli sources, the most recent information for each year has been used.

12. For population: *Statistical Abstract of Israel*, 1972, p. 25; 1971, p. 43; 1969, pp. 40-41; 1968, pp. 37-38; 1966, pp. 38-39; 1964, pp. 40-41; 1962, pp. 45-49; 1957/58, pp. 19-20; and 1956/57, pp. 12-13. The figures quoted refer to population as of December 31 of the second year under "year" column, except for 1960/61, for which the figure refers to the census taken on May 22, 1961. For students in secondary school: *Statistical Abstract of Israel*, 1972, p. 580; 1970, p. 545; 1969, p. 550; 1967, p. 525; 1966, p. 587; 1965, p. 575; 1964, p. 503; 1963, p. 634; 1962, p. 484; and 1961, p. 450. For students attaining diploma: *Statistical Abstract of Israel*, 1972, p. 593; 1971; p. 561; 1970, p. 564; 1968, p. 542; 1966, p. 604; 1964, p. 517; 1963, p. 648; 1962, p. 494; and 1961, p. 459.

Some of the noticeable increase in the number of Arab students and holders of the *Baghrot* diploma in 1968/69 is due to the inclusion of Arab students living in the Old City of Jerusalem in the number of Arab students in Israel, there being no separate information on them.

13. *Statistical Abstract of Israel*, 1972, pp. 314-15; 1969, pp. 260-64; and 1963, pp. 498-501.

14. For crop tonnage: *Statistical Abstract of Israel*, 1972, p. 352; 1971, p. 326; 1970, pp. 322-23; 1969, pp. 324-25; 1967, pp. 330-31; 1963, pp. 234-37; 1962, pp. 200-5; and 1961, pp. 188-93. For crop values: *Statistical Abstract of Israel*, 1972, p. 353; 1971, p. 327; 1970, pp. 324-25; 1969, pp. 326-27; 1967, pp. 332-33; 1963, pp. 240-43; 1962, pp. 206-11; and 1961, pp. 194-99.

15. For crop tonnage: *Statistical Abstract of Israel*, 1972, p. 352; 1971, p. 326; 1970, pp. 322-23; 1969, pp. 324-27; 1962, pp. 200-5; and 1961, pp. 188-93. For crop values: *Statistical Abstract of Israel*, 1972, p. 353; 1971, p. 327; 1970, pp. 324-25; 1969, pp. 326-27; 1967, pp. 332-33; 1963, pp. 240-43; 1962, pp. 206-11; and 1961, pp. 194-99.

16. *Statistical Abstract of Israel*, 1972, p. 342; 1971, p. 513; 1970, p. 309; 1969, p. 313; 1968, p. 313; 1967, p. 319; 1964, p. 314; 1963, p. 216; 1962, p. 148; 1961, p. 172; and 1958/59, p. 131. The Arabs own about half of the total cultivated Arab area; the rest is leased to them by government departments or Jewish settlers.

17. For area under cultivation: *Statistical Abstract of Israel*, 1972, p. 342; 1971, p. 315; 1970, p. 309; 1969, p. 313; 1968, p. 313; 1967, p. 319; 1964, p. 314; 1961, p. 172; and 1958/59, p. 131. For value of crop: *Statistical Abstract of Israel*, 1972, p. 353; 1971, p. 327; 1970, pp. 324-25; 1969, pp. 326-27; 1968, pp. 326-27; 1967, pp. 332-33; 1964, pp. 328-31; 1963, pp. 240-44; and 1961, pp. 194-99.

18. *Statistical Abstract of Israel*, 1972, p. 36; 1967, p. 34; and 1963, pp. 590-91.

19. *Statistical Abstract of Israel*, 1972, p. 36; 1967, p. 34; and 1963, pp. 590-91. The 1971 Arab figures do not include Arabs in the Old City of Jerusalem.

Temple Israel

Minneapolis, Minnesota

IN HONOR OF THE BAT MITZVAH OF
DAPHNE FRUCHTMAN
FROM
DEENA FRUCHTMAN